SIX PERSPECTIVES ON THEORY *for* THE PRACTICE OF OCCUPATIONAL THERAPY

B. Rosalie Johanna Miller, PhD, OTR
Assistant Professor, Department of Occupational Therapy
School of Education, Health, Nursing and Arts Professions
New York University

Kay W. Sieg, MEd, OTR
Associate Professor and Chairperson
Department of Occupational Therapy
College of Health Related Professions
University of Florida

Ferol Menks Ludwig, MS, OTR
Private Practitioner and Consultant
Phoenix, Arizona

Susan Denegan Shortridge, MHS, OTR
President, Developmental Healthcare Services, Inc.
Gainesville, Florida

Julia Van Deusen, PhD, OTR, FAOTA
Associate Professor, Department of Occupational Therapy
College of Health Related Professions
University of Florida

AN ASPEN PUBLICATION®
Aspen Publishers, Inc.

1988

Rockville, Maryland
Royal Tunbridge Wells

Library of Congress Cataloging-in-Publication Data

Six Perspectives on Theory for the Practice of
Occupational Therapy

"An Aspen publication."
Includes bibliographies and index.
1. Occupational therapy—Philosophy. I. Miller, B.
Rosalie Johanna. [DNLM: 1. Occupational Therapy.
2. Occupational Therapy—United States—biography.
WB 55 T396]
RC487.T48 1988 615.8'515 87-35156
ISBN: 0-87189-754-7

Editorial Services: Marsha Davies

Library of Congress Catalog Card Number: 87-35156
ISBN: 0-87189-754-7

Printed in the United States of America

1 2 3 4 5

*To Gail Fidler, Anne C. Mosey, Lela A. Llorens,
A. Jean Ayres, Mary Reilly, and Gary Kielhofner
whose commitment and courage
provided the inspiration for this book.*

Table of Contents

Preface

The goal of this book is to provide a thorough review of selected theorists whose lives and works have influenced the direction and development of clinical practice in occupational therapy. Two assumptions have guided the development of the book. First, careful study of existing theoretical material is needed to provide a knowledge base for the refinement of current theories and for the development of new theories. Second, the clinical relevance of a theory can be enhanced when that theory is studied in the context of the individual theorist's attempts to solve clinical problems or address professional issues that the theorist has encountered in her or his own career.

We felt that such a book was needed in the occupational therapy profession. Practicing therapists can use it to develop a frame of reference for a clinical setting, to review theory related to a new job area, to formulate justifications for practice decisions to other professionals and to third party payers, to establish a rationale for research, or to prepare for continuing education workshops.

For the increasing numbers of therapists returning to school to obtain graduate degrees, a book was needed to provide an overview of theorists and exhaustive bibliographies for more indepth study. Graduate students also need to identify research questions that can add to the body of knowledge and theory base for the profession.

This book is designed to help the undergraduate or basic master's student who is in the process of formulating a professional identity. This book can help them begin to understand the common themes and the differences among the basic theories, which so often seem elusive in this diverse profession. And, because the book identifies a heritage of the outstanding ideas and exemplary careers of some of the people in the profession, it can aid the development of professional self-esteem and confidence.

The book can assist educators to provide a broader conceptual base for course content and curriculum planning, as well as help them to impart to students an appreciation of the richness of theoretical ideas in the profession. It also can provide educators with an additional stimulus for their own scholarly research endeavors.

It is hoped that this book will also inspire all its readers by "demythologizing" the major theorists. Each theory chapter begins with a biographical sketch that describes factors that influenced and motivated the theorist's growth as therapist and theorist. Theory is enlivened in the context of each theorist's personal and professional efforts to solve practical and realistic problems that confront occupational therapists.

In Chapter 1, theory is defined and its relevance to occupational therapy issues is addressed. The core of the book is organized around six theorists, with a chapter devoted to each. These chapters follow a similar format: (1) a biographical perspective of the theorist, (2) an objective review of that person's theory, and (3) the use of that theory in occupational therapy. The impact of each theory on OT practice is revealed through the presentation of subsequent research and application of the theory by others. Comprehensive bibliographies of each theorist's works are provided to lead readers to a deeper understanding of the theorists' concepts and ideas. In the final chapter, the major themes that run through the theories are analyzed, and future theory development needs are identified.

The six theorists included here were selected because of the impact that their work has had on the overall conceptualization and practice of occupational therapy. Certainly, there are many other people who have made and are making significant contributions to our growing theory base. It is hoped that this book will provide support and stimulus to those individuals who have already presented their ideas on OT theory and that it will inspire others in the profession to join in this exciting search for ever greater understanding and clarity about occupational therapy.

Throughout the writing of this book the authors have kept in mind Yerxa's statement that "we deal with enormous complexity which we tend to simplify rather than clarify" (1986, p. 211). It has not been possible to address all the complex issues behind the theories presented, a reality that readers must keep in mind when reading this book. We *do* hope that the work we have done adds more to clarity than to simplification.

REFERENCE

Yerxa, E.J. (1986). Target tomorrow. In *Occupational therapy education: Target 2000* (pp. 209–213). Rockville, MD; American Occupational Therapy Association.

Acknowledgments

This book has its roots in the occupational therapy department at the University of Florida where the ideas for its birth were stimulated in the academic climate first created there by Alice C. Jantzen. It could not have been completed without the assistance and cooperation of many people. Gail Fidler, Anne C. Mosey, Lela A. Llorens, A. Jean Ayres, and Gary Kielhofner provided photographs, generously shared details of their lives and ideas with us and edited the biographies we wrote from that material. Cheryl Salz King, Wilma West, and Mary Donahue reviewed portions of the manuscript and provided valuable feedback. Deborah R. Labovitz, the first author's chairperson, gave much appreciated support and encouragement. Also, the students who spurred us on to explore, synthesize, and write about these issues played a crucial role.

June Chukwumah and Brenda Wise each typed sections of the manuscript. Vivian Moore and Susan Chasin not only typed large portions of manuscript but each also made other invaluable contributions of time and effort toward its completion.

We are indebted to Margaret Quinlin, our senior editor at Aspen Publishers, who prodded us with important questions early on and who has been solidly behind us ever since. This book would never have come to print were it not for the competence and patience of the editorial staff assigned to it.

Last but not least, we acknowledge and thank our families of loved ones and friends who have nourished us and helped us with perspective throughout this and the other projects of our lives.

Chapter One

What Is Theory, and Why Does It Matter?

Rosalie J. Miller

WHAT IS THEORY?

There are many theories about what a theory is, partly because a theory is not a concrete thing or even an observable behavior. A theory is a way of thinking about something. In a conversation about politics, the economy, or a life experience it is common to hear someone say, "My theory about that is . . ." That person then goes on to make a statement about the relationship between two or more concepts. For instance, she or he might say, "My theory about the welfare system is that it adds to the problems of the poor by reducing their motivation to work and hence their self-esteem." The elements of that theory are the *concepts* of "welfare," "problems," "poor," "motivation," and "self-esteem" and a statement of *relationships* among those concepts of "adds to," "by reducing," and "and hence." *A theory, then, is a logically derived statement of the interrelationships between two or more concepts.*

Our unique human ability to use symbols through language enables us to develop concepts. The young child sees something unfamiliar and asks, "What is that?" and the child is told, "That's a cow" or "That's a pan." Through these experiences categories are formed into which one organizes things from the environment. These categories are *concepts* (Duldt & Giffin, 1985, p. 46).

As one grows, one develops more concept categories, relates more and more things to them, and subdivides levels of concept categories in one's mind. For instance, the large concept category of animals is then subdivided into cows, dogs, cats, horses, and so on. The child learns that food is subdivided into fruits, vegetables, grains, etc., which are then further subdivided—fruits into apples, pears, grapes, and so on. So one learns "to recognize things as belonging to certain categories; thus one develops a notion of concepts" (Duldt & Giffin, 1985, p. 46).

Language enables conceptualization. And because of language, we can conceptualize things that we cannot see, whether because we are out of sight of the physical thing itself, as in "cow," or "the pyramids," or because there is no *physical* reality to the concept, as in "self-esteem" or "motivation." Concepts, such as these latter two, that have no physical referent but rather are labels for intangible ideas are often called *constructs*.

As one learns more about concepts one also learns about ways in which concepts relate to one another. Relationships between concepts are called *principles*. For instance, once one learns the concepts of 2 and of 4, one learns the *principle* that if 2 is *added to* 2, the result is 4. Once one has learned the concepts of cat, petting, and enjoyment one can put together the *principle* that the cat enjoys being petted. One also learns reverse consequences of principles: 4 minus 2 equals 2, if one strokes the cat against the lay of the hair it objects, and so on. In all these examples one is using language symbolically to think about the relationships between concepts, and in so doing one is deriving principles (Duldt & Giffin, 1985).

Concepts and principles serve two important functions. First, they "help us understand or explain what is going on around us" (Duldt & Giffin, 1985, p. 47). For example, beginning OT students are usually somewhat confused about "what occupational therapy is." In the course of their education they learn new *concepts* that are used in the field, such as "neurodevelopment" and "occupation" and how to categorize other things and ideas (subconcepts) into these major concepts. For example, subconcepts of "ADL," "work," and "play/leisure" are categorized under the major concept of "occupation." Then the student learns *principles* governing the relationships among concepts, i.e., *involvement in* occupation is *essential to* normal neurodevelopment. Through this process of learning concepts and principles, students grow to better understand what occupational therapy is.

Second, according to Duldt and Giffin, established principles also help us predict future events.

> Some concepts relate to one another so consistently that predictions about future outcomes are relatively simple. For example, when we see dark clouds with lightning and we hear thunder, we know from experience that rain is approaching. We can make this prediction because we understand the relationship between the three concepts—clouds, lightning, and thunder—and because we know they usually combine in such a way that a fourth concept, rain, occurs. Using our knowledge, we can exert some control over the situation by wearing raincoats and using umbrellas. . . . In developing theories, similar relationships are established between concepts. (1985, p. 33)

These relationships can be stated as *correlational*—dark clouds are often accompanied by rain—or *causal*—if you stand in the rain without a raincoat or umbrella you get wet.

From the OT principle stated earlier one can predict future events. For example, given the principle that involvement in occupation is essential to normal neurodevelopment, one can predict that a child who is in a body cast and kept in an isolated environment for a period of time will suffer setbacks in neurodevelopment. This combination of concepts and principles that predicts outcome is an example of *theory*.

Theory is defined in slightly different ways by different people. Duldt and Giffin define it this way: "A theory is a *related set of principles*, each principle being a statement that ties two or more concepts together, usually in a correlational or casual way" (1985, p. 47).

Reed states it somewhat differently, yet she incorporates the same elements. "A theory is defined as a set of interrelated assumptions, concepts, and definitions that presents a systematic view of phenomena by specifying relationships among variables, with the purpose of explaining and predicting the phenomena" (1984, p. 677).

In this definition Reed raises a very important issue—that of *assumptions*. No theory is totally value-free. Every person brings to the task of explaining her or his observations a particular perspective and certain basic values. Certainly most of us share the assumption that the world exists and that we can accurately perceive it through our senses. This may or may not be ultimately true, but most theories are based on these assumptions.

In occupational therapy certain assumptions are generally considered basic to the profession and influence the types and direction of theories that are introduced. In 1919 William Rush Dunton, Jr. published the *Credo for Occupational Therapists*, which delineated the following basic assumptions:

> That occupation is as necessary to life as food and drink.
> That every human being should have both physical and mental occupation.
> That all should have occupations which they enjoy, or hobbies. . . .
> That sick minds, sick bodies, sick souls may be healed through occupation. (p. 10)

The "Philosophical Base of Occupational Therapy" adopted by the Representative Assembly (RA) of the American Occupational Therapy Association (AOTA) in 1979 states very similar assumptions in different words:

> [Humans are] active beings whose development is influenced by the use of purposeful activity. Using their capacity for intrinsic motivation, human beings are able to influence their physical and mental health and their social and physical environment through purposeful activity. . . .
>
> Occupational therapy is based on the belief that purposeful activity (occupation), including its interpersonal and environmental components, may be used to prevent and mediate dysfunction, and to elicit maximum adaptation. (Hopkins & Smith, 1983, p. 27)

It is important to be aware of the assumptions underlying a particular theory so that one may evaluate it thoroughly, rather than accepting it at face value. For instance, a theory may seem quite logical at first, but an examination of the assumptions on which it is based may give one cause to reject it as incompatible with one's own world view. At the same time, it is important to maintain an attitude of flexibility about one's assumptions and realize that the results of truth-seeking might lead one to change an assumption from time to time.

RELATIONSHIP OF RESEARCH TO THEORY

The way one determines whether the principles relating concepts in any particular theory are valid or not is through the process called research. There are many legitimate ways to go about this process, a fact that even many previously "hard-line" experimental research protagonists are beginning to acknowledge. As Ottenbacher recently put it:

> Many investigators (myself included) have displayed a tendency to be overzealous in their use and promotion of experimental methods, much like the young child who, when first given a hammer, finds that everything he encounters needs pounding. The evolving discussion concerning the relative merits of various research strategies makes it clear that traditional designs are a valuable and viable empirical option, but that they are not the absolute ideal in every situation. The debate also helps legitimize and increase the acceptance of qualitative, idiographic, and other alternative research and evaluation strategies. It has forced investigators to focus not only on outcome but also on process, holism, ecology, and other attributes not generally afforded a high priority in the traditional experimental paradigm. (1985, p. 203)

As a practice profession OT's research laboratories are the practice settings in which therapists interact with patients and clients. Those therapists who use theoretical principles to make practice decisions and then observe the results are engaging in a process of testing those theories and, in so doing, may also generate new ones.

Ottenbacher's statement illuminates the fact that there are many exciting ways to go about this process of both testing and generating theory. The development of a solid theoretical and concrete knowledge base of the profession requires only that occupational therapists become more knowledgeable about theory and more conscious and deliberate about the kinds of thinking and problem solving in which they are already engaged and that they then record and share their findings.

DEVELOPMENT OF THEORY

Stages

Theory is constantly revised as new knowledge is discovered through research. Any new science, according to Lewin (1947), goes through three stages in theory development.

The first stage is the *speculative* period, in which the field puts forth theoretical models to attempt to explain phenomena. The second stage is the *descriptive* one. In this period the field gathers facts through research to describe what really is happening and to test the theoretical models. Lewin calls the third stage the *constructive* period. During this time old theories are revised and new ones developed that are grounded in facts, rather than based on speculation.

Any science must and does go through these stages. Occupational therapy seems to have developed speculative theories and has begun the process of gathering facts through research.

Process

Theory is generally developed in one of two ways. An individual may have many facts and then develop a theory to explain relationships among them. Darwin was a scientist who knew the facts that had been gathered up to his time about different species and their description and classification. He posited his theory of evolution as a way of explaining how these many species were related one to another and to human beings (Ostrow, 1980).

Or a person may have a flash of insight that suddenly gives him or her a whole new perspective about the relationship of certain concepts. An example of this type of theory development is Einstein's theory of relativity, which opened up new areas of research and inquiry that had not existed before because no one had ever conceptualized the possibility that energy, matter, and time could be related in the way Einstein suggested.

The way that Jean Ayres' theory of sensory integration was derived combined these two processes. She saw certain developments in the cognitive, perceptual, and motor functioning of the children with whom she worked. After extensive observation and testing she presented her theory of sensory integration. Like Darwin she had accumulated a good deal of knowledge and was a scholar in her area. Also like Einstein, she went beyond the proven, the tested, the observable to develop her theory. Ayres states:

> Exactly how SI occurs in the brain remains elusive, but that lack of knowledge should not be an excuse for avoiding an issue basic to all learning. She challenges that this lack of knowledge "must be faced and dealt with in as adequate a manner as possible with full recognition of the limitations involved and with the realization that any conceptual framework is in some aspects erroneous and will require constant revision as new knowledge unfolds." (1968, p. 43)

This willingness to take risks is an essential quality in any theorist.

Complexity and Scope

Theories range in complexity and scope along a continuum; at one end lie those that are narrow in focus and deal with specific phenomena that are fairly easily defined, and at the other end are those that are very broad and complex and attempt to explain major areas within a discipline. The latter theories often incorporate numerous more specific theories within them (Marriner, 1986).

Parham defines this continuum as ranging from scientific theories to conceptual frameworks and says they are:

> different kinds of thinking tools for the therapist. An overarching conceptual framework allows the therapist to frame the context for intervention by sketching a general configuration of the situation, while a scientific theory leads the therapist to specify technical details of how to act on a problem once it is selected as a target for intervention. It is likely that, in the best instances of competent clinical practice, both kinds of thinking are involved. (Parham, 1987, p. 558)

Kielhofner's model of human occupation is an example of an overarching conceptual framework that provides a perspective from which the therapist can evaluate and determine areas of function and dysfunction in a given patient or client. Ayres' theory of sensory integration is a scientific theory that guides the therapist's intervention once it has been determined that lack of sensory integration is a probable contributor to dysfunction.

The major theories in occupational therapy fall at different points along this continuum of complexity and scope, and very often in a clinical situation a therapist will use more than one theory. This is often necessary because of the complexity of the problems faced by disabled individuals. However, one must be certain when utilizing multiple theories that they are based on compatible assumptions and that their concepts fit together logically.

> Often the therapist will have to choose between competing theories that offer different points of view for understanding a single clinical situation. An appreciation of the different kinds of theories available and what each can bring to the understanding of the problem is required if a wise decision is to be made. (Parham, 1987, p. 557)

An obvious example would be a theorist working from a psychoanalytic theory base with a disturbed child, encouraging her to express her anger. It would greatly confuse that child if she were also treated from a behavioral perspective and rewarded for "good" behavior.

One of the dangers in our field today is the potential for proponents of one or another theoretical perspective to claim authority (Grady, 1987). No one theory or conceptual framework in occupational therapy has yet been subjected to enough *clinical* research to make such a claim. Each of the theories presented in this book offers important perspectives for the problems faced in OT practice. Familiarity with these theories and methods for applying their principles helps therapists to meet the occupational needs of their patients.

WHY DOES IT MATTER?

The therapist who is working in a clinical setting using tools learned in school to evaluate and treat patients and seeing some progress as a result may ask, "So why do we need theory anyway? I'm doing pretty well without thinking much about it, thank you, and besides I don't have the time."

There are many good reasons why it is important for occupational therapists to become conscious of, interested in, and competent with the use of theory. These reasons are described below.

To Validate and Guide Practice

The following excerpt from a 1938 editorial in the journal, *Occupational Therapy and Rehabilitation*, illustrates that the need for theory and research to justify our practice is not a new concern:

> The following list of questions was recently sent to us by a therapist connected with one of our large state hospitals, [the questions] having been given her by the psychologist connected with that institution. It can be recognized that they are questions which are often asked by physicians and sometimes we do not have a ready answer for them so that it is desired to hold a symposium upon them in order that all therapists may be prepared.
>
> 1. What is the occupational therapist's theory as to how occupational therapy proves of assistance in bringing about recovery? 2. What are the statistics upon which is based the statement that occupational therapy does aid recovery? (Editorial, 1938, p. 127)

These remain, today, two of the major issues in promoting and justifying the use of occupational therapy. The first question can be addressed by the therapist familiar with theories of occupational therapy, and the second question can be answered by the occupational therapist who is familiar with the information derived from research in the profession.

As Clark has stated:

> The development and use of theory and theory-testing in practice can and will define the validity of occupational therapy as a professional service. The theories developed for and through practice may be evaluated in terms of their capacity to define and describe that practice, including actions and technology; and their predictive value for the outcome of practice. (Clark, 1979, p. 508)

The theories that guide everyday practice may be used unconsciously. It is critical to bring those theories into the light of consciousness because they may be incomplete, contradictory, or inconsistent. Although it may at first seem threatening to risk discovering that such is the case, concern for providing the best possible care for patients and acceptance of the reality that we are all always learning should provide the necessary motivation to examine the theories one uses in making practice decisions.

As Parham put it:

> Theory is a key element in problem setting and in problem solving. It is a tool that enables the therapist to "name it and frame it." Both language and logic are needed to identify a problem (name it) and to plan a means for altering the situation (frame it). Theory provides these by giving us words or concepts for naming what we observe, and by spelling out logical relationships between concepts. This allows us to explain what we see and to figure out how to manipulate a situation to cause change. (1987, p. 557)

To Justify Reimbursement

Validation of practice is directly tied to reimbursement. Those who pay for OT services are ever more demanding of substantive justification for what occupational therapists do that both *explains* why something is being done and *demonstrates* that what is being done works. The explanation is provided through theory, the demonstration through research.

Baum has stated that in today's changing health marketplace it is not only important to develop cost-effective programs but also to "document program effectiveness using standard and reliable measures of patient/client performance" (1985, p. 24). In a recent article, Baum writes:

> Is occupational therapy cost-effective? Can occupational therapy influence performance? The public expects answers to these questions, and the profession bears the responsibility for providing the answers. In the past OT has relied on the medical and basic sciences for knowledge generation and scientific inquiry. But if our contribution to health care is to be unique, it is up to us to address the important questions about health, occupation, and human performance. (Baum, 1987, p. 145)

To Clarify Specialization Issues

The issue of specialization is related to theory, as occupational therapists need to be able to balance the technical aspects of practice with underlying theoretical explanations that reflect their basic assumptions and identity as occupational therapists. Otherwise, how can one explain the differences between an occupational therapist who specializes in hand therapy and a physical therapist who also specializes in hand therapy? Or, how does one explain the common connections between an occupational therapist who works with adolescent drug abusers and another one who works with elders afflicted with Alzheimer's disease?

To Enhance the Growth of the Profession and the Professionalism of Its Members

One of the major attributes of a profession is that it has a distinctive theoretical base. In 1982 the AOTA stated that one of its missions was "to encourage the development and testing of theories that contribute to the knowledge base, which will enhance the growth of the profession" (Foundation, 1982, p. 116).

> The theoretical systems that comprise the body of knowledge of OT are generated within the profession, as well as drawn from the academic disciplines (e.g., the social and biological sciences) and other professional fields (e.g., medicine). Theories are selected, formulated, and adapted to have specific meaning to the profession's practice. So constituted, they form the body of knowledge or theoretical foundation of the profession. The body of knowledge is unique in its entirety but not in its component parts. The challenge to OT is to identify a body of knowledge that reflects its scientific base and philosophical assumptions in order to organize this knowledge in ways that serve clinical practice. (Williamson, 1977, p. 718)

The use of a theory base to guide decision making is much of what distinguishes a professional person from a technician. As Williamson goes on to state:

> Therapists vary in their level of awareness regarding the philosophical assumptions and theoretical foundations of their practice and their ability to communicate them to others. A professional is distinguished from a technician by knowledge of the propositions that guide his or her actions and the conscious selection of those propositions to influence change. In a practice based on theory, the therapist is able to ascertain the relationship between a client's need and a theoretical principle, and apply intervention procedures on the basis of accurate prediction of outcome. (1977, p. 722)

Although development of a strong theory base will not guarantee occupational therapy's acceptance and recognition by others as a profession, such acceptance and recognition will certainly not come *without* such a base. What seems most important in the entire controversy about professionalism is that to deliver the best service—both directly to patients and clients and indirectly through communication with other members of the health care system—occupational therapists need to feel *confident* about what they are doing and about their ability to communicate why they are doing it. This confidence requires a solid theoretical foundation, as well as the ability to apply that theory to facilitating the functional needs of individual patients and clients.

To Educate Competent Practitioners

In addition to practitioners' need to study, understand, and consciously utilize theory, students and educators must also be actively involved in this process. Yerxa and Sharrott state, "The person who graduates from an occupational therapy program needs to be an independent, critical thinker who is at home with principles and interrelationships among concepts; acts from a knowledge base and can articulate the theoretical support for what he or she does" (1986, p. 155). According to Shapiro and Shanahan, "One of the primary goals for educators of OT's is the preparation of independent practitioners—persons who will be able to use accepted theories, and when necessary, to generate new theories to guide their practice" (1976, p. 217).

Once they leave the classroom, students need to work with fieldwork supervisors who provide positive role models for using theory in everyday practice.

> The application of theory to practice in fieldwork education cannot occur without strong collaborative partnerships between education and practice. We must do all we can to build and reinforce an atmosphere of working together toward the same goal of a profession with strong theoretical bases and practical techniques that are adaptable in a world of changing health care systems. (McGourty, 1986, p. 128)

THEORY AS UNIFYING FOUNDATION

Our theoretical base should and can provide major connections among the various aspects of our field. One certainly should be able to explain best those theories that one uses most often. Yet, possessing an understanding of the major theories that influence practice in the field is a goal to which each occupational therapist can aspire—not only in order to be well educated and better able to communicate but also to be better able to define oneself as an occupational therapist and have confidence that what one is doing with patients, with students, and in research is well founded.

One must take care, however, in using any theory without adequate knowledge. Attempts to apply theories with only a cursory understanding of concepts and principles can lead to inaccurate assumptions and potentially harmful practice with contradictory and confusing outcomes.

SEMANTIC ISSUES

One of the major difficulties in understanding, analyzing, and comparing theories in occupational therapy is that different theorists use different words to discuss similar concepts. The same theorist may even use such terms as theory, model, and paradigm interchangeably. This can be very confusing to the reader. This problem is not unique to occupational therapy, but efforts need to be made to clarify labels, particularly at this time when the importance of understanding and utilizing theory is of such concern.

The process of clarifying and comparing these labels in a way that is consistent and true to theorists' meanings will be a lengthy one. However, it is important that the effort be made. What is presented here is merely a beginning step that, it is hoped, will assist readers to apply their own critical reasoning faculties to the effort to sort out and understand the complexities, similarities, and differences behind the labels.

Highest Levels of Conceptualization

Four of the six theorists in this book present recommendations for conceptualizing what occupational therapy is about. The terms used to describe these overarching conceptualizations differ; consider Reilly's paradigm, Kielhofner's paradigm, Mosey's model, and Llorens' schematic.

The term "paradigm" can be

> used to denote the prevailing network of science, philosophy, and theory accepted by a discipline. . . . The prevailing paradigm directs the activities of a discipline. As such, it is accepted by the majority of individuals within the discipline and suggests the areas of study of interest to the discipline and the means to study them. (Marriner, 1986, p. 22)

The concept of paradigm is much more complex than the scope of this chapter can encompass, and the reader is referred to Kuhn (1970) for greater understanding of its significance.

Reilly was the first occupational therapist to write about paradigm. Her citation as a charter member of the American Occupational Therapy Foundation (AOTF) Academy of Research lauded her "exemplary contributions to the development of a generic paradigm for practice." She is still engaged in scholarly work on this complex concept.

Gary Kielhofner has expanded on the occupational behavior paradigm and has diverged from it in some significant ways. In the book, *Health Through Occupation* (1983), Kielhofner presented contributions from many writers in the field on issues involved in paradigm development for occupational therapy.

Mosey uses the term "model" in the sense of

> the typical way in which a profession perceives itself, its relationship to other professions, and its association with the society to which it is responsible. The model of a profession is characterized by a description of the profession's philosophical assumptions, ethical code, theoretical foundation, domain of concern, legitimate tools, and the nature of and principles for sequencing the various aspects of practice. (Mosey, 1981, p. 50)

And though not quite so global, Llorens' use of a three-dimensional schematic for organizing the body of knowledge in the field bears resemblance to the above conceptualizations. Reilly and Kielhofner took the idea of paradigm from Kuhn, a pure sociologist; Mosey took her concept of model from the literature of the sociology of professions; and Llorens' schematic cubic representation is similar in structure to Guilford's "Structure of Intellect" model (Guilford, 1977).

Levels of Theory

Fidler, Mosey, Ayres, and Llorens each use the label "theory" to refer to a conceptual framework when trying to explain, describe, or predict phenomena of concern to occupational therapy.

Kielhofner uses the term "model" to mean a conceptual framework or theory that is at the broad and complex end of the theory continuum. As Parham states, "A good conceptual framework enables the therapist to cope with the many details of a human problem by synthesizing them into a perspective of the whole" (1983, p. 121). This obviously is quite different from the way Mosey uses the term "model".

Linking Theory to Practice

"Traditionally, the function of theory is to explain, describe, and predict phenomena. Control of events is not a primary aim of scientific knowledge, although it may be a desirable outcome. . . . In the applied professional fields one is concerned with the nature of the change process and the means to influence it. Two approaches are commonly used to relate theoretical systems to intervention—practice theories and frames of reference. They are two systematic ways of organizing and applying knowledge to effect change. Both . . . are similar since they share a common goal and use components of a theory. Practice theories and frames of references serve as linking structures between theory and practice" (Williamson, 1977, p. 718). Ayres' theory is an example of a practice theory, and Mosey has widely articulated frames of references for occupational therapy.

As was stated previously, there obviously are very important differences among these concepts that one must take great care not to oversimplify or gloss over. It is hoped that this brief beginning will stimulate others to further clarify and differentiate concept labels.

The next six chapters describe the lives and works of six major theorists in occupational therapy. Each chapter begins with a photograph and a biographical sketch of the theorist. The intent of these is to place the person in social and professional contexts, to identify influences on her or his theory development, and to "demystify" by presenting the person behind the ideas. It is hoped that this will both enlighten the reader as to the theorist's perspective and inspire the reader to see his or her own practice and potential within a broader historical and professional context.

REFERENCES

Ayres, A.J. (1968). Sensory integrative processes and neuropsychological learning disability. In *Learning disorders. Vol. III* (p. 43). Seattle, WA: Special Child Publication.

Baum, C.M. (1985). The evolution of the U.S. health care system. In *The occupational therapy manager* (pp. 3–26). Rockville, MD: American Occupational Therapy Association.

Baum, C.M. (1987). Nationally speaking: Research: Its relationship to public policy. *American Journal of Occupational Therapy, 41,* 143–145.

Clark, P.N. (1979). Theoretical frameworks in contemporary occupational therapy practice, Part 1. *American Journal of Occupational Therapy, 33,* 505–514.

Duldt, B.W. & Giffin, K. (1985). *Theoretical perspectives for nursing.* Boston: Little, Brown & Co.

Dunton, W.R. (1919). *Reconstruction therapy.* Philadelphia: W.B. Saunders Co.

Editorial (1938, April). *Occupational therapy and rehabilitation,* p. 127.

Foundation (1982). A long-range research plan for occupational therapy. *American Journal of Occupational Therapy, 36,* 116–118.

Grady, A.P. (1987). Nationally speaking: Research: Its role in enhancing the professional image. *American Journal of Occupational Therapy, 41,* 347–349.

Guilford, J.P. (1977). *Way beyond the IQ.* Buffalo, NY: Creative Education Foundation and Bearly Limited.

Hopkins, H.L., & Smith, H.D. (Eds.) (1983). *Willard and Spackman's occupational therapy* (6th ed.). Philadelphia: J.B. Lippincott Co.

Kielhofner, G. (1983). *Health through occupation: Theory and practice in occupational therapy.* Philadelphia: F.A. Davis.

Kuhn, T. (1970). *The structure of scientific revolutions* (2nd ed.). Chicago: University of Chicago Press.

Lewin, K. (1947). *Principles of topological psychology.* New York: McGraw-Hill.

Marriner, A. (Ed.) (1986). *Nursing theorists and their works.* St. Louis: C.V. Mosby.

McGourty, L.K. (1986). Applying theory to practice: Fieldwork education. In *Occupational therapy education: Target 2000* (pp. 126–128). Rockville, MD: American Occupational Therapy Association.

Mosey, A.C. (1981). *Occupational therapy: Configuration of a profession.* New York: Raven Press.

Ostrow, P.C. (1980). The foundation: The care and feeding of theories. *American Journal of Occupational Therapy, 34,* 272–273.

Ottenbacher, K.J. (1985). The foundation: Ritual, rigor, and relevance: The design of clinical research. *American Journal of Occupational Therapy, 39,* 202–203.

Parham, L.D. (1987). Toward professionalism: The reflective therapist. *American Journal of Occupational Therapy, 41,* 555–561.

Reed, K.L. (1984). Understanding theory: The first step in learning about research. *American Journal of Occupational Therapy, 38,* 677–682.

Shapiro, D., & Shanahan, P.M. (1976). Methodology for teaching theory. *American Journal of Occupational Therapy, 30,* 217–224.

Williamson, G.G. (1977). A heritage of activity: Development of theory. *American Journal of Occupational Therapy, 36,* 716–722.

Yerxa, E.J., & Sharrott, G. (1986). Liberal arts: The foundation for occupational therapy education. *American Journal of Occupational Therapy, 40,* 153–159.

Chapter Two

Gail Fidler

Ferol Menks Ludwig

Gail Fidler

BIOGRAPHICAL SKETCH

Gail Fidler was born in Spencer, Iowa, in 1916. She is the first of four children and lived with her family in South Dakota and later in Lebanon, Pennsylvania. Her father was a high school teacher and coach who fostered her avid interest in sports. She played varsity basketball and field hockey in high school and college and later used her certification as a basketball referee to help support herself during occupational therapy school. Fidler was also actively involved in the high school debating team and in writing.

She earned her Bachelor of Arts degree from Lebanon Valley College in 1938 with a double major in education and psychology. After graduation, she worked for 6 months as a high school history teacher, but she found the school system to be too constricting for her (G. Fidler, personal communication, May 13, 1982). At that time, limited financial resources prevented her from pursuing graduate work in psychology or attending medical school to become a psychiatrist. So, to earn the tuition for graduate school, she worked as a hospital attendant at Wernersville State Hospital where she discovered occupational therapy. She described the director of occupational therapy as an interesting and well-educated person with whom she felt that she could connect and she appreciated the normalizing, pleasant atmosphere of the OT clinic.

She enrolled in the OT Certificate Program at the University of Pennsylvania in 1940 and, while attending the program, was employed as a group worker at Smith Memorial Settlement House in Philadelphia until her graduation in 1942. During a summer break she returned to work at the Wernersville State Hospital where she met a medical student who was to become her husband in 1941.

Her first position as an occupational therapist was in 1942 at the Norristown State Hospital. She described this experience as "disturbing."

> It was quite different than my experiences with OT as a student. I had high expectations and what I was seeing in practice was certainly different. I suddenly had to confront reality in comparison to my expectations, knowing that I could not stay in OT if it was no more than I was seeing. It was quite upsetting to suspect that I had made an error in choosing occupational therapy as a career. (G. Fidler, personal communication, May 13, 1982)
>
> In retrospect the department of OT at Norristown was probably the most comprehensive and best organized one that I have seen. It was highly respected and acknowledged as a valuable service to patients.
>
> What was lacking, and disturbing to me, was a rationale for practice. The why's were not being asked and the challenge of

> hypotheses—of theoretical explanation—was simply not being faced. (G. Fidler, personal communication, November 3, 1987)

She decided, however, that it was not wise to make a decision on the basis of sheer emotion, so she entered into a year's contract with herself to study and explore thoroughly the potential of occupational therapy in psychiatry. She clearly defined the procedures that she would follow to answer the question, "Is this all that there is to OT?" She decided that if at the end of a year she discovered that occupational therapy was no more than what was reflected in current practice, she would leave the field. During the following year she methodically attempted to find some rationale for what her 60 patients were doing and how the activities were or were not helpful. It was during this time that she conceived the idea of her activity analysis.

> Midway through my searches I was hooked and felt that at this time I could not pursue medical school or any other career. I had hold of this idea and I needed to see it through. It has been almost 40 years of seeing it through. (G. Fidler, personal communication, May 13, 1982)

During that year she also had the opportunity to know and learn from Dr. Alfred Noyes, a renowned psychiatrist and Superintendent of Norristown State Hospital. "It was a rare privilege to see this man in action and my commitment to psychiatry and to the pursuit of a rationale for occupational therapy was reconfirmed" (G. Fidler, personal communication, May 1, 1987).

Fidler wanted to pursue graduate education in occupational therapy, but at the time no such program existed. She enrolled in the graduate clinical psychology program at New York University, but withdrew after one semester because it was not relevant to the questions that she had nor to what she wanted to do. Several years later she enrolled in social work and discontinued that for similar reasons.

> Mainly my motivation has come from a very fundamental itch that began during that first year of inquiry. This thesis is that there has to be some relationship among what people do, their interests, how they occupy their time, their state of health, and their characteristic personality patterns. (G. Fidler, personal communication, May 13, 1982)

From 1944–1946 she worked as the Chief of Occupational Therapy at the Army Hospital at Fort Story in Virginia, and from 1946–1950 she was employed as a staff therapist at the Veterans' Hospital in Lyons, New Jersey. She furthered her education in psychiatry by attending the William Alanson White Institute of Psychiatry and Psychology in New York City from 1947–1951. It was during this time that she was significantly influenced by the work of Harry Stack Sullivan, particularly his interpersonal theory and hypotheses regarding ego development, self-esteem, and competence (1953). From 1952–1955 she was an instructor with the Pennsylvania Department of Mental Health Training Programs; in that capacity she assumed a major teaching and consultant role in implementing an ongoing series of training institutes for program staff throughout the Pennsylvania mental health system.

From 1955–1957 she was the coordinator of the AOTA Psychiatric Study Group, which was funded by an NIMH grant to examine, assess, and define the current concepts and practice of occupational therapy in psychiatry and to find ways to improve the preparation of future occupational therapists in this specialty area. This study culminated in the *Allenbury Workshop Conference on the Function and Preparation of the Psychiatric Occupational Therapist.* The proceedings of this workshop conference were published in the book, *Changing Concepts and Practices in Psychiatric Occupational Therapy,* which was edited by Wilma West (1959). Fidler served as one of the editorial consultants for this book.

During this period she also taught a summer session at the Philadelphia School of Occupational Therapy and lectured on occupational therapy theory in psychiatry at New York University. She served as Member-at-Large for the AOTA Board of Management from 1957–1963.

She next served as Director of Professional Education, Department of Occupational Therapy at the New York State Psychiatric Institute from 1959–1968. In that position Fidler developed and directed clinical field work study for occupational therapists and students; provided inservice education to physician residents, social workers, and nurses; supervised OT staff; initiated prevocational and work rehabilitation programs; developed patient evaluation and diagnostic measures; and collaborated with the sociology department to research and measure the nature and effect of change within institutional systems.

As director of the Activities Therapy Department at Hillside Hospital during the years from 1968–1971, Fidler was responsible for administration, coordination, and management of a staff consisting of occupational therapists, vocational counselors, therapeutic recreators, secondary school teachers, music and dance therapists, and volunteers. She designed and implemented new service programs for the day hospital, aftercare, and acute admission center. She served as liaison between the city school system and the school at Hillside Hospital and planned inservice education for teachers on working with the emotionally disturbed adolescent. She also developed undergraduate and graduate field work experiences with ten curricula and collaborated to develop a community outreach rehabilitation grant.

While working at the New York State Psychiatric Institute and Hillside Hospital, Fidler directed the master's degree program in psychiatric occupational therapy at New York University and Columbia. She also served as a consultant to several state and hospital programs. During this time her civic activities included involvement with the League of Women Voters, United Fund Council, Visiting Nurse Association Homemakers Program, Education Committee for Teachers and Parents, Plainfield Public Schools, and the Union County Aftercare Program.

From January 1971–1975, Fidler served as associate executive director of the AOTA, directing its practice, education, and research divisions. She wrote several grants that enabled AOTA to offer a series of training institutes for practitioners and educators. She was instrumental in obtaining a grant to support graduate traineeships, and she helped AOTA secure grants totaling over $500,000 to conduct several major studies.

From March 1975 to October of the same year, she was the interim executive director of the AOTA. In October 1975 she became coordinator of AOTA's Educator Training Institutes. She planned, organized, and implemented regional institutes for OT academic and clinical faculty from all of the professional and technical programs. These institutes focused on curriculum design, teaching methods, and competency-based learning.

During the 1970s and 1980s, Fidler continued her consultative services to several psychiatric hospitals where she planned and organized OT services and activity therapy programs and coordinated these services with vocational rehabilitation. The Department of Rehabilitation Services developed by her at Springfield Hospital Center in Maryland was subsequently used as a model for service delivery in mental health hospitals throughout the state.

From 1980–1982 she served as the Assistant Hospital Administrator for Programming at Greystone Park Psychiatric Hospital in New Jersey. Since 1980 she has been a consultant in curriculum development to the New York University Department of Occupational Therapy and in 1982 she was appointed Rehabilitation Consultant to the New Jersey Division of Mental Health Hospitals.

During Fidler's tenure as rehabilitation consultant, she developed and had approved state standards for rehabilitation programs in mental health facilities and agencies and established staffing standards and quality assurance monitoring.

In 1984 she was appointed chief executive officer of the Hagadorn Center for Geriatrics, a New Jersey state facility. In 1987 she completed a major reorganization of the Center from a long-term nursing care facility to a to a geropsychiatric rehabilitation center that would provide community-based day treatment and housing programs in order to sustain the elderly in the community. According to Fidler, "Hagadorn Center operates on those fundamental constructs of occupational therapy which emphasize and prioritize the meaning and value of human performance and the ability 'to do' as the quality of life and as characterizing health" (G. Fidler, personal communication, May 1, 1987).

Throughout her career, Fidler has displayed a strong dedication and enthusiasm for the education of the young professional. She introduced occupational therapists to supervision as a tutorial learning process and offered the first workshops in supervision at Columbia University in the 1950s. During the 1970s, she was a visiting professor at, University of California at San Jose, Kean College, University of Pennsylvania, and Boston University. She continues to teach and lecture on management, the meaning and uses of activities, group process, and program design.

Because of her firm commitment to the development of occupational therapy as a profession, Fidler has been very active in professional activities from the beginning of her career. She has chaired numerous task forces within AOTA and has served on many of its committees. She has also served on the board of directors of the AOTF and on the advisory board of the *American Journal of Occupational Therapy*.

Fidler is also a member of a number of professional organizations. She has served on the Advisory Board of Kean College, on the Board of the Coalition for the Reform of the New Jersey Mental Health System, and on the Board of Directors of the Union County Mental Health Association and its Professional Advisory Committee. She was also a member of the New Jersey Rehabilitation Committee and was the Chair of the Monitoring Committee in the Office of the Public Advocate for the State of New Jersey.

Fidler's work has been recognized by the profession. She was the AOTA Eleanor Clarke Slagle Lecturer in 1965 and received the AOTA Award of Merit in 1980. She is also a Fellow of the AOTA.

Fidler has written many articles and one book and co-authored two books with her husband, Jay Fidler. She continues to give presentations, institutes, and workshops.

Fidler is the mother of two children, a daughter Dagny, and a son Eric, and is the wife of psychiatrist Jay Fidler. She resides in New Jersey.

Fidler believes that some of the obstacles to theory development in occupational therapy stem from the profession's minority position in the health care system and its subsequent difficulty in influencing the medical model of human functioning with its own concepts and constructs.

> I've always said that what we really have to deal with is double

> indemnity. What we theorize and practice is not in the top priority of the medical and health care delivery system structure. It is so "mundane" and seemingly obvious that it carries very little glamour, and it is hard to convince people of the value of something that is part of their everyday life. It is hard to maintain one's professional self-respect when references are continually made to psychology, the psychiatrist, the nurse, the social worker and "others." I was an "and others" for so long it became difficult to maintain a level of ego strength and self-respect in the practice arena. (G. Fidler, personal communication, May 13, 1982)

Any success or contributions that she made were often credited to her personally, rather than to the profession. This angered her, because she experienced it as a criticism of the profession.

According to Fidler, another barrier to the development of the OT profession is attitudes about its predominantly female composition, which tend to perpetuate its minority status and is the other half of the "double indemnity" concept.

> We are many times our own worst enemy and there is a critical need to develop more assertive behaviors and attitudes among our members. We need to state what we do, write it, and publicize it. We need to educate and socialize students into professional behaviors, rather than reinforcing female stereotypical behaviors. (G. Fidler, personal communication, May 13, 1982)

She sees the need to recruit young, bright, and ambitious women and men and to stimulate them by providing an assertive career role model within the profession.

Because occupational therapy is a very complex profession, Fidler believes that a master's degree should be a prerequisite for entry-level positions in the field. To understand the constructs of the art and science of the field requires a longer term of educational socialization than is provided by the baccalaureate programs. Other bona fide professions are built on graduate level work, and their entry into practice is at the graduate level (G. Fidler, personal communication, May 13, 1982).

Her future goals for her theory development are to reach a sophisticated understanding of the nonhuman environment and nonhuman objects, the complex process of engagement with and manipulation of the environment, and the "doing" process as a facilitative process. She encourages occupational therapists to go out into the community and create environments that are less stressful and more supportive of the individual. She is convinced that our future is dependent on fuller development of these constructs through doctoral and postdoctoral studies and research.

> Being at the beginning of the development of a profession is both exciting and scary. It means admitting that there is much that we cannot know, and acknowledging that many years of arduous development of research and of educational preparation of the professional occupational therapist may be required. I really believe that it is going to take as many years to begin to move toward realizing this potential and generating a knowledge base as it has taken medicine and law. But search and discovery are incredibly exciting. (G. Fidler, personal communication, May 1982)

Fidler is disturbed by the devaluation of activities in OT practice and their replacement with "talking groups" in mental health and with physical therapy modalities in physical dysfunction. She feels that the mimicking of other professions brings the field very close to losing what is essential and critical to occupational therapy (G. Fidler, personal communication, May 13, 1982).

On the other side of the ledger, balancing out the obstacles to her work in occupational therapy is the support she has received from others in and outside the profession.

> I was indeed fortunate to have been able to work with and learn from so many very talented and famous persons in the field of psychiatry, such as Nathaniel Apter, Elvin Semiad, Alfred Noyes, and Lawrence Kolb. Another strong incentive has been the positive, challenging responses of the many young, bright occupational therapists with whom I've been privileged to work. Certainly the most positive force has been the interest and support of my husband. He has continued to be my finest advocate, teacher, and friend. (G. Fidler, personal communication, September 24, 1984)

She stated that many persons influenced her thinking and motivation (G. Fidler, personal communication, May 1, 1987). She credits her father with teaching her the values and attitudes of critical thinking and creative and logical problem solving. He taught her to understand that only she can be responsible for herself. Her husband, Jay Fidler, immeasurably shaped her thinking, sparked her motivation and "clarified realities with loving care" (G. Fidler, personal communication, May 1, 1987). She credits Helen Willard with teaching her about "integrity and dignity without ever once threatening the spontaneous fun in me." She mentions Elizabeth

Ridgway, whose understanding and sensitivity about the schizophrenic patient impressed her and taught her so much.

Fidler describes her current viewpoint on occupational therapy.

> I have not become disenchanted nor have I had any questions about the fundamental concept of OT. The longer I have looked and worked with it, the more convinced I am that there is a credibility and relevance to this perspective of human functioning that is unique and different from any other perspectives about human behavior. I have no question about that. I *do* have a question about how we pursue development and how we do not pursue it. (G. Fidler, personal communication, September 24, 1984)

This last statement is of great concern to her. She feels that the fundamental concept underlying occupational therapy is a viable one and that if the profession does not develop it and use it, other professions will.

THEORETICAL CONCEPTS

Since she entered the field of occupational therapy in 1942, Gail Fidler has consistently believed that purposeful planned activity is the very core of the OT therapeutic process. Although her theories were derived from psychoanalytic concepts and during the first half of her career were mainly applicable to psychosocial function and dysfunction, she has continued to expand them to include new knowledge and developments in related basic and applied sciences and in occupational therapy. Likewise, she has influenced the development of other theories and theorists, such as Anne Mosey.

Currently her theory concerning activity addresses the physical, neurobehavioral, cognitive, psychological, and sociocultural aspects of the individual and how purposeful activity and objects in the human and nonhuman environment might best match the needs of the individual. She believes that the meaning of activities cannot be reduced to one or two factors, but instead interact with each other at many levels. The following subsections examine these factors and their hypothesized relationships.

Nonhuman Environment and Object Relations

Searles' (1960) work on the human and nonhuman environment strongly supported Fidler's early formulations of the meaning of activity. They described how persons develop object relationships with the nonhuman environment from infancy through adulthood. These interactions serve many functions. Symbolically and realistically, they are a means of communicating feelings, needs, and ideations; they mediate between the inner and outer world; and they also help one achieve a sense of self. One uses object relations to differentiate self from oneself and to learn more about both. The nonhuman environment is a source of need gratification. Ego functions are developed and strengthened by realistic encounters with objects.

Object relations and their symbolic meaning and unconscious processes (Azima, 1961; Azima & Azima, 1959; Wittkower & Azima, 1958) are key elements of Fidler's early theories. She outlined procedures for evaluating and measuring clients' responses to objects, which included responses to the therapist, the activity, and the group. Such responses provide diagnostic information regarding clients' basic needs, if and how these are being gratified, and their development of adequate ego defenses and strengths. Since this initial formulation, little has been done to develop or define these constructs and concepts further in OT evaluation and treatment. This is of great concern to Fidler (Fidler & Fidler, 1954, 1963).

Communication Process

Another purpose of activity is to express thoughts and feelings nonverbally. "Occupational therapy is in effect another language for communication with the patient" (Fidler & Fidler, 1963, p. vi). In their 1954 and 1963 texts, Gail and Jay Fidler describe some of the characteristics of this language as an expression of needs, attitudes, and emotion and explain their reasoning behind this application. "As a communication process occupational therapy is concerned with action, the meaning of action, its use in communicating feelings and thoughts, and the use of such nonverbal communication for the benefit of the patient" (Fidler & Fidler, 1963, p. 19).

Action of the patient involved in occupational therapy is more likely to reveal the unconscious. The therapist will use things such as uncovering, supporting, or directing to help the patient to communicate (Fidler & Fidler, 1963).

Activity Analysis

A central theme of Fidler's work throughout her career has been the analysis of the components of activities and the correlation of these components with the specific needs, interests, and abilities of the client in order to provide action-oriented learning experiences to facilitate needed skill acquisition. Her early activity analysis (Fidler, 1948; Fidler & Fidler, 1954, 1963) focused mainly on the psychodynamic properties of activities as a guide for the therapist in evaluation and treatment. Motion, procedures, materials, creativity, symbols, hostile and aggressive components, control, predictability, narcissism, sexual identification, dependence, reality testing, and group relatedness are examined because she felt that these factors provide valuable clues to what emotional needs and drives might be encouraged by particular activities. Activities should be selected that correlate with the specific needs of the client, and then the performance of those activities should be controlled and guided in order to increase their therapeutic value.

Subsequently, she expanded the analysis of activities to include motor, sensory integrative, psychological, sociocultural, cognitive, and interpersonal skills (Fidler, 1958, 1981a, 1982a). Activities need to be matched to the individual's readiness to learn or to receive stimuli, to personal characteristics, to interests and abilities, and to sociocultural values and norms. The real and symbolic meanings of activities used to promote acquisition of these essential skills also need to be explored (1981a). This concept is further developed in the Fidlers' constructs of "doing" (Fidler & Fidler 1978).

Doing

The Fidlers (Fidler & Fidler, 1978) use the term "doing" to connote performing, producing, or causing purposeful action in order to (1) test a skill, (2) clarify a relationship, or (3) create an end product. The process of doing enables the development and integration of the sensory, motor, cognitive, and psychological systems; is a socializing agent; and verifies one's efficacy as a competent contributing member of one's society. Thus, the occupational therapist uses doing to enable patients to learn the performance skills that they will need to care for and maintain themselves more independently, to satisfy their personal needs for intrinsic gratification, and to contribute to meeting the needs and welfare of others within an appropriate cultural context.

At any given point in time, the level and type of performance skills and the balance among them are determined by the individual's age, developmental level, unique biology, and culture. The balance among these skill clusters is critical to a lifestyle that is health sustaining and satisfying to oneself and to significant others (Fidler & Fidler, 1978).

According to the Fidlers (Fidler & Fidler, 1978), the acquisition of skills needed to perform one's life tasks and roles is influenced both by factors in the external environment and by internal systems. Such variables as culture, economics, family constellation, social class, housing, geographical surroundings, and architectural structures affect the external environment. They can inhibit or facilitate performance skill development.

Internal systems refer to the individual's unique biology; that is, his or her sensory, motor, physical, cognitive, and psychological systems. Maturational or developmental delays or deficits caused by trauma affect these systems and thereby influence the development of performance skills learning (Fidler & Fidler, 1978).

Competence and Mastery

Fidler's hypotheses concerning the relationship of purposeful activity to competence were influenced by the works of Sullivan (1953), Arieti (1962), White (1959, 1971), and other ego psychologists who proposed that there is an innate drive to master and explore the environment, which results in survival and a sense of competence from direct successful encounters with it. The reward is intrinsic, and reinforcement from others is not necessary. Fidler (1981a), Fidler & Fidler (1983) suggests that the more masteries one has, the stronger is one's sense of competence. Each success then reinforces more attempts to develop skills and competencies further. Thus, "doing" facilitates one's sense of competence and efficacy by creating experiences with human and nonhuman objects in one's environment. One learns about one's potential and limitations through these direct, action-oriented experiences.

Fidler (1981a) believes that the profession of occupational therapy must work to relate competence, mastery, adaptation, and self-esteem to OT practice. She views competence, mastery, achievement, self-esteem, self-value, and self-worth as interrelated states that are derived from direct encounters with and successful management of elements in the environment. When each of these experiences is verified both by the resulting intrinsic gratification and positive feedback from significant others, one's value is enhanced (1981a, 1981b). Fidler emphasizes that the feedback that one receives from the process of doing is essential to learning about the realities of the self and the world. People learn about reality and test their perception of reality from predictable learned interactions with it (1981a), Fidler & Fidler (1983). Until one acts on an idea or thought there can be no distinction between reality and nonreality. It is necessary to test one's ideas and thoughts through action in order to ascertain their validity, efficacy, and relevance to one's life.

Fidler (Fidler & Fidler, 1978) considers the social feedback from doing to be important because it provides consensual validation of masteries and competencies by their value to others. Another hypothesis that she offers is germane to the meaning and use of activities and their social relevance. That is, the values and norms of a society place higher status on certain tasks and activities than on others. Some activities may have high social significance and priority, whereas others may be less important or even be seen as having negative significance or value (Fidler, 1981a). Thus, when one successfully performs an activity valued by society, one's sense of esteem and value as a human being are enhanced. Likewise, when one senses a risk of failure, doing in the presence of others is threatening and may be inhibited. Activities that are not valued by society may adversely affect one's sense of worth and competence (Fidler & Fidler, 1983).

Her advocacy of the use of task groups in occupational therapy is based on the hypothesis that the task selected within a group context will meet the social, developmental, and learning needs of the participants by providing feedback on the efficacy of the action within sociocultural norms. By working within the context of a task group, the patient has a chance to learn constructive and rewarding behavior patterns. Opportunities arise for the development of several different roles, and a variety of individual needs can be met simultaneously (Fidler, 1969). The client learns to use his or her existing integrative assets and capacities to develop and improve skills necessary for the assumption of successful economic and social roles in everyday life outside the hospital. Age-appropriate social skill development is a critical component of performance and is facilitated or impaired by factors in both the external environment and by internal processes.

Integrative Process

Gail Fidler (1982a) hypothesizes that activities are an integral part of human development, represent real-life situations, and are valuable and realistic vehicles to use to acquire or redevelop skills necessary to fulfill life roles and to provide a source of satisfaction. The acquisition of these functional skills is a developmental process and progresses in a hierarchical manner. Certain behaviors are prerequisite to more mature and complex performance skills.

Specific actions of an activity or task elicit distinguishable and measurable sensory integrative, motor, cognitive, psychological, and social behaviors. When these are matched with the individual's needs and capacities, opportunities are provided to learn skills and develop more functional abilities in sensorimotor integration, self-maintenance, task behaviors, and leisure skills. Thus, by engaging in purposeful activity, the development and in-n of internal sensory, motor, cognitive, and psychological process are facilitated (1982a).

Health and Illness

Health is viewed as the ability to perform those roles and tasks of living throughout the life cycle that are essential to care for and to maintain the self in an independent manner, satisfy one's personal needs and thus provide intrinsic gratification, and contribute to the needs and welfare of others within a socially and age-appropriate context (Fidler, 1981a, 1981b, 1982a; Fidler & Fidler, 1978, 1983). A sense of competence and social efficacy is basic to the ability to cope and adapt. This sense of the self as competent is largely achieved through successful doing experiences that carry social value and indicate mastery and achievement.

Dysfunction results when physical, social, cognitive, and/or psychosocial problems or trauma impede development and/or impair functions and adaptations that are fundamental to daily living skills for self-maintenance, work, and leisure (Fidler, 1984; Fidler & Fidler, 1978, 1983).

APPLICATION TO OCCUPATIONAL THERAPY PRACTICE

Fidler's theories and hypotheses were derived from and directed toward clinical practice. She developed several assessment tools to explore the meaning and use of activities and the nature and quality of the processes in occupational therapy. Her initial contribution was the "Activity Analysis," which was created to examine the psychodynamics of activity (Fidler, 1948; Fidler & Fidler, 1963). Fidler wrote that a thorough understanding of each component of the OT experience was essential to become more skilled in its use. "We believe that the nature or characteristics of the action experience are of primary importance. Involvement in an activity can be either therapeutic or damaging to the patient" (Fidler & Fidler, 1963, pp. 72–73). The purpose of this activity analysis was to guide one toward an understanding of the basic and fundamental psychodynamic characteristics of a selected activity.

Assessment

Her "Outline for Evaluation" (Fidler & Fidler, 1963, pp. 104–107) guides the therapist by raising questions about the psychodynamics manifested by the patient in relationship to the therapist, activity, and group. It is psychoanalytically oriented, as was most of her work until the early 1970s.

Her "Diagnostic Battery" (Fidler, 1968) is made up of a drawing, a finger painting, and a clay sculpture. The client is asked to comment on each production after it is completed. The productions and responses are interpreted and used in total treatment team planning.

In 1965, she further refined this tool, adapting it for use within a group context. This instrument, the "Activity Laboratory" (Fidler, 1982a, pp. 195–207), has been used since 1965 with a wide variety of clients, with numerous students, and with interdisciplinary staffs. During that time, it has undergone many refinements to enable its tasks to elicit important areas of skill components and performance more effectively. Fidler does not propose that this be the only instrument used for evaluation to determine treatment planning. Rather, it is intended to be used as an "initial tentative behavioral profile" (Fidler, 1982a, p. 196). It also explores how strengths and characteristic styles of organizing and responding can be capitalized on in treatment intervention. How the individual handles the five tasks in the "Activity Laboratory" indicates his or her predominant sensory, motor, cognitive, psychological, and social behavior needs.

In collaboration with Susan Fine in 1970, she developed the "Object History" (unpublished manuscript) to help people learn about and understand the importance of objects. Fidler feels that every occupational therapist should complete an "Object History" as part of his or her education. This instrument provides a descriptive account of the ways in which certain nonhuman objects are significantly linked with phases of an individual's growth and development. The participant selects an object that has had or continues to have special meaning during a particular part of his or her life. Objects might be toys, animals, household items, nature objects, clothing, or food. The participant is then asked to describe the object, identify how it came to be his or hers, how it was used, its meaning and importance, how family and friends were aware of or involved with the object, and how the object relationship was ended (Activity workshop, Galveston, Texas, September 22–23, 1983).

Her "Play History" (1971, unpublished manuscript) is intended to develop an individual's appreciation for cultural and sexual differences in one's play history and to help him or her understand better the real and symbolic meanings of these activities. The person is asked to identify and briefly describe those games or activities in which he or she engaged during the childhood and adolescent years. Next, the individual is asked to identify who taught him or her the game, what was the most enjoyable aspect of the game, with whom it was most frequently shared, and the extent to which it was part of his or her family's culture. Next, the person describes the specific practice and/or learning that the game provided in such areas as sensory/perceptual, motor, self-identity, reality orientation, cognitive, dyadic, and group skills. Aspects felt to be most and least enjoyable are then explored. The next section examines the strategies involved, the game's aesthetic elements, and the role played by chance in determining the game's outcome. Competitive elements, and the game's symbolic, creative, structured, and unstructured properties are analyzed. Three hobbies or activities that are an important part of the individual's present lifestyle are then identified and compared with those from earlier years. These are then compared to one's present job or career choice (Activity workshop, Galveston, Texas, September 22–23, 1983).

More recently, Fidler developed "The Lifestyle Performance Profile" (1982b, pp. 43–48) as part of a conceptual model that describes adaptive performance as a fundamental concern of OT practice that builds on her concepts of "doing" and competence. According to Fidler, OT practice is primarily concerned with skill development and the achievement of a satisfying, health-sustaining lifestyle. To achieve those goals, one has to evaluate the individual's existing strengths and skill deficits, developmental levels, and external barriers and resources (Fidler, 1982b, pp. 43–48). The "Lifestyle Performance Profile" provides a structure to identify and organize the person's sensorimotor functions and cognitive, psychological, dyadic, and group social skills within the context of his or her sociocultural milieu and characteristic response patterns and management of life tasks. It also describes sociocultural and environmental resources that support skill development and those external forces that interfere and impede it. The therapist must assess what work, play, and self-care activities are required of this individual in his or her given environment and which of these are intact or dysfunctional. This information may be obtained from existing records, interviews, standardized tests, and observation of the patient in specifically planned tasks and activities that involve sensorimotor, cognitive, and social behaviors.

Patient evaluations and assessments are fundamental means of providing data needed to plan and set priorities among treatment goals, to measure progress, and to plan for discharge. From the evaluation and assessment information, the therapist obtains an overview of the patient's strengths and deficits in managing the everyday tasks of his or her world and of performance patterns and related functional deficits that impair coping and adaptation (Fidler, 1984, pp. 33–36).

Intervention

Fidler's early theories about intervention and application were derived mainly from a psychoanalytical frame of reference. According to that perspective, the occupational therapist is a valuable member of the psychotherapeutic process because of her or his use of the combination of activities, the dyadic relationship, and groups. Specific treatment guidelines, rationale, and case histories were described in several publications (Fidler, 1958; Fidler & Fidler, 1954, 1963, 1978). The Fidlers felt, and still feel, that nonverbal techniques, the use of objects, and object relationships are very effective treatment methods to incorporate into the total treatment regimen for many patients.

In their second book the Fidlers (1963) developed these concepts further, describing occupational therapy as a communication process in terms of the action itself, objects used in the action process, and the end products of those actions and interpersonal relationships. The therapeutic process, goals, and case examples are described in that book as consistent with the psychodynamic theoretical constructs described earlier in this chapter.

The idea of the dyadic or therapeutic relationship (discussed as therapeutic use of self by Fidler) is based on Harry Stack Sullivan's work on interpersonal theory (1953). Therapeutic use of self involves the therapist using actions that will be helpful to the patient. According to the Fidlers, "the problem in therapy is to anticipate the degree and type of response that will help the patient" (Fidler & Fidler, 1963, p. 41).

Group phenomena in occupational therapy are an essential part of intervention. The group leader is responsible for the emotional atmosphere of the group. He or she sets the tone and the expectations for group behavior. Important social roles and behaviors are learned in the context of task-oriented group activity (Fidler, 1969; Fidler & Fidler, 1963).

Fidler's conceptualization of the rehabilitative process is built on her theories of meanings, both real and symbolic, of activity, and of involvement with objects. Activities are used to explore and express the unconscious, provide gratification of needs, teach adaptive ego defenses and functional skills, provide a base for reality testing, and explore interpersonal relationships (Fidler, 1948, 1957, 1966; Fidler & Fidler, 1963; Ridgway & Fidler, 1955). Activities may also be used to sustain and protect intact functions and abilities and to prevent further disability. The therapist selects those that provide experiences that enable the individual to use existing interests and skills for personal growth, to experience intrinsic gratification, and to meet needs for acceptance, achievement, creativity, autonomy, and social relationships. Activities and tasks are also chosen that will promote and enhance work skills and habits and teach and encourage independent functioning in activities of daily living. The therapist also introduces new activities that will provide compensatory learning and practice for the skills the patient needs to assume for his or her roles in community life. The individual is able to develop new interests and explore potentials because of his or her new experiences with activities. The client comes to see himself or herself as the doer, and the end product is tangible evidence of his or her ability to achieve (Fidler, 1981a).

As the Fidlers developed their theory further to include new developments in the art and science of occupational therapy, more implications for practice emerged. Purposeful activity is an organizing construct for practice and the distinguishing characteristic of occupational therapy (Fidler, 1981b). Purposeful activity, as expanded into concepts of "doing" and competence, became an essential link in the treatment process. They moved from the term "treatment" because it connoted changing and altering pathology and preferred the terms of "habilitation" or "remediation" (Activity workshop, Galveston, Texas, September 22–23, 1983).

When pathology is identified, doing must be used in the service of personality integration via performance skill development and reinforcement with treatment modalities that are adaptive and relevant to the performance skill demands and expectations of the home setting. An understanding of the nature and complexity of these performance skills and their interrelationship with internal and external processes is required. These skills are needed to enable one to feel that one is a productive, contributing, and needed member of society. (Activity workshop, Galveston, Texas, September 22–23, 1983).

Action is directed toward (1) testing a skill, (2) clarifying a relationship, or (3) creating an end product. As discussed earlier, activities and doing experiences must be analyzed and matched to the individual's developmental needs and skill readiness in motor, sensorimotor integration, cognitive, pyschological, and interpersonal components as is relevant and significant to the needs and values of the person's sociocultural group and as is satisfying to the self (Fidler & Fidler, 1983, pp. 267–280). The fit between the individual and an activity is crucial if (1) integration of these systems and an adaptive response are to occur and (2) if choices of leisure, work, and self-maintenance activities are to result in intrinsic gratification, pleasure, and social efficacy of the individual (Fidler & Fidler, 1978).

Fidler wrote *Design of Rehabilitation Services in Psychiatric Hospital Settings* (1984) as a result of her work as a consultant with the Mental Hygiene Administration of the Maryland State Department of Health and Mental Hygiene at Springfield Hospital Center and at Greystone Park Psychiatric Hospital in New Jersey. The book is a comprehensive guide to program design of rehabilitation services primarily for public psychiatric hospitals, but it is also relevant to private hospitals and community mental health centers. It shows how rehabilitation services can be integrated into the program of a psychiatric hospital by describing policies and procedures for rehabilitation services, clarifying the rationale and focus of the program design, and giving guidelines for practice and administration of a rehabilitation program. The goal of rehabilitation services is to develop and support functional skills that patients need to perform basic everyday living tasks and social roles as independently as possible so that they can cope with their environmental demands in ways that are satisfying to themselves and to significant others. Fidler describes in detail how to organize a number of specialized services to achieve this goal, focusing on program principles, staffing and supervisory patterns, referral guidelines, evaluations and assessments, programs evaluation, budget, planning, and task and activity group programs and protocols.

APPLICATION TO THE OCCUPATIONAL THERAPY PROFESSION

Fidler has posed many hypotheses and raised numerous questions about OT.

> I have always believed that defining the question and pursuing the question is far more important than coming up with an answer. The writing that I have done has pushed for clarifying the question because I think that once the question is clarified, this will inevitably lead to answers. (G. Fidler, personal communication, May 13, 1982)

She has spent most of her professional life pursuing these questions through her writings, grants, workshops, seminars, and clinical and educational activities. She has taught and challenged others to clarify and search out the questions and answers. She has affected the practice and education of occupational therapists in their everyday activities, as well as the work of other theorists by her relentless search for the meaning of activities and their application in occupational therapy. With her husband she wrote the first major texts for occupational therapists in psychiatric settings. For almost 20 years these works remained as the only texts. She educated therapists about object relationships and developed several assessment tools and guides for treatment planning. Her conceptualization of doing further supported the importance of activities as therapeutic agents and their relationship to competence, mastery, self-worth, and achievement.

The many questions raised by Fidler about the OT process and the nature of purposeful activity have been the subject of very little subsequent research. She wrote:

> To date, there has been very little effort to study activities with a standardizing process to list the most common types of response.

> It is possible to give people a variety of activities and have them express their subjective experience while they are involved in the activity. (Fidler & Fidler, 1963, p. 36)

She urged that research be done with many people in a variety of settings as she has been doing with her "Activity Laboratory" since 1965.

Each of Fidler's many hypotheses regarding doing are awaiting validation through further research and empirical testing. Each construct and theory of "doing" needs to be translated into researchable questions and hypotheses and systematically developed and pursued. "There is a need to pursue investigation into the neurologic, perceptual, and social components of action in relation to mental health" (Fidler & Fidler, 1983, p. 273).

One hallmark of a good theory is that it is flexible enough and internally consistent so that it can allow new information to be incorporated into it. Fidler has consistently incorporated new information into her theories and consistently expanded them to include a more comprehensive view of occupational therapy.

Another feature of a good theory is that it enables one to organize phenomena and make predictions. Fidler's work has provided a structure for conceptualizing the OT process that has many direct applications to practice. What is needed is empirical testing of these hypotheses and constructs. Such research will be long term and will require many investigators to do empirical work and replication. Each study will need to focus on only a small part of Fidler's theories. Yet, the gratification from such a task is long term and builds upon itself and the work of others. It is essential to test hypotheses generated by her work and the predictions of her theory to measure its significance.

REFERENCES

American Occupational Therapy Association. (1958). *The objectives and functions of occupational therapy.* Dubuque, IA: William Brown.

Arieti, S. (1962). Psychotherapy of schizophrenia. *Archives of General Psychiatry, 6,* 232–239.

Azima, H. (1961). Dynamic occupational therapy. *Diseases of the Nervous System Monograph Supplement, 22,* 138–142.

Azima, H., & Azima, F. (1959). Outline of a dynamic theory of occupational therapy. *American Journal of Occupational Therapy, 13,* 215–221.

Fidler, G.S. (1948). Psychological evaluation of occupational therapy activities. *American Journal of Occupational Therapy, 2,* 284–287.

Fidler, G.S. (1957). The role of occupational therapy in a multidisciplinary approach to chronic illness. *American Journal of Occupational Therapy, 11,* 8–12.

Fidler, G.S. (1958). Some unique contributions of occupational therapy in the treatment of a schizophrenic. *American Journal of Occupational Therapy, 12,* 9–12.

Fidler, G.S. (1966). A second look at work as a primary force in rehabilitation. *American Journal of Occupational Therapy, 20,* 72–74.

Fidler, G.S. (1968). Diagnostic battery-scoring and summary. In *Final report* (Rehabilitation Services Administration Grant No. 123-T-68 for Field Consultant in Psychiatric Rehabilitation). Washington, DC: U.S. Government Printing Office.

Fidler, G.S. (1969). The task-oriented group as a context for treatment. *American Journal of Occupational Therapy, 23,* 43–48.

Fidler, G.S. (1981a). From crafts to competence. *American Journal of Occupational Therapy, 35,* 567–573.

Fidler, G.S. (1981b). *Overview of occupational therapy in mental health.* Prepared by the American Occupational Therapy Task Group of the American Psychiatric Association on Psychiatric Therapies.

Fidler, G.S. (1982a). The activity laboratory: A structure for observing and assessing perceptual, integrative, and behavioral strategies. In B. Hemphill (Ed.), *The Evaluation Process in Psychiatric Occupational Therapy* (pp. 195–207). Thorofare, NJ: Charles B. Slack.

Fidler, G.S. (1982b). The lifestyle performance profile: An organizing frame. In B. Hemphill (Ed.), *The Evaluation Process in Psychiatric Occupational Therapy* (pp. 43–47). Thorofare NJ: Charles B. Slack.

Fidler, G.S. (1984). *The design of rehabilitation services in psychiatric hospital settings.* Laurel, MD: Ramsco.

Fidler, G.S., & Fidler, J.W. (1954). *Introduction to psychiatric occupational therapy.* New York: Macmillan.

Fidler, G.S., & Fidler, J.W. (1963). *Occupational therapy: A communication process in psychiatry.* New York: Macmillan.

Fidler, G.S., & Fidler, J.W. (1978). Doing and becoming: Purposeful action and self-actualization. *American Journal of Occupational Therapy, 32,* 305–310.

Fidler, G.S., & Fidler, J. W. (1983). Doing and becoming: The occupational therapy experience. In G. Kielhofner (Ed.), *Health through occupation: Theory and practice in occupational therapy,* (pp. 267–279). Philadelphia: F.A. Davis.

Fidler, G.S., & Fine, S.B. (1962). The occupational therapist and psychotherapy. In *Transitional programs in psychiatric occupational therapy.* Dubuque, IA: William Brown.

Ridgway, E.P., & Fidler, G.S., (1955). Occupational therapy: Laboratory for living. *Mental Health Views, 3,* (3).

Searles, H. (1960). *The nonhuman environment.* New York: International University Press.

Sullivan, H.S. (1953). *The interpersonal theory of psychiatry.* New York: W.W. Norton.

West, W.L. (Ed.). (1959). *Changing concepts and practices in psychiatric occupational therapy.* New York: American Occupational Therapy Association.

White, R.W. (1959). Motivation reconsidered: The concept of competence. *Psychiatric Review, 66,* 297.

White, R.W. (1971). The urge toward competence. *American Journal of Occupational Therapy, 25,* 271–274.

Wittkower, E.D., & Azima, H. (1958). Dynamic aspects of occupational therapy. *Archives of Neurology and Psychiatry, 79,* 706–710.

BIBLIOGRAPHY

1948

Fidler, G.S. (1948). Psychological evaluation of occupational therapy activities. *American Journal of Occupational therapy, 1,* 284–287.

1953

Fidler, G.S. (1953). Comments on a study of a task directed and a free choice group. *American Journal of Occupational Therapy, 7,* 124, 130.

1954

Fidler, G.S., & Fidler, J.W. (1954). *Introduction to psychiatric occupational therapy.* New York: Macmillan.

1955

Ridgway, E., & Fidler, G.S. (1955). Occupational therapy: Laboratory for living. *Mental Health Views, 3* (3).

1957

Fidler, G.S. (1957). The role of occupational therapy in a multidisciplinary approach to chronic illness. *American Journal of Occupational Therapy, 11,* 8–12.

1958

Fidler, G.S. (1958). Some unique contributions of occupational therapy in the treatment of the schizophrenic. *American Journal of Occupational Therapy, 12,* 9–12.

1962

Fidler, G.S., & Fine, S.B. (1962). The occupational therapist and psychotherapy. In *Transitional programs in psychiatric occupational therapy* (pp. 14–20). Dubuque, IA: William Brown.

1963

Fidler, G.S. (1963). Educational experiences for the occupational therapist. *Journal of the South African Occupational Therapy Association.*

Fidler G.S., & Fidler, J.W. (1963). *Occupational therapy: A communication process in psychiatry.* New York: Macmillan.

1964

Fidler, G.S. (1964). A guide to planning and measuring growth experience in the clinical affiliation. *American Journal of Occupational Therapy, 18,* 240–243.

1966

Fidler, G.S. Learning as a growth process: A conceptual framework for professional education. *American Journal of Occupational Therapy, 20,* 1–8.

Fidler, G.S. (1966). A second look at work as a primary force in rehabilitation. *American Journal of Occupational Therapy, 20,* 72–74.

1968

Fidler, G.S. (1968). Diagnostic battery-scoring and summary. In *Final report* (Rehabilitation Services Administration Grant No. 123-T-68 for Field Consultant in Psychiatric Rehabilitation). Washington, DC: U.S. Government Printing Office.

Fidler, G.S. (1968). The task-oriented groups as a context for treatment. In *Final report* (Rehabilitation services administration Grant No. 123-T-68 for Field Consultant in Psychiatric Rehabilitation). Washington, DC: U.S. Government Printing Office.

1969

Fidler, G.S. (1969). The task-oriented group as a context for treatment. *American Journal of Occupational Therapy, 23,* 43–48.

1970

Fidler, G.S., & Fine, S.B. (1970). Object history. Unpublished manuscript.

1971

Fidler, G.S. (1971). Play/activity history. Unpublished manuscript.

1977

Fidler, G.S. (1977). From plea to mandate. *American Journal of Occupational Therapy, 31,* 653.

1978

Fidler, G.S., & Fidler, J.W. (1978). Doing and becoming: Purposeful action and self-actualization. *American Journal of Occupational Therapy, 32,* 305–310.

Fidler, G.S. (1978, November). Professional or non-professional. In *Occupational Therapy: 2001 AD.* Rockville, MD: American Occupational Therapy Association.

1979

Fidler, G.S. (1979). Specialization. *American Journal of Occupational Therapy, 33,* 34.

1981

Fidler, G.S. (1981). From crafts to competence. *American Journal of Occupational Therapy, 35,* 567–573.

Fidler, G.S. (1981). *Overview of occupational therapy in mental health.* Prepared by the American Occupational Therapy Task Group of the American Psychiatric Association on Psychiatric Therapies.

1982

Fidler, G.S. (1982). The activity laboratory: A structure for observing and assessing perceptual, integrative, and behavioral strategies. In B. Hemphill (Ed.), *The Evaluation Process in Psychiatric Occupational Therapy* (pp. 195–207). Thorofare, NJ: Charles B. Slack.

Fidler, G.S. (1982). The lifestyle performance profile: An organizing frame. In B. Hemphill (Ed.), *The evaluative process in psychiatric occupational therapy* (pp. 43–48). Thorofare, NJ: Charles B. Slack.

1983

Fidler, G.S., & Fidler, J.W. (1983). Doing and becoming: The occupational therapy experience. In G. Kielhofner (Ed.), *Health through occupation: Theory and practice in occupational therapy* (pp. 267–280). Philadelphia: F.A. Davis.

1984

Fidler, G.S. (1984). *The design of rehabilitation services in psychiatric hospital settings.* Laurel, MD: Ramsco.

Chapter Three

Anne Cronin Mosey

Ferol Menks Ludwig

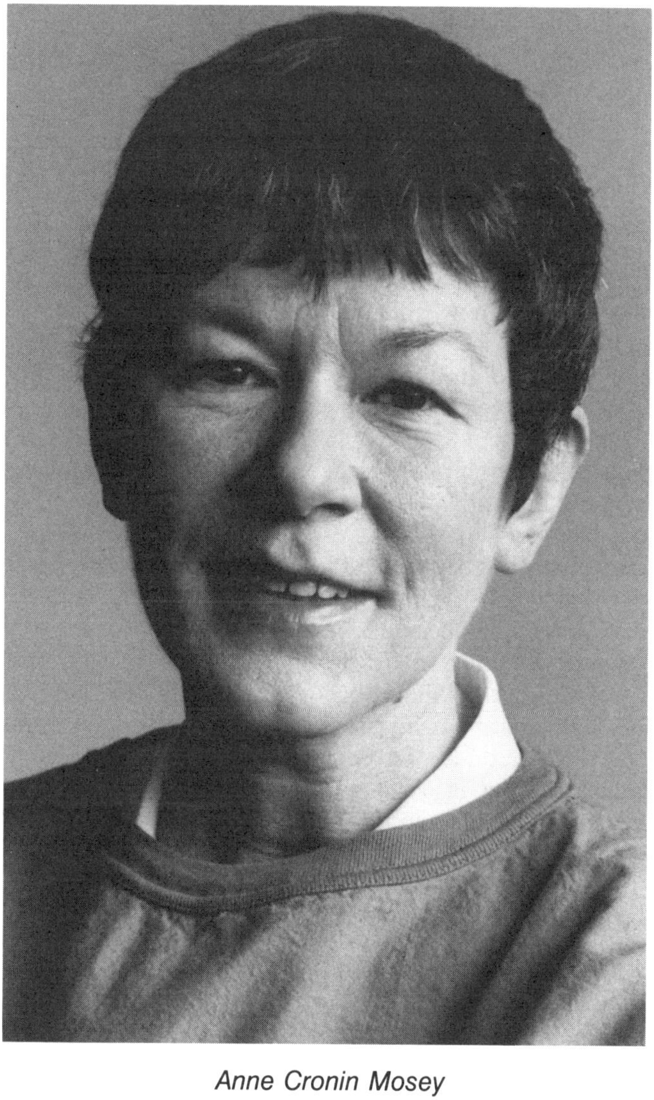

Anne Cronin Mosey

BIOGRAPHICAL SKETCH

Anne Cronin Mosey was born in 1938, and was raised in Minneapolis, Minnesota. She is the third of seven children. As a child, she read extensively, helped with cooking for nine people and had long talks with her father about the state of the world. She stated that "life picked up" when she discovered boys and she began to date (A. C. Mosey, personal communication, August 4, 1985).

On graduation from high school, she attended the University of Minnesota where she pursued a double major in sociology and psychology. Her Irish family background did not permit young ladies to work, so during the summer of her junior year she did volunteer work at the Veteran's Hospital in Minneapolis. On the suggestion of the coordinator of volunteer services, she worked in the OT department of the psychiatric unit.

Not really understanding what occupational therapy was about, but having enjoyed the work, she changed her major to occupational therapy when she returned to college. In 1961, she earned her B.S. degree in occupational therapy from the University of Minnesota, School of Medicine. Anne Mosey credits Marvin Lepley, her advisor at the University of Minnesota, with playing an important role in her professional development through his confidence in her and his encouragement (A. C. Mosey, personal communication, October 4, 1984).

After graduation, Mosey worked for several months at Glenwood Hills Hospital in Minneapolis. She then moved to New York City to work with and to learn from Gail Fidler. She joined the OT department at New York State Psychiatric Institute where she remained for 5 years, until August 1966. As her supervisor, Fidler encouraged Mosey to think, read, and broaden her horizons about clinical practice and to focus on patient needs.

Mosey decided after a few years that she wanted to be an educator. She began graduate studies in occupational therapy at New York University and earned her M.A. degree in 1965. She then enrolled in Human Relations and Community Studies at New York University where she earned her Ph.D. in 1968. Professor Lloyd Barenblatt, one of her instructors and Chair of her dissertation committee, helped her "to refine skills in critical thinking" (A. C. Mosey, personal communication, October 4, 1984).

From 1966–1968, she was on the faculty of Columbia University as an instructor in occupational therapy. During this period she (1) realized that "teaching is something one must learn how to do and is a difficult task" (A. C. Mosey, personal communication, May 3, 1987), (2) developed the idea and structure of the frame of reference, (3) wrote *Three Frames of Reference for Mental Health* (1970), and (4) completed her dissertation. She then joined the faculty at New York University and moved upward through the academic ranks to her current status as Professor of Occupational Therapy with tenure. From 1972–1980 she served as department chairperson and in 1977 was the acting head of the Division of Health.

Mosey has served the AOTA in several leadership capacities on the state and national levels. Since 1979 she has been a continuous reviewer of proposed presentations for the AOTA Annual Conferences. She is a research consultant for the AOTF, and since 1984 has been a member of the Panel of Experts of the AOTA Continuing Education Program in Mental Health. Dr. Mosey has also shared her experience and knowledge by serving as a consultant to several hospitals and state mental health systems.

From 1966–1969 she was a consultant to the VRA-OTA Project for the Massachusetts Department of Mental Health. She was a faculty member for the AOTA Regional Institutes from 1966–1967. As an invited participant, she was involved with the Theory Building Seminar for AOTA in 1967. She served as consultant to the Division of Rehabilitation Education at New York University, Hillside Hospital Professional Examination Services, Family Centered Research Project, Institute of Pennsylvania Hospital, Greater Trenton Mental Health Center, and Christopher House.

Mosey has published 11 papers and 5 books and given numerous presentations and workshops. One of her articles was a collection of four poems about the thoughts of an occupational therapist who arrived home late on a dark winter night after a long and exhausting day (Mosey, 1976). As the therapist looks out the window at the blinking city lights below, she tries to put into words the thoughts and feelings of four patients. These sensitive and insightful poems demonstrate empathy, understanding, and caring. "To me, this is a statement that I needed to make . . . forget the papers and books" (A. C. Mosey, personal communication, May 3, 1987).

Numerous students and therapists have learned from her and sought her guidance. She has supervised masters and doctoral research projects since 1968. Recently, Mosey has also taught international students, which she finds to be "a tough, fun, insightful, and interesting learning experience" (A. C. Mosey, personal communication, August 4, 1985).

Her profession honored her in 1973 by naming her a Fellow of the AOTA. In 1975 she received the Distinguished Service Award from the National Association of Activity Therapy, and in 1985, she was awarded the AOTA's Eleanor Clarke Slagle Lectureship.

Mosey lives in Greenwich Village. She is divorced and has one son, now in college, whom she considers to be her best critic (A. C. Mosey, personal communication, May 3, 1987). She is interested in history and anthropology and enjoys the theater, concerts, being with friends, and being alone to think, read, and "contemplate the nature of the world" (A. C. Mosey, personal communication, August 4, 1985). Her current professional concerns are helping junior faculty become educators, teaching international students, continuing to explore and learn through reading, writing, and teaching, and "only maybe, to write another book" (A. C. Mosey, personal communication, May 3, 1987).

The major obstacles to her theoretical and professional development were Mosey's perception that no one seemed to understand what she was talking about and the subsequent lack of support (A. C. Mosey, personal communication, October 7, 1984). She felt that she was standing alone, yet she tenaciously went ahead because she felt deeply that her work was important to the profession and it was exciting to her to put ideas together. However, she found writing to be difficult (A. C. Mosey, personal communication, August 4, 1985).

THEORETICAL CONCEPTS

Throughout her career, Mosey has been concerned with laying the groundwork for the OT evaluation and intervention process. She has searched for answers to the questions of where are we now and how did we get here. She has investigated the building blocks of the profession in a scholarly manner and has organized them into a taxonomy of the profession. Three main themes can be seen in her work: (1) the articulation of frames of references for occupational therapy in mental health, (2) how one structures and translates theories of psychosocial dysfunction into frames of reference to apply to practice, and (3) the development of a taxonomy that identifies the various elements of the profession and their relationship to each other.

Frames of Reference for Mental Health

One of the three main strands of Mosey's work, that of articulating frames of reference for occupational therapy in mental health, began with her development of the recapitulation of ontogenesis frame of reference. She later developed an activities therapy frame of reference.

Recapitulation of Ontogenesis

In "Recapitulation of Ontogenesis: A Theory for Practice of Occupational Therapy" (1968b) Mosey proposes a developmental frame of reference for evaluation and treatment. Its theoretical base is derived from a variety of personality and developmental theories proposed by Sullivan (1953), Piaget (Flavell, 1963), Bruner (1966), Sigmund Freud (1949), Anna Freud (1965), Llorens (Llorens & Beck, 1966), Schilder (1950), Searles (1960), Sechehaye (1951a, 1951b), Ayres (1958, 1961, 1963, 1964) and

Hartman (1958). Her clinical work with Fidler also was influential in this frame of reference's development. Recapitulation of ontogenesis is a biological concept that refers to the repetition of the evolutionary stages of a species during the embryonic development of an individual organism. To developmental theorists this means that the individual sequentially progresses through developmental stages. Recapitulation of ontogenesis is concerned with the development of adaptive skills needed for successful participation in occupational performance (Mosey, 1986).

Mosey (1968b) proposes that the individual is a being who seeks equilibrium. Disequilibrium results from changing psychological and physical needs and new environmental demands. It motivates one to learn adaptive skills needed to reestablish a state of equilibrium. Mosey describes seven adaptive skills—each of which has component subskills—in the sequential order in which they are learned: (1) perceptual-motor, (2) cognitive, (3) drive object, (4) dyadic interaction skills, (5) primary group interaction skill, (6) self-identity skill, and (7) sexual identity interaction skill. When all of the component subskills have been integrated, the person has achieved full maturity in that skill.

A state of function is characterized by integrated learning of those adaptive skill components that are needed for successful participation in the social roles expected of the individual in his or her usual environmental setting. Minimal and maximal limits are usually set by one's cultural group. Adaptive skill performance enables one to obtain self-gratification and to meet environmental demands.

Dysfunction results when these necessary skill components are not learned because of (1) abnormalities or lack of maturation of physical structures, (2) severe environmental stress, or (3) lack of environmental elements necessary for the development of these skill components. When skill components needed for the fulfillment of social roles are not learned, interaction with the social system may be unproductive and/or learned maladaptive behaviors may be exhibited. For example, these learned patterns may be displayed as depression or hyperactivity (Mosey, 1968b). There is a continuum of function/dysfunction.

To evaluate the client, one must observe him or her in roles and activities that will elicit these adaptive skills and then identify whether particular skill components are present or absent. The therapist needs to collaborate with the patient and other staff to learn more about what skills are needed in the person's expected environment.

The individual is able to move from a state of dysfunction to a state of function through activities that are similar to those object interactions believed responsible for normal skill development. Activities are chosen that require the performance of selected adaptive skill components. The therapist helps the patient grow from where normal development ceased by providing experiences that take the person through the developmental stages of the adaptive skill components; these experiences facilitate learning of the skills and abilities needed. Learning occurs through interaction with objects, which will vary according to the component that needs to be learned. Activities have a "doing" nature. The manner in which the person responds to the activity will depend on the elements of the activity, past experiences, and skills previously learned.

Adaptive skill components need to be learned sequentially. The more elementary component must be learned before the next and so on, in a consecutive order. Thus, Mosey proposes a developmental approach (1968b).

The long-term goal of this developmental approach is to help the person participate fully in his or her expected social roles and environment. The short-term goal is to learn the skill component. Activities are analyzed, synthesized, and/or selected that contain elements needed for learning the skill components. Symbolic activities may be used, but reality and the here-and-now are stressed. In particular, the more mature skill components must employ reality-oriented activities (Mosey, 1968b).

Mosey's next publication (1969), provides a developmental frame of reference for the evaluation and treatment of pathological distortion of body image. This is consistent with her recapitulation of ontogenesis frame of reference (1968b) but is delimited to a specific dysfunction. It gives the reader specific examples of the application of the frame of reference. It is based on the theory that defective experiences during the developmental process may lead to pathological distortion of body image. Drawing on the work of Schneider (1960), Ayres (1958, 1961, 1963, 1964), Schilder (1950), Sigmund Freud (1949), Anna Freud (1965), Pearce and Newton (1963), Sechehaye (1951a,b), and the Fidlers (1963), Mosey proposes that the transition from an undifferentiated body image to an adult body image is a complex process that can be disrupted by factors both internal and external to the self. The ability to perceive and organize sensory stimuli is crucial to the control and development of normal motor behavior, purposeful movement and body mastery. It also determines whether one is accepted or rejected by one's peers. The parents' idiosyncratic and/or cultural norms, values, and attitudes about the body or any of its parts are incorporated by the child. As a result, the body or any of its parts may either be valued or be seen as dirty or have other negative connotations. Body parts may be excessively focused on or denied.

Acceptance of sexuality and sexual parts of the body is important to the attainment of a mature body image. Investing a lot of libidinal energy to control internal conflicts may cause de-egotization of the body or any of its parts, which may result in depersonalization. Self-mutilation, perception of the self as a tree, or egotization of less threatening objects may be seen when the person rejects his or her sexuality. An external factor, such as physical trauma that causes loss of function of a body part or parts, may also result in distortion of the body image.

Evaluation of the client is based on observation and interpretation of behavior to identify whether body image distortion is present and, if so, the type and extent. Such distortion is expressed by the client's wearing clothes that are too large, too tight fitting and revealing, childish, or sexually undifferentiated; covering the face with hair and excessive makeup; emphasizing, denying, or rejecting a body part; and making rigid uncoordinated or stylized movements (1969).

Treatment is based on the theory that distortion of body image may be corrected by providing similar experiences to those believed responsible for the normal development of body image.

Again using recapitulation of ontogeny as the theoretical base, Mosey proposes the use of developmental groups for persons who lack primary group interaction skills (1970a). Where a client falls on the function/dysfunction continuum is determined by his or her achievement of primary group interaction skills and its components. Developmental groups are defined as groups that are structured to simulate the various types of nonfamilial groups that are usually experienced in the normal developmental process. The postulates regarding change are consistent with those of recapitulation of ontogeny. Five levels of developmental groups are delineated and described, which are intended to lie on a continuum and are sequential and hierarchical. These are: (1) parallel group, (2) project group, (3) egocentric group, (4) cooperative group, and (5) mature group. Learning occurs as the individual experiences the consequences of his or her behavior in the structured group setting. The type of behavior to be learned is clearly spelled out; adaptive behavior is reinforced and maladaptive behavior is not.

Developmental groups may also be used to treat deficiencies in other adaptive skill components that may only be partially or completely learned through nonfamilial groups. The group must be structurally similar to the type of group in which these components are normally acquired. Developmental groups can also be used to satisfy mental health needs (1970a).

Activities Therapy

Activities Therapy (Mosey, 1973a) was written to describe a type of therapy that uses immediate, action-oriented interactions to help persons designated as mentally ill learn to be a part of their community and to cope with the stresses of daily life. This book is based on the assumption that psychosocial dysfunction is due to a lack of one or more of the following abilities: to plan and carry out a task, to interact comfortably in a group, to identify and satisfy needs, to express emotions in an acceptable manner, to attain a fairly accurate perception of the self and the human and nonhuman environment, to establish a value system that allows the person to meet his or her needs without infringing on the rights of others, to perform activities of daily living skills, to work at a relatively satisfying job, to enjoy avocational and recreational activities, and to interact comfortably in family and friendship relationships. Any deficits in these abilities limit one's effective performance in the community. Deficit learning or inappropriate learning of behaviors can be treated by learning more effective behaviors.

Here again Mosey (1973a) stresses the importance of here-and-now, action-oriented experiences that involve learning through doing. Activities are used to provide realistic situations to help participants learn new skills and identify faulty patterns of behaviors and the feelings and values that support these maladaptive patterns. The therapist is concerned with the (1) greater understanding of the self and (2) development of skills.

Human beings have three facets: basic skills, the private self, and the public self. Basic skills are those that a person must have to function satisfactorily in the community with others. They include task and group interaction skills. The private self is composed of those aspects that cannot be directly seen or experienced by others, such as cognitive processes, needs, emotions, and values. The public self involves aspects of the individual that can be observed by others and can be a point of contact. Activities of daily living, work, recreation, and intimacy are essential components of the public self (1973a).

The teaching-learning process and group dynamics that use action-oriented experiences help the client learn necessary skills. The teaching-learning process, which is fundamental, is described in detail. The sequence, principles, and case examples of the evaluation and treatment process are discussed and are consistent with Mosey's *Three Frames of Reference for Mental Health* (1970b). In *Activities Therapy* (1973a) she also describes the various types of psychiatric treatment centers in which this frame of reference might be applicable.

Three Frames of Reference

The three frames of reference that Mosey initially categorized and described were (1) developmental, (2) analytical, and (3) acquisitional (1970b). The developmental frame of reference is derived from "Recapitulation of Ontogenesis: A Theory for the Practice of Occupational Therapy" (1968b). Freud's stages of psychosexual development and Erickson's eight stages are classified here. Skills in the developmental frame of reference are interdependent, qualitative, and stage specific. They are usually acquired in the normal developmental process in growth-facilitating environments.

The analytical perspective is concerned with concepts of need fulfillment, expression of primitive impulses, and control of inherent drives. It is based on the theories of Sigmund Freud (1949), Anna Freud (1965), Maslow (1962), Erikson (1950), and Jung (1933, 1964). The acquisitional frame of reference considers various skills and abilities that the individual needs for adequate and satisfying interaction with the environment. These skills are independent of each other, quantitative, and nonstage-specific, which is primarily what delineates them from the developmental frame of reference. The acquisitional frame of reference is based on learning theories, such as those of Bandura (1969), Wolpe and Lazarus (1966), Dollard and Miller (1950), and ego theorists, such as Sullivan (1953). Such occupational therapists as Sieg (1974), Diasio (1968), and Smith and Tempone (1968) are also resources.

Mosey still regards these three as the major current frames of reference in occupational therapy in psychosocial dysfunction. She has refined and added to her earlier works to "provide an adequate blueprint for evaluation and intervention" (Mosey, 1986, p. vii). In her most recent book, *Psychosocial Components of Occupational Therapy* (1986), Mosey's frames of reference are more clear and integrated and their application is further developed. She has also added a critical analysis of the works of Fidler, King, Llorens, Reilly, and Kielhofner, and she has integrated their thinking into the corresponding frames of reference.

Theory and Frame of Reference

The second strand of her work entwines with the development of specific frames of reference for occupational therapy in mental health since it explores how she structured and translated theory into frames of reference for use in practice.

The book, *Three Frames of Reference for Mental Health,* was written "to plead a case for the conscious use of theoretical frames of reference as a basis for the treatment of psychosocial dysfunction" (1970b, p. v). This book has served for many years as a basic text on the treatment of psychosocial dysfunction. Mosey begins by defining theory and discusses the process of theory building. A theory describes the relationship among events and makes predictions about these events. A theoretical frame of reference is deduced from theory and makes use of concepts, definitions, and postulates from a theory or theories. It is composed of principles to guide action that are deduced from scientific postulates regarding change.

In contrast to a theory, which is merely descriptive, a theoretical frame of reference provides principles for action and is prescriptive. It applies to daily situations and can guide the actions of the practitioner.

Frames of reference should be comprehensive, internally consistent, and stated in an organized and logical manner (Mosey, 1970b, p. 9). Mosey uses a four-part structure for a frame of reference that she derived from Ford and Urban (1963). The first part is a theoretical base that is drawn from theory or theories from a variety of fields such as psychology, sociology, or neuroscience. It specifies the nature of human beings, of the environment, and their relationship to each other and identifies the parameters of the frame of reference. It is the basis from which all other parts are deduced.

The second part is the delineation of function and dysfunction continua, which is derived from the theoretical base and its view of health and dysfunction. Operational definitions of verbal and nonverbal behavior that are indicative of function or dysfunction are included in this part. These behaviors are what the therapist will assess in the evaluation process.

Evaluation, which comprises the third part of the frame of reference, is the process of identifying whether an individual is in a state of function or dysfunction. It is used as a basis for treatment. The particular frame of reference selected determines which verbal and nonverbal behaviors constitute function and dysfunction. Evaluation tools and techniques are selected that will serve as stimuli to elicit these behaviors that are to be observed and measured to differentiate between function and dysfunction. Procedures and rules to interpret the data are determined by the frame of reference selected. Reliability and validity are important considerations in the evaluation process (Mosey, 1970b).

Prescriptive statements that are deduced from the postulates of the theoretical base make up the fourth part of the frame of reference (Mosey, 1970b). They state the principles by which an individual is aided in moving from a state of dysfunction to one of function. They guide the therapist in arranging his or her interaction with the client and the nonhuman environment. Ideally, these postulates have been empirically tested. Similar activities may be used with different frames of reference or postulates, but how they are structured and utilized will differ. For example, task groups may be analytical or they may be developmental, and both could use fingerpainting. However, the analytical group may be using fingerpainting to express primitive impulses, whereas the developmental group may be working on primary social skill interaction.

Treatment is aimed at effecting predetermined change in the patient's limitations so that he or she may be a more productive member of a social system. It is a planned collaborative interaction between the patient, therapist, and nonhuman environment (Mosey, 1970b).

The criteria for a frame of reference are stringent and are a statement of the ideal, rather than the actual. Mosey has bravely and painstakingly synthesized theories and developed them into three frames of reference according to this four-part structure. She does not consider them to be complete, rather they were proposed to stimulate thinking about frames of reference and what they should and should not include, to identify a goal for continued work in the area, and to give an orientation for classification of frames of reference that are currently available.

Taxonomy of the Profession

Mosey's position as program director of the OT curriculum at New York University led her to widen her focus to the profession of occupational therapy as a whole. She began to search for its common elements in order to describe and analyze the profession's form and structure and the ways in which these parts relate to one another (A. C. Mosey, personal communication, October 4, 1984). This is the third main theme of her work.

Biopsychosocial Model

In 1974 she developed a biopsychosocial model as an alternative to the medical or health models for occupational therapy. The content of the medical model is not relevant to the OT process because therapists are not concerned with diagnosis of disease nor with the elimination of pathology. The health model is too vague. Because it focuses primarily on assets, rather than limitations or dysfunction, the health model is useful for prevention and community practice, but is too limiting for remediation. Neither model permits the complete organization of the theoretical base of occupational therapy.

The biopsychosocial model (Mosey, 1974) focuses on the body, mind, and environment of the individual. It views the individual as a physical being who suffers the effects of illness and injury; a person with thoughts, emotions, needs, and values; and a player of many and varied social roles. This model is concerned with the skills, knowledge, abilities, and values that need to be learned by the individual in order to function productively within his or her expected environment with others. Change in the individual is primarily brought about through delineating learning needs and the teaching-learning process. The teaching-learning process, which was a central theme in treatment in her earlier works (1968b, 1970b, 1973b), is described in the 1981 book, *Occupational Therapy: Configuration of a Profession*. The therapist, as the teacher, begins where the learner is and moves at a rate that is comfortable for the learner. Opportunities for trial and error, imitation, repetition, and practice in different situations must be provided through which the learner can observe and experience the consequences of an action. He or she needs to understand both what is to be learned and the rationale for learning. The teaching-learning process may be based on any of a variety of theories about learning, such as operant conditioning and social learning theory.

Mosey (1974) initially felt that this model would be useful for practice because it (1) provides a method to systematize OT knowledge, (2) provides a holistic statement of the profession's goals and theories of change, (3) is oriented to the development of skills needed by the client or patient for fuller participation in the community setting, (4) helps clarify the role of occupational therapy in relationship to medicine and the other health-related professions, and (5) is well suited to community-based programs and the meeting of health needs.

However, 6 years after presenting the biopsychosocial model, she wrote that "it became evident that the biopsychosocial model did not provide sufficient structure and content to give a holistic view of occupational therapy" (1980, p. 11). She continued with her quest for a model for the profession, refining the biopsychosocial model in an attempt to provide a holistic or generic approach to the philosophical and scientific foundation for the practice of occupational therapy. "My goal was and remains the identification of those factors which give unity to the profession and a firm base for the further development of areas of specialization" (Mosey, 1980, p. 11).

Characteristics of a Professional Model

Mosey further researched the occupational therapy literature and primary sources most frequently cited by occupational therapists, and discussed this issue with faculty, students, and clinicians. Based on this further study, she defined and described the structure, function, and characteristics of a model for professions in general and one specific to occupational therapy (1980, 1981, 1986). She drew on philosophical and sociological literature of what constitutes a profession. A model for a profession describes the particular way in which a profession perceives itself, its relationship to other professions, and to society to which it is responsible, as well as the profession's responsibility to society, methods, and rationale. A model applies to the entire profession, rather than to any particular area of specialization. A model defines and delineates the nature of the profession and is accepted by its members and by society. It is dynamic, and its content is continually changing. Some of the changes result from changes in the body of knowledge and expertise of the profession, the domain of concern of other professions, and the needs, mandate, and/or acceptance of society. Each part of the model is interrelated, and a change in one part effects change in others. Mosey cautions that a profession takes great risks in expanding its model beyond the limits of its present theoretical foundation and domain of concern. More may be claimed than can be delivered, which may result in a loss of respect for the profession (Mosey, 1981, pp. 52–57).

The structure and characteristics of a model seem to be similar for all health professions. Some content, such as theories of human growth and development, may be shared by several professions. However, it is the specific content of each profession's model that differentiates each model. A profession's model is composed of the following six elements: (1) philosophical assumptions basic to practice, (2) ethical code, (3) theoretical foundation (later referred to as a body of knowledge), (4) domain of concern, (5) nature of and principles for sequencing the various aspects of practice, and (6) legitimate tools. Mosey (1980, 1981, 1986) describes each of these components in detail in terms of its composition and structure and how they relate to and influence each other.

In the model for occupational therapy, the first element—*philosophical assumptions*—contains seven basic beliefs about the individual, his or her relationship with the human and nonhuman environment, and the profession's goals or purpose. They are as follows:

1. Each individual has the right to a meaningful existence; to an existence that allows one to be productive; to experience pleasure and joy; to love and be loved; and to live in surroundings that are safe, supportive, and comfortable.
2. Each individual is influenced by stage-specific maturation of the species, the social nature of the species, and the cognitive structure of the species.
3. Each individual has inherent needs for work, play, and rest that must be satisfied in a relatively equal balance.
4. Each individual has the right to seek his or her potential through personal choice within the context of some social constraints.
5. Each individual is only able to reach his or her potential through purposeful interaction with the human and nonhuman environment.
6. Each individual is only able to be understood within the context of his or her environment of family, community, and cultural group.
7. Occupational therapy is concerned with promoting functional independence through intervention directed toward facilitating

> participation in major social roles (occupational performances) and the development of the physical, cognitive, psychological, and social skills (performance components) that are fundamental to these roles. The extent to which intervention is focused on occupational performances or performance components is dependent on the needs of a particular client at any given point in time (Mosey, 1986, p. 6).

These humanistic and developmental assumptions are derived primarily from the philosophical literature in occupational therapy (1980, 1981, 1986).

The profession's *ethical code* comprises principles of human conduct regarding what is moral behavior toward clients, students, and colleagues. Mosey refers the reader to AOTA's Code of Ethics (1981, pp. 64–70).

The profession's *body of knowledge,* which is also referred to as its theoretical foundation, contains the scientific basis for the profession. It is derived from an ordered set of selected theoretical systems from a variety of different disciplines, as well as from the profession itself. These are selected, formulated, and adapted to the individual profession. Each profession's body of knowledge is unique because what is selected and the way in which it is combined are of particular relevance to it. Occupational therapy's body of knowledge comes from the biological sciences, behavioral sciences, the arts, medicine, and occupational therapy (1980, 1981, 1986).

The *domain of concern,* the fourth element, concerns areas of expertise of the profession. Though the concept of domain of concern and the subconcepts of performance components and areas of occupational performance had been identified and labeled by an AOTA task force, Mosey conducted her own survey of the literature to identify those areas of human function that occupational therapists believed they could successfully influence. She examined the writings of Reilly (1962, 1974), Llorens (1966, 1976), Kielhofner (1977, 1983), and many others. She lists the components of performance as motor function, sensory integration, visual perception, cognitive function, psychological function, and social interaction. She considers occupational performances to include family interaction, activities of daily living, school/work, play, leisure, recreation, and temporal adaptation. The clients' chronological and developmental age and cultural, social, and physical environment are also essential components. (See Figure 3-1.)

Fifth are the *nature of and principles for sequencing the various aspects of practice* (1980, 1981, 1986), which describe the problem-identification and problem-solving processes used to evaluate and treat clients. Mosey wrote about these in her earlier works (1970b, 1973a) mainly as applicable

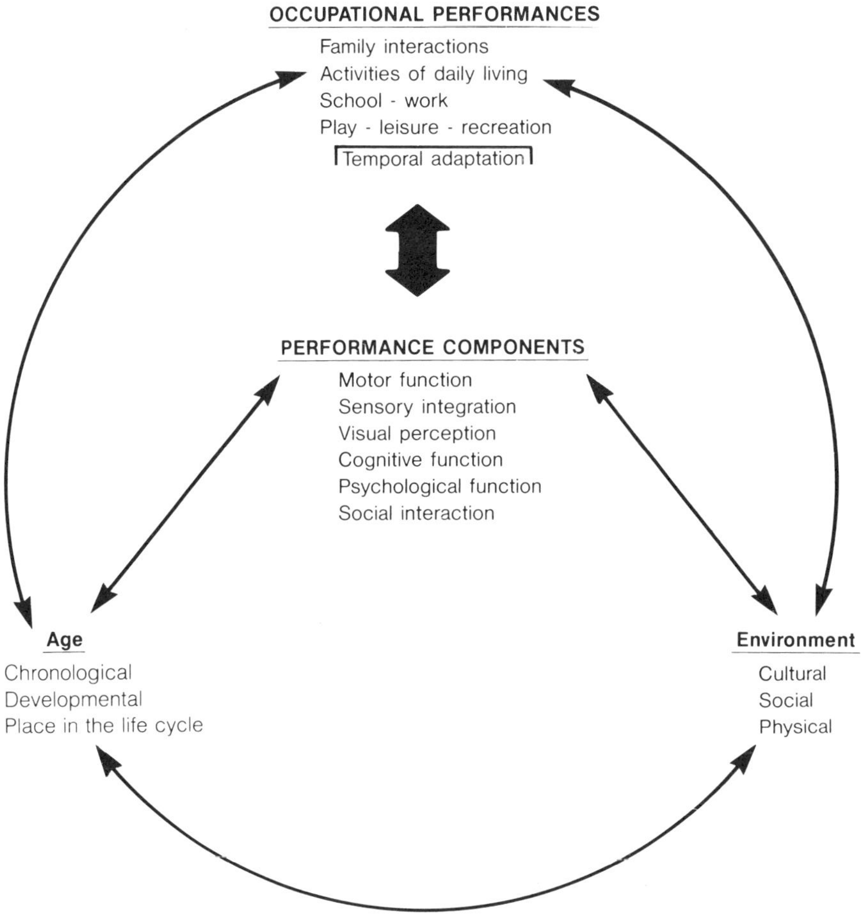

Figure 3-1 Domain of concern for occupational therapy. *Source:* From *Occupational Therapy: Configuration of a Profession* (p. 75) by A.C. Mosey, 1981, New York: Raven Press Ltd. Copyright 1981 by Raven Press Ltd. Adapted by permission.

to frames of reference. In *Occupational Therapy: Configuration of a Profession* (1981) and in *Psychosocial Components of Occupational Therapy* (1986) she builds on and integrates these principles into the larger concept of a model.

Legitimate tools, the sixth part of the model, are the modalities that the profession uses to achieve its goals. From her review of the OT literature she identified the following six tools: (1) nonhuman environment, (2) conscious use of self, (3) the teaching-learning process, (4) purposeful activity, (5) activity groups, and (6) activity analysis and synthesis (1981, 1986).

Frames of Reference

Frames of reference are derived from the model of the profession and offer a variety of approaches to the evaluation and intervention process. Mosey defines a frame of reference as a set of interrelated, internally consistent concepts, definitions, and postulates derived from or compatible with empirical data that provide a systematic description of, or prescription for, a practitioner's interaction within a particular aspect of a profession's domain of concern for the purpose of facilitating evaluation and effecting change (1986, p. 376). The professional model provides the linkages among the various frames of reference to the profession as a whole.

Frames of reference are derived from a model, but are more limited. They link theory and practice in only a small area of the profession's body of knowledge and domain of concern, whereas a model defines the whole profession. A model is almost universally accepted by the profession and the society to which it is responsible. In contrast, a frame of reference has more limited acceptance by practitioners, and more than one frame of reference may be applied to the same portion of the domain of concern in the profession. Conflict and disagreement may ensue, which might lead to clarification of concepts and further research. Whereas a model gives overall direction to the profession, a frame of reference guides the practitioner in his or her daily interaction with clients, is prescriptive in nature, and delineates interactions considered effective in decreasing dysfunction.

A profession may have many frames of reference. Mosey's three major frames of reference in occupational therapy still remain analytic, acquisitional, and developmental. She considers Reilly (1962, 1974), Banus (1979), Llorens (1976), Kielhofner (1977, 1983), Rood, Brunnstrom, and Bobath to be contributors to the developmental frame of reference. She added the biomechanical and rehabilitative approaches as outlined by Trombly and Scott (1977) to the acquisitional frame of reference.

Professional Configuration

Her research into the literature and conceptualizations about professional models and frames of reference provided some basic elements of her configuration of the profession. This configuration is composed of a loop with six parts: (1) philosophical foundation, (2) model, (3) frames of reference, (4) practice, (5) data, and (6) research (Mosey, 1981, 1986) (See Figure 3-2).

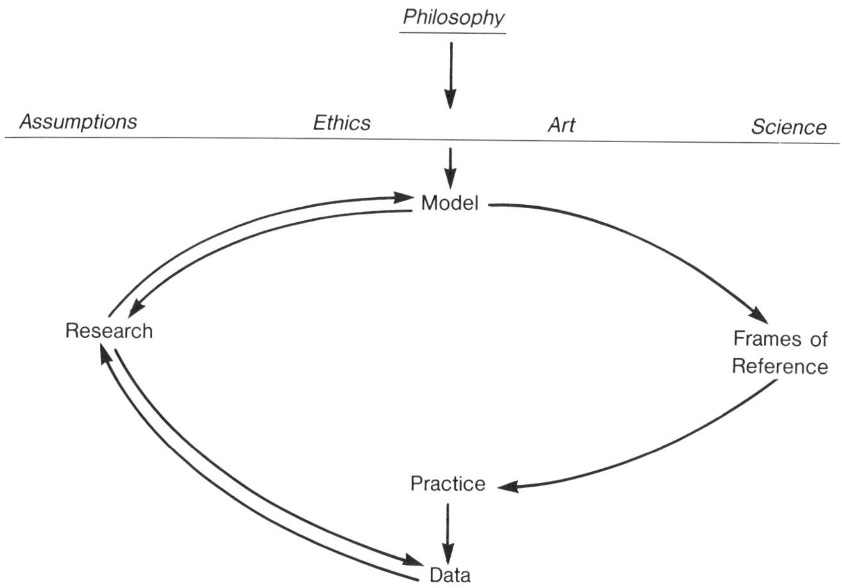

Figure 3-2 Occupational Therapy Loop. *Source:* From *Occupational Therapy: Configuration of a Profession* (p. 42) by A.C. Mosey, 1981, New York: Raven Press Ltd. Copyright 1981 by Raven Press Ltd. Reprinted by permission.

Philosophical assumptions, ethics, art, and science are basic elements of all professions. It is from each profession's particular philosophical foundation that a unique professional model develops. Various frames of reference are deduced from this model and serve as a guide for practice. Practice then produces data that enables one to evaluate its effectiveness and to refine the profession's body of knowledge. Thus the arrows flow in two directions among data, research, and model. In her configuration, there is no direct relationship between research and practice or between research and frames of reference. Research only directly influences the body of knowledge component of the model by modifying or supporting its theoretical base. When a theory is altered by research findings, changes are then effected in frames of reference that utilize that base. These in turn lead to changes in practice. Thus, research can influence practice only after it is integrated into the professional model and relevant frames of reference. The professional model also influences research because a theoretical foundation should be continually evaluated (Mosey, 1981, 1986).

Her next scholarly task was to further review, synthesize and systematize the literature basic to psychosocial occupational therapy from this field and from those disciplines and professions from which we select relevant theories. This work is embodied in her book, *Psychosocial Components of Occupational Therapy* (1986). She wrote that, "Its purpose is to provide an overview of the psychosocial components—both the body of knowledge and approaches to evaluation and intervention" (Mosey, 1986, p. vii).

Mosey feels that psychosocial components are applicable to all areas of specialization because they are "fundamental to the understanding of our clients, ourselves as therapists, and the tools that we use in practice" (Mosey, 1986, p. vii). She examines the knowledge, skills, and attitudes basic to adaptation regardless of the person's current physical condition. Consistent with her thinking is the pluralistic approach and use of a variety of frames of reference. These are presented and reviewed. She encourages occupational therapists to select frames of reference best suited to their own theoretical and philosophical positions and consistent with their clients' needs.

This book synthesizes the three strands of her work—theories of psychosocial dysfunction, frames of reference for occupational therapy in mental health, and development of a taxonomy for the profession—into a unifying whole.

Her Historical Perspective chapter (1986, pp. 16–37) is a very scholarly work that traces the evolution of the various types of intervention, frames of reference, and tools of occupational therapy in the psychosocial components of occupational therapy in both physical medicine and psychiatry. She discusses the profession's "search for identity" from its initial reliance on medicine to formulating its development of frames of reference.

She devotes considerable attention to the domain of concern and integrates the professional knowledge in this area. She also discusses the five areas of specialization recognized by AOTA: (1) mental health, (2) physical disabilities, (3) developmental disabilities, (4) gerontology, and (5) sensory integration. She integrates and applies all of the previously discussed concepts into the special problems of each of these areas.

APPLICATION TO OCCUPATIONAL THERAPY

Use of Theory

Mosey (1973) regards clinical practice as the process of using science and applying theories. The therapist must consciously select theories and use them as a guide for action. The therapist's actions may be guided by one or more theories. Such an eclectic approach is acceptable, but the postulates need to be logically compatible. She objects to therapists doing what they feel is right intuitively without reference to any particular theoretical system.

Until more refined techniques of measurement are developed and researched, no one frame of reference can claim authority. Therefore, she encourages therapists to develop their own individual frame of reference and techniques for patient care to suit their style of practice. The frame of reference needs to be a part of the self in order to be a useful guide for action, which is impossible if it is incompatible with the self. The frame of reference selected also needs to be appropriate to the client's cultural norms and background. She suggests that the beginning therapist study and use a variety of frames of reference with a nonjudgmental attitude. Initial efforts to apply frames of reference should be done under competent supervision.

In Mosey's (1971) review of the growth of the rehabilitation movement from 1942–1960, she concludes that during that period occupational therapists functioned primarily as technicians, rather than as professionals. Emphasis was placed on technique, not on theory. She further stated that she saw little change as of 1970. Practice continues without the conscious use of a theoretical base. She feels that it is imperative that the considerable amount of available knowledge basic to practice be systematically organized. Doing so will enable us to eliminate the irrelevant and help us identify what knowledge is lacking and what is available, thereby facilitating the organization of theory and research.

Health Needs

Mosey, using a conceptualization similar to that of Maslow, defines health needs as "inherent human requirements that must be met for an individual to experience a sense of physical, psychological, and social well-being" (Mosey, 1973b, p. 14). All persons, regardless of their state of health, have these needs. Mosey encourages therapists to re-emphasize the importance of meeting health needs in occupational therapy, the institution, and the community. This becomes increasingly important as therapists move into community-based practice. The occupational therapist's knowledge of human growth and development and recognition of the individual's need for satisfying interaction with the human and nonhuman environment provide excellent support for this focus. The occupational therapist needs to ask whether this environment (the occupational therapy clinic, the institution, the community) seems to offer the opportunity for those types of need satisfaction that the patient requires. Further study of the process of meeting health needs is required (Mosey, 1973b, 1986).

The book, *Psychosocial Components of Occupational Therapy* (Mosey, 1986), provides the practitioner with an excellent synthesis of the theoretical base of the profession as a whole, as well as a taxonomy of its specific parts. The therapist is provided with the structure needed to make the transition from theory to practice.

APPLICATION TO THE OCCUPATIONAL THERAPY PROFESSION

Mosey has sought to identify those common elements of the profession that would provide a sense of unity to occupational therapy. The increasing specialization that is occurring in practice makes it even more essential to answer the question of what is common to all areas that makes each a part of occupational therapy. "The self-questioning of a profession occurs in cycles and provides a healthy means for re-examination, revitalization, and change" (Mosey, 1981, p. 120).

In her Eleanor Clarke Slagle lecture in 1985, Mosey once again bravely undertook the task of helping us further develop and articulate our professional identity and how this influences our practice. Monism and pluralism are two approaches that professions can take to form their identity. Monism is an attempt to define a profession by one of its elements or a facet of an element that is considered primary and that governs all other elements. A pluralistic approach is much broader and takes into consideration all of the elements of a profession. The whole is defined by the totality of its parts, and each of these parts is distinct and different.

A monistic approach usually takes the form of a comprehensive theory (Mosey, 1985). The profession has one theoretical base and one method for applying it to its domain of concern. Some of the approaches that have been considered for a comprehensive theory for occupational therapy have been developmental theory as proposed by Llorens (1976), occupational behavior as described by Reilly (1962, 1974), purposeful activity as discussed by the Fidlers (1978), King's theory of adaptive response (1978), and human occupation as proposed by Kielhofner et al. (1983). Mosey states (1985) that a monistic approach may tend to be exclusionary, and so important facts may not be included. Members may be placed in a rigid, constricted position, and creative, divergent thinking may not be tolerated. New knowledge and the needs of society may be ignored and not included or added to the theory. A comprehensive theory may oversimplify our body of knowledge, domain of concern, and practice, or it may be too complex and intricate to be easily understood. It may also inhibit research if the concepts cannot be operationalized and made into variables for empirical testing to assess the theory's validity or the effectiveness of interventions derived from that theory.

Therefore, Mosey has consistently advocated a pluralistic approach in her development of frames of reference. The pluralistic approach regards all the elements of a profession as being of equal importance. The legitimate tools of the profession are as important as the theories that underlie their application and vice versa. A profession shares part of its knowledge, skills, and philosophical beliefs with other professions or fields, but it is its total content that is unique and different. She feels that the pluralistic model is more flexible and can more readily allow for change as new ideas, knowledge, and beliefs emerge to meet the changing needs of society. Diversity in orientations is healthy and potentially more adaptive (Mosey, 1985, 1986).

After discussing monistic and pluralistic approaches, Mosey suggests a taxonomy for the articulation of a pluralistic identity that classifies and orders phenomena (1985). Each of the elements of the profession—philosophical assumptions, ethical code, theoretical foundation, domain of concern, principles for sequencing various aspects of practice, and legitimate tools—would be clearly defined and the various contents outlined. By making clear the content of each element, this taxonomy would readily identify incongruences among them. Content could be added or deleted as appropriate. Professional identity would be derived from all of our elements. This pluralistic approach would provide a structure to enable us more readily to analyze critically our philosophical assumptions, select or develop new theories, make changes in our domain of concern, consider alternative legitimate tools, and formulate more definitive and additional frames of reference. Further, there is a need to examine how we as occupational therapists can use current theories generated by such disciplines as neurophysiology and integrate them into occupational therapy.

SUBSEQUENT RESEARCH AND APPLICATION BY OTHERS

Mosey's work has contributed immeasurably to an understanding of the profession's parts and wholeness. However, because her major work has been to develop a taxonomy, it is difficult to evaluate subsequent research and application of her work.

Too, the structure of a frame of reference is hard to live within, and many therapists are generally more comfortable operating intuitively. It is also difficult to work with and combine various frames of reference, rather than just using one, which is an issue in the debate over monistic or pluralistic models for the profession. She has received support for the pluralistic model. Whether researchers will build upon her work remains to be seen.

> It takes a long time for professions to change and I present my ideas and people can accept or not accept them. I have no driving need for people to accept my ideas. I am not a public person. The thrill and reward come from playing with ideas and putting ideas together and knowing that eventually it will help our patients. (A. C. Mosey, personal communication, August 4, 1985)

Mosey has repeatedly stated that there is a strong need to test the theories and theoretical foundations that we have and use as a basis for practice, to translate them into frames of reference, and to evaluate their effectiveness (1968a, 1968b, 1970b, 1980, 1981, 1986). She has painstakingly given us the framework with which to do this. Using the research process, data generated from practice can systematically lead to tentative hypotheses that will refute, develop, refine, or verify the theoretical bases. This can help us evaluate frames of reference and the theoretical base. According to Mosey (1986) when the theoretical base is altered by research findings, changes in frames of reference result, which leads to changes in practice. The researcher finds fertile ground in Mosey's works in which to engage in this process.

REFERENCES

Ayres, J. (1958). The visual-motor function. *American Journal of Occupational Therapy, 12,* 130–139.

Ayres, J. (1961). Development of body scheme in children. *American Journal of Occupational Therapy, 15,* 99–102.

Ayres, J. (1963). The development of perceptual motor disabilities. *American Journal of Occupational Therapy, 17,* 221–225.

Ayres, J. (1964). Tactile function. *American Journal of Occupational Therapy, 18,* 6–11.

Bandura, A. (1969). *Principles of behavior modification.* New York: Holt, Rinehart, & Winston.

Banus, B. (Ed.). (1979). *The developmental therapist.* Thorofare, NJ: Charles B. Slack.

Bruner, J. (1966). *Studies in cognitive growth.* New York: John Wiley & Sons.

Diasio, K. (1968). Psychiatric occupational therapy: A search for a conceptual framework in light of psychoanalytic, ego psychology, and learning theory. *American Journal of Occupational Therapy, 22,* 400–407.

Dollard J., & Miller, N. (1950). *Personality and psychotherapy.* New York: McGraw Hill.

Erikson, E. (1950). *Childhood and society.* New York: Norton.

Fidler, G., & Fidler, J. (1963). *Occupational therapy: A communication process in psychiatry.* New York: Macmillan.

Fidler, G., & Fidler, J. (1978). Doing and becoming: Purposeful action and self-actualization. *American Journal of Occupational Therapy, 32,* 305–310.

Flavell, J. (1963). *The developmental psychology of Jean Piaget.* New York: D. Van Nostrand.

Ford, D., & Urban, H. (1963). *Systems of psychotherapy.* New York: John Wiley & Sons.

Freud, S. (1949). *An outline of psychoanalysis.* New York: Norton.

Freud, A. (1965). *Normality and pathology in childhood.* New York: International University Press.

Hartman, H. (1958). *Ego psychology and the problems of adaptation.* New York: International University Press.

Jung, C. (1933). *Modern man in search of a soul.* New York: Harcourt, Brace and World.

Jung, C. (1964). *Man and his symbols.* New York: Doubleday.

Kielhofner, G. (1977). Temporal adaptation: A conceptual framework for occupational therapy. *American Journal of Occupational Therapy, 31,* 235–242.

Kielhofner, G. (Ed.). (1983). *Health through occupation: Theory and practice in occupational therapy.* Philadelphia: F. A. Davis.

King, L.J. (1978). Towards a science of adaptive responses. *American Journal of Occupational Therapy, 32,* 429–437.

Llorens, L. (1976). *Application of a developmental theory for health and rehabilitation.* Rockville, MD: American Occupational Therapy Association.

Llorens, L., & Beck, G. (1966, March). Training methods for cognitive-perceptual-motor dysfunction. *Therapy Seminar* on *Normal Growth and Development With Deviations,* St. Louis.

Maslow, A. (1962). *Toward a psychology of being.* Princeton, NJ: D. Van Nostrand.

Mosey, A. (1968a). *Occupational therapy: Theory and practice.* Medford, MA: Pothier Brothers Press.

Mosey, A. (1968b). Recapitulation of ontogenesis: A theory for the practice of occupational therapy. *American Journal of Occupational Therapy, 22,* 426–432.

Mosey, A. (1969). Treatment of pathological distortion of body image. *American Journal of Occupational Therapy, 23,* 413–416.

Mosey, A. (1970a). The concept and use of developmental groups. *American Journal of Occupational Therapy, 24,* 272–275.

Mosey, A. (1970b). *Three frames of reference for mental health.* Thorofare, NJ: Charles B. Slack.

Mosey, A. (1971). Involvement in the rehabilitation movement 1942–1960. *American Journal of Occupational Therapy, 25,* 234–236.

Mosey, A. (1973a). *Activities therapy.* New York: Raven Press.

Mosey, A. (1973b). Meeting health needs. *American Journal of Occupational Therapy, 27,* 14–17.

Mosey, A. (1974). An alternative: The biopsychosocial model. *American Journal of Occupational Therapy, 28,* 137–140.

Mosey, A. (1976). The night of January twenty-seven. *American Journal of Occupational Therapy, 30,* 648–649.

Mosey, A. (1980). A model for occupational therapy. *Occupational Therapy in Mental Health, 1,* 11–32.

Mosey, A. (1981). *Occupational therapy: Configuration of a profession.* New York: Raven Press.

Mosey, A. (1985). A monistic or a pluralistic approach to professional identity. Eleanor Clarke Slagle Lecture. *American Journal of Occupational Therapy, 39,* 504–509.

Mosey, A. (1986). *Psychosocial components of occupational therapy.* New York: Raven Press.

Pearce, J., and Newton, S. (1963). *The conditions of human growth.* New York: The Citadel Press.

Reilly, M. (1962). Occupational therapy can be one of the greatest ideas of the twentieth century. *American Journal of Occupational Therapy, 16,* 1–9.

Reilly, M. (Ed.) (1974). *Play as exploratory learning.* Beverly Hills: Sage Publications.

Schilder, P. (1950). *The image and appearance of the human body.* New York: John Wiley & Sons.

Schneider, A. (1960). *Personality development and adjustment in adolescence.* Milwaukee: Bruce Publishing Company.

Searles, H. (1960). *The nonhuman environment.* New York: International University Press.

Sechehaye, M. (1951a). *Symbolic realization.* New York: International University Press.

Sechehaye, M. (1951b). *A new psychotherapy in schizophrenia.* New York: Grune & Stratton.

Sieg, K. (1974). Applying the behavioral model to occupational therapy. *American Journal of Occupational Therapy, 7,* 421–428.

Smith, A., & Tempone, V. (1968). Psychiatric occupational therapy within a learning theory context. *American Journal of Occupational Therapy, 22,* 415–425.

Sullivan, H.S. (1953). *The interpersonal theory of psychiatry.* New York: Norton.

Trombly, C., & Scott, A.D. (1977). *Occupational therapy for physical dysfunction.* Baltimore: Williams & Wilkins.

Wolpe, J., & Lazarus, A. (1966). *Behavior therapy techniques.* New York: Pergamon Press.

BIBLIOGRAPHY

1968

Mosey, A.C. (1968), *Occupational therapy: Theory and practice.* Medford, MA: Pothier Brothers.

Mosey, A.C. (1968). Recapitulation of ontogenesis: A theory for the practice of occupational therapy. *American Journal of Occupational Therapy, 22,* 426–432.

1969

Mosey, A.C. (1969). Treatment of pathological distortion of body image. *American Journal of Occupational Therapy, 23,* 413–416:

1970

Mosey, A.C. (1970). The concept and use of developmental groups. *American Journal of Occupational Therapy, 24,* 272–275.

Mosey, A.C. (1970). *Three frames of reference for mental health.* Thorofare, NJ: Charles B. Slack.

1971

Mosey, A.C. (1971). Involvement in the rehabilitation movement 1942–1960. *American Journal of Occupational Therapy, 25,* 234–236.

1973

Mosey, A.C. (1973). *Activities therapy.* New York: Raven Press.

Mosey, A.C. (1973). Meeting health needs. *American Journal of Occupational Therapy, 27,* 14–17.

1974

Mosey, A.C. (1974). An alternative: The biopsychosocial model. *American Journal of Occupational Therapy, 28,* 137–140.

Corry, S., Sebastian, V., & Mosey, A.C. (1974). Acute short-term treatment in psychiatry. *American Journal of Occupational Therapy, 28,* 401–406

1976

Mosey, A.C. (1976). The night of January twenty-seven. *American Journal of Occupational Therapy, 30,* 648–649.

1980

Mosey, A.C. (1980). A model of occupational therapy. *Occupational Therapy in Mental Health, 1,* 11–32.

Katz, G.M., & Mosey, A.C. (1980). Fieldwork performance, academic grades and pre-selection criteria of occupational therapy students. *American Journal of Occupational Therapy, 34,* 794–800.

1981

Mosey, A.C. (1981). The art of practice. In B.C. Abreu (Ed.), *Physical disabilities manual* (pp. 1–3). New York: Raven Press.

Mosey, A.C. (1981). *Occupational therapy: Configuration of a profession.* New York: Raven Press.

1985

Mosey, A.C. (1985). A monistic or a pluralistic approach to professional identity. Eleanor Clarke Slagle Lecture. *American Journal of Occupational Therapy, 39,* 504–509.

1986

Mosey, A.C. (1986). *Psychosocial components of occupational therapy.* New York: Raven Press.

Chapter Four

Lela A. Llorens

Susan Denegan Shortridge

Lela A. Llorens

BIOGRAPHICAL SKETCH

Lela A. Llorens was born in Shreveport, Louisiana in 1933 during an era when women were not expected to have careers. In addition to the cultural stereotypes of the times, Llorens' heritage as a black woman in a Southern community made it difficult for her to break away from the environmental barriers surrounding her. Llorens' parents recognized these barriers and moved the family to Michigan in search of a better education than was available to black children in the South at that time.

A natural inclination toward art and crafts and an interest in medicine led Llorens to explore occupational therapy as a career choice. Her initial contact with the profession of occupational therapy was through a curriculum description in a college catalog. She decided to enter the OT program at the University of Puget Sound in 1949. In 1950, she transferred to Western Michigan University in conjunction with another family move.

While attending Western Michigan University (1950–1953), Llorens was a student of Marion R. Spear, chairperson and founder of that department. That department held high leadership expectations for its graduates. Five future OT department chairpersons graduated in the years immediately before and after Llorens' graduation. Llorens was recognized early as an outstanding student and received the Marion R. Spear Scholastic Award.

Llorens' main areas of interest in occupational therapy were in mental health and pediatrics, and her career moves were chosen to enable her to develop her skills in these areas. Mentors seemed to have played an important part in shaping her career, and in each position she sought significant people within the work setting from whom to learn. As she stated, "The positions I've held have contributed to my continued growth, interest, and direction in the field. This has been partly deliberate and partly opportunity" (L.A. Llorens, personal communication, September 2, 1983).

Llorens' first position as an occupational therapist was as a staff therapist at the site of one of her internships—Wayne County General Hospital. As a student, she had been concerned about not being able to explain satisfactorily what occupational therapy was. As a new therapist, she identified many therapists who could "demonstrate" the value of occupational therapy, but could not articulate frames of reference or theory related to it.

Llorens was enthusiastic about program development for adult psychiatric patients within a general hospital setting. Mae McGiverin, head of the occupational therapy department at Wayne County General Hospital, became a significant person in Llorens' career development. Within this setting, Llorens began to develop programs and to articulate what occupational therapy was providing through these programs. Llorens remained in this position for 4 years (1953–1957).

Despite a decrease in salary and an increase in travel time, Llorens accepted a staff position at Northville State Hospital in Michigan because it enabled her to increase her patient contact with children. Although she was there for only 1 year (1957–1958), this experience confirmed Llorens' interest in pediatrics. As she stated:

> I really was fascinated with emotionally disturbed children and what occupational therapy could do for them. There was not very much in the literature regarding pediatrics . . . it was a matter of figuring out what the profession had to offer based on what was already known about adults. (L.A. Llorens, personal communication, September 2, 1983)

Llorens' next professional move was to the Lafayette Clinic (1958–1968). She started as supervisor of children's OT services and gradually moved up to become head of the OT clinic. As a practicing occupational therapist in child psychiatry and as a supervisor of therapists practicing with adult psychosocial and neurological patients, Llorens felt a need to be more conversant with psychology and research methodology. Within this work setting, Llorens was trying to delineate the role of occupational therapy in a psychotherapeutic setting. In order to support her practice goals with educational advancement, Llorens pursued an M.A. degree in vocational rehabilitation from Wayne State University in Detroit, Michigan. She chose this degree program because its flexibility enabled her to choose course work that complemented her effectiveness as a therapist and as a supervisor. School became the arena where Llorens could explore the questions that were uncovered during her working day. She stated:

> Term papers that I was doing for classes were essentially significant learning experiences. They were not just papers that were handed in to fulfill an assignment or requirements for a degree. (L.A. Llorens, personal communication, September 2, 1983)

It was during this exploration-learning phase of Llorens' early career that a strong collaborative relationship developed with Eli Rubin, Ph.D., then coordinator of children's services at the Lafayette Clinic. Dr. Rubin provided a sounding board for her early thoughts on emotionally disturbed children. It was during the beginning of this working relationship that Llorens' first article, "Psychological Tests in Planning Treatment Goals" was published (Llorens, 1960). This first work revealed the importance of

Llorens' relationship with Dr. Rubin and the impact of her schooling on her professional work. As she said:

> My first publication resulted from a term paper that I did for my masters degree. Although I was the single author on this paper, Eli contributed a great deal to the structure and the content. He helped me to organize—which was probably the beginning of a framework or orientation to organize behaviors that we were seeing in occupational therapy. I initially used more of a psychological framework because that seemed to offer some way of beginning to look at the behaviors that we were seeing clinically. (L.A. Llorens, personal communication, September 2, 1983)

While at the Lafayette Clinic, Llorens worked with a research team, an experience that added a new dimension to her writing and treatment capabilities. Members of the interdisciplinary team who were involved in patient care and research included two special educators, a recreational therapist, and two psychologists. After establishing professional relationships with members of this team, Llorens' publications reflected a stronger base in psychology, improved skills in traditional research methodology, and a more distinct view of occupational therapy. Her early article, "Psychological Tests in Planning Treatment Goals," was an attempt to integrate evaluation data gathered from psychological testing with behavior observations made in occupational therapy. As stated by Llorens (1960):

> For occupational therapy to contribute to the therapeutic community it must be capable of contributing a specific commodity . . . participate cooperatively . . . and must be capable of a collaborative relationship. For many years, occupational therapy has maintained a dependent role to medical staff and a rivalrous, conflicting role to nursing . . . . Occupational therapy has a specific contributive function which can be realized through effective evaluation and comprehensive programming. (p. 89)

Llorens was awarded the AOTA Eleanor Clarke Slagle Lectureship in 1969. This award stimulated the emergence of Llorens' own developmental theory. The lecture created a time-pressure and as Llorens (1970) explicitly stated at the time of its presentation:

> Preparing for this moment has been an arduous task. Many of my colleagues and friends have checked on my progress during

> the year and the answer most given was "We're living with it." We, including my family, have literally lived with the "Lecture" this year and the breakthrough that I was struggling for did not come until late summer during our trip to West Africa. When it did, it came in the form of ten premises which express a developmental theory of occupational therapy. (p. 93)

Almost 15 years passed between Llorens' first position as an occupational therapist and her written conceptualization of a developmental theory for the practice of occupational therapy. Three significant accomplishments were achieved during this phase of Llorens' career. First, receiving the Eleanor Clarke Slagle Lectureship indicated recognition of her expertise in the practice of occupational therapy by the profession as a whole. Second, Llorens' written publications confirmed her abilities in the treatment of emotionally disturbed children. Third, the completion of an M.A. degree in vocational rehabilitation confirmed her commitment to higher education and provided important academic credentials. The time period following the presentation of the Eleanor Clarke Slagle Lectureship was a quieter professional phase for Llorens.

Throughout Llorens' career, she has been inspired by Wilma West, who has served as a important mentor. West was long active in the AOTA and worked in administration, education, research, and consultation. According to Llorens, "Wilma West's vision, her ability to articulate the promise of occupational therapy, and her belief in my ability to make a significant contribution to the profession were inspirational to me" (L.A. Llorens, personal communication, September 2, 1983). On West's suggestion, Llorens moved to Mount Zion Hospital in San Francisco to become a member of the Comprehensive Child Care Project (1968–1971). This project enabled Llorens to explore diverse roles for the profession, particularly the expansion of OT services into community and nontraditional settings. While working on this project Llorens began to address cultural variables in health care delivery. She also explored the limits of occupational therapy's effectiveness in a pediatric population. The significance of this work experience was that it confirmed that occupational therapy had a knowledge base that could expand and remain viable in diverse settings, such as public schools, community agencies, and outpatient clinics.

Llorens served primarily as a consultant in the Mount Zion Project. This was a new role for occupational therapists. However, it did not satisfy Llorens' desire to develop stronger research skills. In 1970, Llorens entered a doctoral program at the University of the Pacific in Stockton, California, but found that the program's emphasis in educational psychology did not satisfy her need to learn more about research while maintaining her commitment to occupational therapy.

At this point in Llorens' career, she began to reflect on her original choice of profession and to explore other vocational possibilities. Llorens went so far as to take vocational tests and found that her test profiles were almost identical to ones from her college years that had confirmed her decision to become a health care professional. From this time of reflection came Llorens' decision that she should change her focus from clinical practice to academia.

Llorens had acquired teaching experience throughout her employment history. For example, one of Llorens' responsibilities during the Mount Zion Project was to teach growth and development to medical pediatric interns and residents. Although the Department of Pediatrics wanted Llorens to continue to do this teaching, she was faced with a career decision.

> I really felt that if I was going to teach full-time, I should be teaching occupational therapists. I had about 18 years experience and there were not many people around with that kind of clinical experience. . . . I felt that it should be passed on. (L.A. Llorens, personal communication, September 2, 1983)

While seeking a teaching position, Llorens investigated many OT programs. Her decision to accept an appointment as an associate professor at the University of Florida was based on several critical factors. These included the opportunity to be involved in the development of a graduate program, the developmental hierarchy inherent in the design of the existing curriculum, and a deep respect for the chairperson, Dr. Alice Jantzen. Llorens' relationship with Dr. Jantzen proved to be a significant factor in guiding her academic career toward success. As she described:

> I would also have to name Dr. Jantzen as one of my mentors. I learned a great deal from her as a strong leader within the profession, as well as in the college and department at the University of Florida. It was important to me that she was planning to remain for a number of years after I arrived. My goals, while they included a future academic administrative position, also included some other things that I thought I needed to learn. (L.A. Llorens, personal communication, September 2, 1983)

This new phase of involvement in academic occupational therapy appeared to be a significant reawakening of ambition and direction for Llorens. From 1971–1974 Llorens was occupied with responsibilities as an associate professor and graduate coordinator. During this phase of her teaching career, she gained invaluable skills and knowledge from Dr. Jantzen.

> I learned about academia from Dr. Jantzen. I learned how to "mentor" young faculty and how to run an academic program as contrasted to a rehabilitative program. I learned about higher education as viewed by the academy, which has a different value system than that held by "helping" professions. I learned how to be an academician, as well as a therapist, teacher, and writer. (L.A. Llorens, personal communication, September 2, 1983)

In 1975, when Jantzen retired, Llorens assumed a new academic role, the position of acting department chairperson. In the next 2 years, she made significant advances in the academic setting. She received her Ph.D. from Walden University, Naples, Florida, was promoted to the rank of professor, and was officially appointed as the chairperson for the Department of Occupational Therapy at the University of Florida.

Llorens maintained this position for 6 years, during which time she contributed greatly to the department's development. She was instrumental in articulating the department's frame of reference for occupational therapy education and practice. She was responsible for refining the graduate program in occupational therapy. In addition to promoting graduate students' interest in research Llorens had a profound influence on the professional development of less experienced faculty.

Llorens' influence in the area of OT education was recognized at university and state levels. One of Llorens' more noteworthy responsibilities was as chairperson for the Research Advisory Committee of the American Occupational Therapy Foundation. Her abilities as a researcher and leader in the field were apparent in her repeated election to this position (1978 to present). Awards granted by the AOTA, in addition to the Eleanor Clarke Slagle Lectureship, include Roster of Fellows in 1973, a Certificate of Appreciation in 1981, and the Award of Merit in 1986.

In 1982, after 10 years at the University of Florida, Llorens made a new career decision. She became Professor and Coordinator of Graduate Studies at the Department of Occupational Therapy, San Jose State University. The following year, she was elected by the faculty to serve as chairperson of that department. In contrast to the department at the University of Florida, which is based in a medical center, San Jose's department of occupational therapy is part of The College of Arts and Sciences, which presented new challenges for Llorens.

THEORETICAL CONSTRUCTS

Dr. Llorens' experiences stimulated her to clarify a theory that would add credibility to her profession and to her role as an occupational therapist. As she states:

> The theory . . . has been an outgrowth of my experiences and research in the field of psychiatry, both pediatric and adult . . . in pediatric general medicine and community health. . . . These experiences have stimulated my desire to think through the function and purpose of occupational therapy as I have experienced it. (1970, p. 93)

The theory advanced by Llorens for the practice of occupational therapy was developed from the following thesis:

> That occupational therapy is a facilitation process which assists the individual in achieving mastery of life tasks and the ability to cope as efficiently as possible with the life expectation made of him through the mechanisms of selected input stimuli, and availability of practice in a suitable environment. (1970, p. 93)

This thesis is based on the following ten premises (Llorens, 1970):

1. That the human organism develops horizontally (simultaneously) in the area of neurophysiological, physical, psychosocial, and psychodynamic growth and in the development of social language, daily living, and sociocultural skills at specific periods of time.
2. That the human organism develops longitudinally (chronologically) in each of these areas in a continuous process as one ages.
3. That mastery of particular skills, abilities, and relationships in each of the areas of neurophysiological, physical, psychosocial and psychodynamic development, social language, daily living, and sociocultural skills, both horizontally and longitudinally, is necessary to the successful achievement of satisfactory copying behavior and adaptive relationships.
4. That such mastery is usually achieved naturally in the course of development.
5. That the fundamental endowment of the individual and the stimulation of experiences received within the environment of the family come together to interact in such a way as to

promote positive early growth and development in both the horizontal (simultaneous) and longitudinal (chronological) planes.

6. That later influences of extended family, community, social, and civic groups assist in the growth process.
7. That physical or psychological trauma related to disease, injury, environmental insufficiencies, or intrapersonal vulnerability can interrupt the growth and development process.
8. That such growth interruption will cause a gap in the developmental cycle, resulting in a disparity between expected coping behavior and adaptive facility and the necessary skills and abilities to achieve the same.
9. That occupational therapy, through the skilled application of activities and relationships, can provide growth and development links to assist in closing the gap between expectation and ability by increasing skills, abilities, and relationships in the neurophysiological, physical, psychosocial, psychodynamic, social language, daily living, and sociocultural spheres of development as indicated both horizontally and longitudinally.
10. That occupational therapy, through the skilled application of activities and relationships, can provide growth experiences to prevent the development of potential maladaptation related to insufficient nurturance in neurophysiological, physical, psychosocial, psychodynamic, social language, daily living, and sociocultural spheres of development both horizontally (simultaneously) and longitudinally (chronologically). (pp. 93–94)*

These premises are based both on her experience and research in the practice of occupational therapy and the OT and human development literature. Llorens specifically cites the literature sources contributing to her theory. However, the clinical and professional experiences that contributed to theory development are less clearly identified. In a retrospective look at her developmental theory, Llorens (1977) describes the subtle influences of her clinical and professional experiences:

> It has been of interest to rediscover the fact that some of the initial work presented in the Eleanor Clarke Slagle Lecture had

*From "Facilitating Growth and Development: The Promise of Occupational Therapy" by L.A. Llorens, 1970, *The American Journal of Occupational Therapy,* 24(2), pp. 93–94. Copyright March 1970 by American Occupational Therapy Association, Inc. Reprinted by permission.

> its roots historically in the (Theory Building Seminar of 1967) and to know that concepts discussed there were interwoven with the author's experience. However, the formulation that resulted for this author could only be articulated as it seemed real and understandable to her personal and professional development at the time. (p. 657)

Elements of Llorens' ten premises can be found in her early written works. Because these concepts were gaining stability during these years, however, it is difficult to isolate the premises in any one article. Llorens' early writings were based on her work with emotionally disturbed children and experience in vocational rehabilitation. From 1960–1964 Llorens focused on her quest for appropriate OT evaluation and treatment procedures. Publications written during those years were generally case studies and descriptions of activity programs (Llorens, 1960, 1961; Llorens & Bernstein, 1963; Llorens, Levy, & Rubin, 1964; Llorens & Rubin, 1961, 1962; Llorens & Young, 1960).

Llorens (Llorens and Rubin, 1961) was quick to recognize that data were needed to support the assumption that OT activities for children were therapeutic. In an attempt to establish baseline data she began to look at the effects of emotional disturbances on the child's development. This idea is perhaps Llorens' first reference to the impact of developmental disruption on the OT client in relationship to the process of occupational therapy. It is the central theme of Llorens' developmental theory and is most clearly expressed in premises 7 and 8, which address the influence of physical or psychological trauma on the developmental process.

The primary impact of Llorens' work in cognitive-perceptual-motor (CPM) dysfunction on her later developmental theory was that it was her first exposure to the effect of adverse conditions on growth and development (Beck et al., 1965). Llorens hypothesized that CPM deficits could create an inability to cope with the demands of the environment (Llorens, Levy, & Rubin, 1964).

Llorens' description of the OT process, later defined as "skilled application of activities and relationships" in premises 9 and 10, was clearly present in her early work (1970, p. 94). Llorens' early conceptualization of "skilled application" emphasized the need for gradation, the presentation of activity at the client's level, and the use of specific activities for specific goals. Because of the stability of these concepts, one can select many of Llorens' early papers to support them (Llorens, 1967; Llorens & Beck, 1966; Llorens & Johnson, 1966; Llorens & Rubin, 1962). For example, in "A Directed Activity Program for Disturbed Children," Llorens (Llorens & Rubin, 1962) emphasized that treatment procedures should be:

> activities beginning at a level commensurate with the child's ability, allowing for successful accomplishment and mastery and presenting opportunities to raise his level of skill. (p. 287)

This developmental approach to treatment is also found in Llorens' publications on vocational rehabilitation. Criteria for selecting patients for a work adjustment program are based on vocational deficits, rather than diagnostic classification (Llorens, Levy, & Rubin, 1964). In Llorens' later work with emotionally disturbed clients and CPM dysfunction, initiation of treatment at the child's level continued to be stressed. However, a more definitive move from the medical model was seen in Llorens' involvement with the Lafayette research team's effort to clarify causes of deficits and put aside classification according to diagnostic category (Braun et al., 1965).

As Llorens continued to clarify the OT evaluation and treatment process, the concept of mastery emerged in her writing. The importance of the concept of mastery was later elaborated on in premises 3 and 4 of her advanced theory. In her early writings on emotional disturbance, Llorens recognized that the absence of emotional problems resulted in the acquisition of skills through practice and mastery. She hypothesized that these skills later became problem-solving methods that directly affected the child's self-confidence, self-concept, and self-esteem (Llorens & Rubins, 1961). As a stronger relationship between emotional disturbance and CPM deficits was expressed in the Lafayette research team's writings, the recognition that mastery should be an integral part of the treatment protocol for CPM dysfunction became apparent. Treatment activities were described as follows (Beck et al., 1965):

> Many of the activities are those which children usually master through maturation and environmental stimulation. However, since some children do not, for a variety of reasons, such as inadequate experiences, master them successfully, the retraining process provides a sequence through which the child can progress artificially, thus enabling him to correct his deficit in primary adaptive functions. (pp. 236–237)

Not only was the need for mastery recognized in treatment but also the concept of mastery as a naturally occurring developmental phenomenon became recognized as CPM training was further defined (Llorens & Beck, 1966).

> CPM training is a learning process concerned with developing areas of functional ability where competency usually develops through maturation and environmental experience. Mastery in such areas is ordinarily achieved naturally without specific attention being paid to it and without the necessity of it being taught. (p. 155)

As Llorens' involvement with CPM research continued, she began to address the relationship of environmental factors to the child's CPM dysfunction. Such factors included parental attitude, early schooling, and environmental feedback (Braun et al., 1967). The effect of the environment on the developmental process is shown in premises 5 and 6.

Llorens did not discuss environmental factors in depth until after the premises had been written and presented in the Eleanor Clarke Slagle lecture. This aspect of development was later emphasized while Llorens was active in the Mount Zion Project. Her following publications (1971–1973) discussed the effect of sociological and cultural variables in health care delivery. For example, in Llorens' (1971a) description of lifestyles in the black community and their relevance to child rearing and health care practices, she stated:

> All children must master specific developmental tasks and ego adaptive skills between infancy and adolescence. . . . Some of these skills will be learned in school. In this society, the combination of financial means, the lifestyle of the family, and its aspirations, along with knowledge of and availability of resources, play a large part in influencing the extent to which black children are able to develop in these areas. (p. 148)

Llorens' conception of the occupational therapist as a health care agent changed as she placed increased emphasis on the cultural aspect of the client's development. In her earliest description, Llorens depicted the therapist as an enabler, helping the client learn new ideas and develop new skills (Llorens & Rubin, 1962). Facilitating the process of enculturation became more important as Llorens gained clinical experience.

Perhaps the key element of Llorens' theory—that growth and development occur simultaneously (horizontally) and chronologically (longitudinally)—is found in her first two premises. These premises do not contain new information; however, it is Llorens' organization of the material that gives them value. Llorens elaborates on the holistic nature of development and cites theorists who support this idea. For example, although Piaget was recognized primarily for his work in cognitive development, he links such development closely to the acquisition of sensorimotor and sociocultural skills.

Not only was Llorens able to present the ten premises in an orderly, understandable sequence but she also went one step further in developing a graphic representation of growth and development concepts for occupational therapy. The *Schematic Representation of Facilitating Growth and Development* was first published in 1970. In 1976 she published an updated version. This schematic presents stage-specific development categories of human growth (Llorens, 1976). References cited in the organization of this chart include Ayres (neurophysiological development); Gesell (physical, social language, sociocultural, and daily living development); Erikson (psychosocial development); Freud (psychodynamic development); Havighurst (developmental tasks); Pearce, Newton, and Mosey (adaptive skills); and Piaget (intellectual development). Although each theorist is recognized for a particular area of expertise, Llorens stressed that these areas of growth "overlap and interweave" and should not be viewed in a "segmental" fashion. The schematic representation expresses growth horizontally and vertically to depict chronological or age-related development. Thus, this chart can be seen as a tapestry. Each area of development overlaps and interweaves horizontally and vertically, creating a stable base for the human organism to mature. If any one area is interrupted, then a thread becomes weakened, and the growth and development process is no longer stable.

The schematic representation is organized into three sections (see Table 4-1). Section I emphasizes developmental expectations, behaviors, and needs. It deals primarily with areas of developmental growth described by Ayres, Gesell, Erikson, and Freud. Chronological growth is depicted vertically with age ranges superimposed; however, Llorens (1970) cautions that these ages are "suggestive rather than absolute" (p. 95). The concept of mastery, first described in premises 3 and 4, is emphasized in the application of this structure for practice. It is mastery of developmental tasks that results in achievement of behavior expectations and adaptive skills described in Section III. Although developmental tasks and behavior expectations are separated in the chart, Llorens feels that they occur simultaneously. Growth in developmental tasks is facilitated by the family, environment, extended family, community, and social and civic groups (premises 5 and 6).

Adaptive skills and behavioral expectations are those coping skills that help the individual deal effectively with life and life roles. The behavior expectations presented in Section III are derived from the works of

Table 4-1 Schematic Representation of Facilitating Growth and Development

SECTION I
Developmental Expectations, Behaviors, and Needs
(Selected for illustrative purposes)

Neurophysiological-Sensorimotor Ayres	*Physical-Motor Gesell*	*Psychosocial Erikson*
0-2 Sensorimotor Tactile functions Vestibular functions Visual, auditory, olfactory, gustatory functions	0-2 Head sags Fisting Gross motion Walking Climbing	Basic Trust vs. Mistrust/Oral Sensory Ease of feeding Depth of sleep Relaxation of bowels
6 mo.-4 Integration of Body Sides Gross motor planning Form and space perception Equilibrium response Postural and bilateral integration Body scheme development	2-3 Runs Balances Hand preference established Coordination	Autonomy vs. Shame and Doubt/ Muscular-Anal Conflict between holding on and letting go
3-7 Discrimination Refined tactile Kinesthetic, visual, auditory, olfactory, gustatory functions	3-6 Coordination more graceful Muscles develop Skills develop	Initiative vs. Guilt/Locomotor-Genital Aggressiveness Manipulation Coercion
3- Abstract Thinking Conceptualization Complex relationships Read, write, numbers	6-11 Energy development Skill practice to attain proficiency	Industry vs. Inferiority/Latency Wins recognition through productivity Learns skills and tools
Continue development Conceptualization Complex relationships Read, write, numbers	11-13 Rapid growth Poor posture Awkwardness	Identity vs. Role Confusion/ Puberty and Adolescence Identification Social roles
Development presumably maintained	Growth established and maintained	Intimacy vs. Isolation/Young Adulthood Commitments Body and ego mastery
Alterations begin to occur in sensory functions, conceptualization, and memory	Alterations begin to occur in motor behavior, strength, and endurance	Generativity vs. Stagnation/ Adulthood Guiding next generation Creative, productive
Alterations in sensory functions, conceptualization, and memory	Alterations in motor behavior, strength, and endurance	Ego Integrity vs. Despair/Maturity Acceptance of own life cycle

Table 4-1 (*Continued*)

SECTION I
Developmental Expectations, Behaviors, and Needs
(Selected for illustrative purposes)

Psychodynamic Hall, Grant, Freud	*Socio-Cultural Gesell*	*Social-Language Gesell*	*Activity of Daily Living Gesell*
<u>0-4 Oral</u> Dependency Initially aggressive Oral erotic activity	Individual mothering person most important Immediate family group important	Small sounds Coos Vocalizes Listens Speaks	Recognizes bottle Holds spoon Holds glass Controls bowel
<u>0-4 Anal</u> Independence Resistiveness Self-assertiveness Narcissism Ambivalence	Parallel play Often alone Recognizes extended family	Identifies objects verbally Asks "why?" Short sentences	Feeds self Helps undress Recognizes simple tunes No longer wets at night
<u>3-6 Genital-Oedipal</u> Genital interest Possessiveness of opposite sex parent Antagonistic to same sex parent Castration fears	Seeks companionship Makes decisions Plays with other children Takes turns	Combines talking and eating Complete sentences Imaginative Dramatic	Laces shoes Cuts with scissors Toilets independently Helps set table
<u>6-11 Latency</u> Primitive struggles quiescent Initiative in mastery of skills Strong defenses	Group play and team activities Independence of adults Gang interests	Language major form of communication	Enjoys dressing up Learns value of money Responsible for grooming
<u>11- Adolescence</u> Emancipation from parents Occupational decisions Role experiment Re-examine values	Team games Organization important Interest in opposite sex	Verbal language predominates	Interest in earning money
Outgrow need for parent validation Identify with others	Group affiliation Family, social, civic interest	Non-verbal behavior also used to communicate	Concern for personal grooming, mate, family
Emotional responsibilities may lessen Physical and economic independence accepted Shift from survival to enjoyment	↓	↓	Accepting and adjusting to changes of middle age
Continued growth after middle age Inner trend toward survival	↓	↓	Adjusting to changes after middle age

Table 4-1 (*Continued*)

SECTION II
Facilitating Activities and Relationships (Selected)

E V A L U A T I O N

Sensorimotor Activities	*Developmental Activities*	*Symbolic Activities*	*Daily Life Tasks*	*Interpersonal Relationships*
Tactile stimulation Visual, auditory, olfactory, gustatory stimulation	Dolls Animals Sand Water Excursions	Biting Chewing Eating Blowing Cuddling	Recognize food Hold feeding equipment Use feeding equipment	Individual Interaction
Physical exercise Balancing Motor planning	Pull toys Playground Clay Crayons Chalk	Throwing Dropping Messing Collecting Destroying	Feeding Dressing Toileting	Individual Interaction Parallel play
Listening Learning Skilled tasks and games	Being read to Coloring Drawing Painting	Destroying Exhibiting	Feeding Dressing Toileting Simple chores	Individual Interaction Play small groups
Reading Writing Numbers	Scooters Wagons Collections Puppets Building	Controlling Mastery	Feeding Dressing Grooming Spending	Individual Interaction Groups Teams Clubs
All of the above available to be recycled	Weaving Machinery tasks Carving Modeling	All of the above to be recycled	Feeding Dressing Grooming Pre-vocational skills	Individual Interaction Groups Teams
	Arts Crafts Sports Club and interest groups Education Work		Feeding Dressing Grooming Life role, skills	Individual Interaction Groups

Table 4-1 (*Continued*)

SECTION III
Behavior Expectations and Adaptive Skills

Developmental Tasks *Havighurst*	*Ego-Adaptive Skills* *Mosey, Pearce, and Newton*	*Intellectual Development* *Piaget*
Learning to: Walk Talk Take solids Elimination Sex difference To form concepts of social and physical reality To relate emotionally to others Right Wrong To develop a conscience	Ability to respond to mothering Mastering of gross motor responses	Motor skills Integrated
	Ability to respond to routines of daily living Mastery of 3 dimensional space Sense of body image	Investigative Imitative Egocentric
	Ability to Follow directions Tolerate frustrations Sit still Delay gratification	Egocentricism reduced, social participation increases Language replaces motor behavior
Learn physical skills Getting along Reading, writing Values Social attitudes	Ability to perceive, sort, organize and utilize stimuli Work in groups Mastery of inanimate objects	Orders experiences Relates parts to wholes Deductive reasoning
More mature relationships Social roles Selecting occupation Achieving emotional independence	Ability to accept and discharge responsibility Capacity for love	Systematic approach to problems Sense of equality supersedes submission to adults
Selecting a mate Starting family Marriage, home Congenial social group	Ability to function independently Control drives Plan and execute Purposeful motion Obtain, organize, and use knowledge Participate in primary group Participate in variety of relationships Experience self as acceptable Participate in mutually satisfactory heterosexual relations	Development established and maintained
Civic and social responsibility Economic standard of living Develop adult leisure activities Adjust to aging parents		Alterations in other areas may affect
Adjust to decreasing physical health, retirement, death Age group affiliation Meeting social obligations		

Source: From *Application of a Developmental Theory for Health and Rehabilitation* (pp. 32–33) by L.A. Llorens, 1976, Rockville, Md.: American Occupational Therapy Association, Inc. Copyright 1976 by American Occupational Therapy Association, Inc. Reprinted by permission.

Havighurst (development tasks); Pearce, Newton, and Mosey (ego-adaptive skills); and Piaget (intellectual development).

The role of occupational therapy (presented in premises 9 and 10)—facilitating activities and relationships—is shown in Section II of the chart. When physical or psychological trauma is experienced in any one of the horizontal or longitudinal parameters, the development cycle is threatened or disrupted (premises 7 and 8). This creates disparity between the developmental expectations (Section I) and behavioral expectations and adaptive skills (Section III). To bridge this developmental gap, Section II illustrates the tools of occupational therapy that are used in the process of facilitating growth and development. As noted by its position in the chart, the first step in the intervention process is evaluation, which includes testing, interviews, record review, and systematic clinical observation. It is from these evaluation procedures that the therapist determines "at what level the individual is functioning in the various aspects along the developmental continuum and to program for facilitating growth and development . . . in accordance with the needs of the individual and the demands of his age" (Llorens, 1970, p. 100). The therapist chooses tasks from sensorimotor activities, developmental play activities, symbolic activities, daily life tasks, and interpersonal relationships to facilitate the growth process and narrow any developmental discrepancy (Llorens, 1970). Llorens emphasizes that, although special attention may be placed on facilitating the process of growth in any one particular parameter, all parameters of development must be acknowledged for an integrating growth experience to occur.

Llorens views human functioning as interrelated in an ongoing developmental continuum, but recognizes that declines in growth and development are normal at certain time periods. The human being is a changing organism, as stated by Llorens (1970):

> The life span of the individual encompasses several phases of physical growth, neurophysiological, psychological, social and emotional development, as well as a gradual decline in many of these processes, particularly physical development . . . (p. 94)

Although different phases of development gain primacy at specific periods of time during the developmental life-span, Llorens (1970) believes that in order to "achieve in the adaptive areas of functioning, it is necessary . . . to experience satisfaction and mastery" in all areas of development (p. 95). Emotional growth requires nurturing, specifically with "affection, understanding, security, and discipline" (Llorens, 1970, p. 95).

This developmental theory is related to the health-illness continuum by its connection to the individual's ability to master developmental tasks successfully and thus achieve appropriate adaptive skills. This achievement is viewed as a healthy state, with recognition of normal deviations that may occur. Illness is seen as either psychological or physical stress that is potentially threatening to a client's wellness and may result in functioning that does not display the client's optimum skill level; specifically, regression to an earlier developmental level may occur.

When disruption in the developmental process has been identified through the appropriate evaluation procedures, it is the task of the occupational therapist to determine at what level the client is functioning on the developmental continuum. An appropriate facilitation program should meet the client's needs and the demands of the client's age and life roles. The intervention process for prevention of health problems is different from that for conditions of acute illness or temporary or permanent disability. Llorens (1970) believes that "intervention at a stage that can be identified before trauma becomes overwhelming will allow the individual to continue his growth process with a minimum of interruption and continue toward the achievement of ego-adaptive skills" (p. 100). In treatment geared toward identifiable acute illness or temporary or permanent disability, facilitation of development tasks and ego-adaptive skills must be viewed in relationship to the client's needs and limitations and geared to a realistic level of attainment.

Later Work

Llorens' theoretical conceptualizations are presented in several major publications, each of which builds on the other, strengthening not only the theory's clarity but also its accessibility to the reader (Llorens, 1970, 1976, 1977). After the theory was first introduced to the OT profession through the Eleanor Clarke Slagle Lectureship, Llorens' concepts were published in the *American Journal of Occupational Therapy* in 1970. The title of this major work was "Facilitating Growth and Development—The Promise of Occupational Therapy" (Llorens, 1970). In the years that followed, work on her developmental theory continued, specifically on its application to health and rehabilitation. The book, *Application of a Developmental Theory for Health and Rehabilitation,* which was published in 1976, was a restatement of her developmental theory that elaborated on its application with clients through the entire developmental spectrum, from pediatrics to old age.

Llorens' theory changed very little between its early presentation and the *Application of a Developmental Theory for Health and Rehabilitation* (Llorens, 1976). As it was refined, new terms were substituted and statements reorganized for improved clarity. For example, the original terms "horizontal" and "longitudinal" development were clarified by the addition of the words, "simultaneous" and "chronological" development, respectively. In defining the areas of development affected by occupational therapy, Llorens added intellectual development to the original list that included neurophysiological, physical, psychosocial, psychodynamic, social language, daily living, and sociocultural skills. The first chart paired Piaget's theory of intellectual development with Ayres' neurophysiological development. In the later formulation of premises 9 and 10, Llorens more distinctly pinpointed when OT services were appropriate: "at the time of growth interruption" (premise 9) and "before the point of overwhelming trauma" (premise 10) (Llorens, 1976, p. 3). Daily life tasks were added to the tools of the occupational therapist in Section II.

CRITIQUE

When Llorens' developmental theory is subjected to critical analysis, several identifiable strengths and weaknesses are found. The theory has clearly withstood the test of time and has made a significant contribution to the field of occupational therapy. Llorens' early publications demonstrate the initial formulation of concepts of development that then blossomed into an organized theoretical conceptualization and credible research. In reviewing the publications of Dr. Llorens, two adjectives come to mind: consistency and common sense.

Llorens' commitment to writing, research, and education has enhanced her theory's credibility by making it accessible to the profession. Through these three modes, Llorens has contributed to making theory development an integral aspect of OT knowledge generation, and practice.

Llorens' developmental theory is an organized one. Although Llorens' writing skills may have been stimulated by her early experiences in psychology and subsequent exposure to an established research style, she demonstrates an intuitive ability to organize material. This ability is manifested in her schematic representation of the theory's conceptualization and in the dissemination process that Llorens has used to make her theory visible. A distinct progression of the theory's early constructs to its systematic application through the Sequential Client Care Record (1982) can be found throughout her numerous publications. Llorens has the ability to derive fresh ideas from her original concepts. She circulates her information to new audiences by selecting a variety of communication methods, such as workshops, journals, newsletters, and lectureships, to convey her concepts.

Llorens' career development is that of an organized and goal-directed professional. A systematic process of educational advances and career moves can be found throughout Llorens' professional development. Preparation, planning, and timetables have been integral parts of Llorens' decision making. These organizational skills have helped Llorens complete numerous publications and participate in a variety of professional activities. Her roles have been varied and have included such titles as: distinguished lecturer, consultant, chairperson, board member, grants reviewer, division editor, visiting scholar, principal investigator, and wife and mother.

The developmental theory provides a frame of reference that is applicable to all clients along the developmental continuum. It does not encourage specialization within the profession, but instead provides a framework for the occupational therapist to coordinate mind and body in holistic treatment fashion.

However, although the theory purports to be applicable to clients of all ages, it can be more easily applied to the younger client. This weakness stems from the lack of human growth and development research that was available on the adult when the theory was first developed. Llorens (1970) alluded to this weakness in the theory's initial presentation as an Eleanor Clarke Slagle lecture quoting Pearce and Newton (1963, p. 119):

> The primary conditions for growth for the adult are crucially different from the conditions of growth of the developmental eras of pre-adulthood. . . . Not enough information has been documented concerning physical growth and development in old age. (1970, p. 95)

She has, however, strengthened her theory as more information has become available. Llorens' developmental theory substantiates the role of the biological and behavioral sciences in the OT profession. In addition to the inclusion of theories that come from a strong scientific base, such as Piaget and Erikson, Llorens also incorporates the concept of activity analysis into her framework. Although activity analysis and the use of activity in the restoration of function have long been accepted by the OT profession, these concepts have not yet been clearly substantiated or refuted through systematic study. An inherent weakness in theory development exists when the hierarchy on which it is built is not scientifically consistent. Llorens chose to include activity analysis because it is readily accepted within the profession. However, a reader outside the profession would clearly pinpoint this weakness.

APPLICATION TO OCCUPATIONAL THERAPY PRACTICE

Llorens' 1976 book made several contributions to increasing the theory's applicability to OT practice. The first was the creation of the Occupational Therapy Development Analysis Evaluation and Intervention Schedule

(DAEIS). This schedule provided a framework for application of her theories.

The second contribution of this text in solidifying the theory was its developmental case analyses. The theory, which presented information on the optimum levels of developmental function, was applied to 15 clients whose growth and development had been adversely affected. These case analyses described clients of all ages and with varied areas of disruption.

Another contribution is the discussion of evaluation and intervention methods that give detailed descriptions of OT tools used in the treatment or facilitation process. Both standardized and nonstandardized procedures are viewed as credible evaluation tools; however, they are described separately so that the therapist can clearly see their differences. Activity analysis is highlighted, with examples that provide insight into the theoretical basis of sensorimotor activities, developmental activities, and interpersonal relationships. Earlier, Llorens (1970) stated:

> Within the practice of our profession, there are predictable aspects relative to cause and effect in the use of activities and the application of relationships which must be identified, applied repeatedly in a systematic manner, analyzed and documented in order to establish their validity. (p. 101)

It was during her doctoral studies in 1976 that Llorens looked more closely at the validity of the DAEIS (1976) as a viable data collection tool for occupational therapy. After further study, she decided to incorporate the Problem-Oriented Medical Record (POMR) (Weed, 1971) with the DAEIS to produce a client care record with a stronger scientific base. This became the Sequential Client Care Record (SCCR) (Llorens, 1982). Subsequent research on the record's usefulness found that the variables of completeness, organizational sequence, and understandability for research and education were statistically significant (Llorens & Schuster, 1977).

The immediate need for the SCCR was to monitor quality care and accountability of OT services. However, the impact of the SCCR proved to be multifaceted. As an organizational tool, it documented the OT process in a systematic fashion while providing a viable communication tool to be used with colleagues, clients, and client's families. The SCCR served as an educational tool and provided a large data base for potential research (Llorens, 1982).

In the 1981 keynote address presented to the New Zealand Association of Occupational Therapists and in a 1983 closing address presented to the AOTA, Llorens emphasized the need to study systematically the OT process. She presented a three-dimensional schematic that categorized information related to age groups, phases of practice, modalities for screening/

evaluation, intervention, and outcomes. The Occupational Therapy Sequential Client Care Record was recommended for data gathering about the process of OT practice.

In addition to tangible evidence of the impact of Llorens' theory on occupational therapy, which is provided by these assessment tools, the theory had two by-products that are more difficult to document. The first significant by-product was that her theory added credibility to the OT profession and the role of a therapist. In one of her first publications, Llorens (1970) stated that conceptualization theory provided a method "to think through the function and purpose of occupational therapy as she had experienced it" (p. 93). Llorens confirmed this function and the attainment of this objective in her later work:

> The theory has served me well as a way to conceptualize occupational therapy and to approach patients, both as practitioner and in attempting to teach the practice discipline to undergraduate and graduate students. (L.A. Llorens, personal communication, September 2, 1983)

The second less tangible by-product of Llorens' theory is the increased awareness by occupational therapists of theory development brought about by Llorens' teaching, publications, and public presentations. The impact that Llorens has had on the OT profession is shown by the OT graduates who have entered practice with an understanding of and commitment to philosophy and theory. As Llorens states:

> It is important for me to have graduate students study theory but not be Llorens duplicates . . . to not just learn about what I knew but to put what I knew into the context of the larger field . . . . (L.A. Llorens, personal communication, September 2, 1983)

APPLICATION TO THE OCCUPATIONAL THERAPY PROFESSION

Llorens (Llorens & Gillette, 1985) believes that the OT profession should be moving to clarify the "knowledge base of occupational therapy and the effectiveness of occupational therapy intervention" (p. 143). This emerging knowledge base or science has been termed "occupationology." As Llorens and Gillette (1985) so clearly state:

> As an academic discipline, the science of occupation is in its formative stages. Because the occupational theory that supports

> the art and science of practice is also still evolving, both these areas of research need to be considered as dual interdependent missions facing the profession. (p. 143)

In speculating on the future direction of occupational therapy, Llorens hypothesizes that occupational therapy will "identify a common core from the numerous formulations that have been advanced . . . synthesized and analyzed . . . (and) will emerge with a universal theory of occupational therapy" (L.A. Llorens, personal communication, September 2, 1983). More than one frame of reference will be applied to different populations. Through this organizational process, the profession will be able to identify and organize evaluation and intervention techniques that are "congruent with the theoretical base and frames that are established" (L.A. Llorens, personal communication, September 2, 1983).

Dr. Lela A. Llorens has contributed greatly to the OT profession through the organization of the principles and concepts found in her conceptualization of developmental theory. Through the Occupational Therapy Sequential Client Care Record, she has provided a solid framework within which to collect data for future OT research. She has identified areas of research that need to be initiated by occupational therapists (Llorens, 1984; Llorens & Gillette, 1985). And she has advanced the philosophical idea for a universal theory for the profession to which she has contributed the developmental aspect. When asked, "What advice would you give to therapists struggling to identify their professional frame of reference," she replied:

> Try to be in touch with what you have been doing right as a practicing therapist . . . recognize the history of occupational therapy and theory development, there is more of that available to look at now, than there was. . . . It is important to struggle with the analysis and synthesis of one's own practice, values, and belief systems and to try to know what those are in relationship to the prevailing theoretical frames of reference, and theory of occupational therapy. What you will find is that the ideas that you have and the values you have shared are common with many who have written or with whom you are working. You will begin to be able to identify with the community of occupational therapy, rather than seeing yourself as an isolated therapist who is in a practice setting. (L.A. Llorens, personal communication, September 2, 1983)

REFERENCES

Beck, G.R., Rubin, E.Z., Braun, I.S., Llorens, L.A., Beall, D., & Mottley, N. (1965). Educational aspects of cognitive-perceptual motor functions in children—A suggested change in approach. *Psychology in Schools, 2*(3), 233–238.

Braun, J.S., Rubin, E.Z., Llorens, L.A., Beck, G.A. (1967). Cognitive-motor deficits—definition and intervention. *Proceedings of the International Convocation on Learning Disabilities.* Pittsburgh: Crippled Children's Home.

Braun, J.S., Rubin, E.Z., Llorens, L.A., Beck, G.A., Beall, D., & Mottley, N. (1965). Cognitive perceptual motor function in school children: A suggested change in approach. *Journal of School Psychology, 3,* 1–5.

Llorens, L.A. (1960). Psychological tests in planning treatment goals. *American Journal of Occupational Therapy 14,* 243–246.

Llorens, L.A. (1961). Bridging the gap: Vocational rehabilitation counseling in a psychiatric setting. *Michigan Rehabilitation Digest 2,* 24–26.

Llorens, L.A. (1967). Project technique in occupational therapy. *American Journal of Occupational Therapy, 21,* 226–229.

Llorens, L.A. (1970). Facilitating growth and development: The promise of occupational therapy. *American Journal of Occupational Therapy, 24,* 93–101.

Llorens, L.A. (1971a). Black culture and child development. *American Journal of Occupational Therapy, 25,* 144–148.

Llorens, L.A. (1971b). Occupational therapy in community child health. *American Journal of Occupational Therapy, 25,* 335–339.

Llorens, L.A. (Ed.). (1973). *Consulting in the Community: Occupational therapy in child health.* Dubuque, IA: Kendall-Hunt Publishing Co.

Llorens, L.A. (1976). *Application of a developmental theory for health and rehabilitation.* Rockville, MD: American Occupational Therapy Association.

Llorens, L.A. (1977). A developmental theory revisited. *American Journal of Occupational Therapy, 31,* 656–657.

Llorens, L.A. (1981). Occupational therapy: State of the art—Potential for development. *Proceedings of New Zealand Occupational Therapy Association.* Auckland, New Zealand.

Llorens, L.A. (1982). *Occupational therapy sequential client care record.* Laurel, MD: Ramsco Publishing Co.

Llorens, L.A. (1984). Changing balance: Environment and individual. *American Journal of Occupational Therapy, 38,* 29–34.

Llorens, L.A., & Beck, G.R. (1966). Treatment methods for cognitive-perceptual motor dysfunction. In M.J. Fehr (Ed.), *Normal growth and development with deviations in the perceptual motor and emotional areas.* (pp. 155–176). St. Louis, MO: Washington University.

Llorens, L.A., & Bernstein, S.P. (1963). Fingerpainting with an obsessive-compulsive, organically-damaged child. *American Journal of Occupational Therapy, 17,* 120–121.

Llorens, L.A., & Gillette, N.P. (1985). Nationally speaking: The challenge for research in a practice profession. *American Journal of Occupational Therapy, 39,* 143–146.

Llorens, L.A., & Johnson, P.A. (1966). Occupational therapy in ego-oriented milieu. *American Journal of Occupational Therapy, 20,* 178–181.

Llorens, L.A., Levy, R., & Rubin, E.Z. (1964). The work adjustment program: a provocational experience. *American Journal of Occupational Therapy, 18,* 15–19.

Llorens, L.A., & Rubin, E.Z. (1962). A directed activity program for disturbed children. *American Journal of Occupational Therapy, 16,* 287–290.

Llorens, L.A., & Rubin, E.Z. (1961). Occupational therapy is therapeutic: A research study with emotionally disturbed children. *Proceedings of 1961 AOTA National Conference.* Detroit, MI: American Occupational Therapy Association.

Llorens, L.A., & Schuster, J.J. (1977). Occupational therapy client care recording system: A comparative study. *American Journal of Occupational Therapy, 31,* 367–371.

Llorens, L.A., & Young, G.G. (1960). Fingerpainting for the hostile child. *American Journal of Occupational Therapy, 14,* 306–307.

Pearce, J., & Newton, S. (1963). *Conditions of human growth.* New York: Citadel Press.

Weed, L.L. (1971). *Medical records, medical education and patient care.* Chicago: Year Book Medical Publishers.

BIBLIOGRAPHY

1960

Llorens, L.A. (1960). Psychological tests in planning treatment goals. *American Journal of Occupational Therapy, 14,* 243–246.

Llorens, L.A., & Young, G.G. (1960). Fingerpainting for the hostile child. *American Journal of Occupational Therapy, 14,* 306–307.

1961

Llorens, L.A. (1961). Bridging the gap: Vocational rehabilitation counseling in a psychiatric setting. *Michigan Rehabilitation Association Digest 2,* 24–26.

Llorens, L.A., & Rubin, E.Z. (1961). Occupational therapy is therapeutic: A research study with emotionally disturbed children. *Proceedings of 1961 AOTA National Conference.* Detroit, MI: American Occupational Therapy Association.

1962

Llorens, L.A., & Rubin, E.Z. (1962). A directed activity program for disturbed children. *American Journal of Occupational Therapy, 16,* 287–290.

1963

Llorens, L.A., & Bernstein, S.P. (1963). Fingerpainting for the compulsive child. *American Journal of Occupational Therapy, 17,* 120–121.

1964

Llorens, L.A., Levy, R., & Rubin, E.Z. (1964). The work adjustment program: A prevocational experience. *American Journal of Occupational Therapy, 18,* 15–19.

Llorens, L.A., Rubin, E.Z., Braun, J.S., Mottley, N., & Beall, D. (1964). Training in cognitive-perceptual-motor functions: A preliminary report. *American Journal of Occupational Therapy, 18,* 202–209.

1965

Llorens, L.A., & Rubin, E.Z., (1965). A directed activity program for emotionally disturbed children. In J.C. Gowan & G.D. Demos (Eds.), *The guidance of exceptional children.* New York: David McKay Company.

Beck, G.R., Rubin, E.Z., Braun, J.S., Llorens, L.A., Beall, D., & Mottley, N. (1965). Educational aspects of cognitive-perceptual motor functions in children—A Suggested change in approach. *Psychology in Schools, 2*(3), 233–238.

Braun, J.S., Rubin, E.Z., Llorens, L.A., Beck, G.A., Beall, D., Mottley, N. (1965). Cognitive perceptual motor function in school children: A suggested change in approach. *Journal of School Psychology, 3,* 1–5.

1966

Llorens, L.A. (1966). Aspects of pre-vocational evaluation with psychiatric patients. *The Canadian Journal of Occupational Therapy, 33,* 5–12.

Llorens, L.A. (1966). Cognitive-perceptual-motor dysfunction, evaluation and training. In J.M. Kiernat (Ed.) *Perceptual motor dysfunction evaluation and training.* (pp. 271–292). Madison, WI: University of Wisconsin.

Llorens, L.A., & Beck, G.R. (1966). Treatment methods for cognitive-perceptual-motor dysfunction. In M.J. Fehr (Ed.), *Normal growth and development with deviations in the perceptual motor and emotional areas.* (pp. 155–177). St. Louis, MO: Washington University.

Llorens, L.A., & Johnson, P.A. (1966). Occupational therapy in ego-oriented milieu. *American Journal of Occupational Therapy, 20,* 178–181.

1967

Braun, J.S., Rubin, E.Z., Llorens, L.A., & Beck, A.R. (1967). Cognitive motor deficits—definition and intervention. *Proceedings of the International Convocation on Learning Disabilities.* Pittsburgh: Crippled Children's Home.

Llorens, L.A. (1967). Cognitive-perceptual-motor dysfunction and training. *Selected papers from professional program segments of United Cerebral Palsy's Annual Conference.* New Orleans: United Cerebral Palsy Association.

Llorens, L.A. (1967). An evaluation procedure for children 6 to 10 years of age. *American Journal of Occupational Therapy, 21,* 64–69.

Llorens, L.A. (1967). Projective technique in occupational therapy. *American Journal of Occupational Therapy, 21,* 226–229.

Llorens, L.A. (1967). Gauging emotional, intellectual and professional growth in students. *Educational Newsletter, 2*(2), 2.

Llorens, L.A. & Rubin, E.Z. (1967). *Developing ego functions in disturbed children: Occupational therapy milieu.* Detroit, MI: Wayne State University Press.

1968

Llorens, L.A. (1968). Changing methods in treatment of psychosocial dysfunction. *American Journal of Occupational Therapy, 22,* 26–29.

Llorens, L.A. (1968). Identification of the Ayres' syndrome in children with behavior maladjustment. *American Journal of Occupational Therapy, 22,* 286–288.

1969

Llorens, L.A. (1969). The occupational therapist in a children and youth project. *Proceedings of the National Conference of Children and Youth Projects.*

Llorens, L.A. (1969). The occupational therapist in a community health program. *Proceedings of SCOTA Annual Conference.*

Llorens, L.A., Rubin, E.Z., Braun, J.S., Beck, G.R., & Beall, C.D. (1969). The effects of cognitive-perceptual-motor training approach on children with behavior maladjustment. *American Journal of Occupational Therapy, 23,* 502–512.

1970

Llorens, L.A. (1970). Facilitating growth and development: The promise of occupational therapy. *American Journal of Occupational Therapy, 24,* 93–101.

1971

Llorens, L.A. (1971). Black culture and child development. *American Journal of Occupational Therapy, 25,* 144–148.

Llorens, L.A. (1971). Occupational therapy in community child health. *American Journal of Occupational Therapy, 25,* 335–339.

1972

Llorens, L.A. (1972). Facilitating growth and development: The promise of occupational therapy. In *The Eleanor Clarke Slagle Lectures, 1966–1972.* Dubuque, IA: Kendall-Hunt Publishing Co.

Llorens, L.A. (1972). Problem-solving: The role of occupational therapy in a new environment. *American Journal of Occupational Therapy, 26,* 234–238.

Rubin, E.Z., Braun, J.S., Beck, G.R., & Llorens, L.A. (1972). *Cognitive-perceptual-motor dysfunction: From research to practice.* Detroit, MI: Wayne State University Press.

1973

Canfield, A.A., Williams, M.R., Llorens, L.A., & Wroe, M.C. (1973). Competencies for allied health educators. *Journal of Allied Health,* Fall.

Llorens, L.A. (Ed.). (1973). *Consulting in the community: Occupational therapy in child health.* Dubuque, IA: Kendall-Hunt Publishing Co.

Llorens, L.A. (1973). A case presentation: Billy. In E.K. Oremland & J.D. Oremland (Eds.), *Effects of hospitalization on children.* Springfield IL: Charles C. Thomas.

Llorens, L.A. (1973). What journal editors want. In M.K. Morgan, D.M. Filson, & A.A. Canfield (Eds.), *Publishing in the Health Professionals.* Gainesville, FL: University of Florida.

Llorens, L.A. (1973). Activity analysis for cognitive-perceptual-motor dysfunction. *American Journal of Occupational Therapy, 27,* 453–456.

1974

Llorens, L.A. (1974). Learning disability, occupational therapy and community programming. *Proceedings of the Sixth International Congress World Federation of Occupational Therapists.*

Llorens, L.A. (1974). The effects of stress on growth and development. *American Journal of Occupational Therapy, 28,* 82–86.

1975

Llorens, L.A. (1975, March). Occupational therapy consultation in community programs for children. *Proceedings from consultation in the community: A conference for occupational therapists.*

Llorens, L.A. (1975). Consultation in occupational therapy programs for children. *Canadian Journal of Occupational Therapy, 41,* 114–116.

Llorens, L.A. & Sieg, K.W. (1975). A profile for managing sensory integrative test data. *American Journal of Occupational Therapy, 29*(4), 205–208.

1976

Llorens, L.A. (1976). *Application of a developmental theory for health and rehabilitation.* Rockville, MD: American Occupational Therapy Association.

Llorens, L.A. & Adams, S.P. (1976). Student learning styles. In M. Morgan & C. Ford (Eds.), *Allied health teacher preparation.* St. Louis: C.V. Mosby.

1977

Llorens, L.A. (1977). A developmental theory revisited, *American Journal of Occupational Therapy, 31,* 656–657.

Llorens, L.A., & Schuster, J.J. (1977). Occupational therapy client care recording system: A Comparative study. *American Journal of Occupational Therapy, 31,* 367–371.

1978

Llorens, L.A. & Adams, S.P. (1978). Learning style preferences of occupational therapy students. *American Journal of Occupational Therapy, 32,* 161–164.

1979

Llorens, L.A. (1979). Thinking research in occupational therapy. *Developmental Disabilities SIS Newsletter, 2,* 1.

1981

Llorens, L.A. (1981). Research in occupational therapy, the need, the response. *The Occupational Therapy Journal of Research, 1,* 3–6.

Llorens, L.A. (1981). On the meaning of activity in occupational therapy. *Journal of the New Zealand Association of Occupational Therapists, Inc., 32,* 3–6.

Llorens, L.A. (1981). Maintaining credibility: The academic occupational therapist. *OT Education Bulletin,* Fall, 10–11.

Llorens, L.A. (1981). The role of occupational therapy in vocational rehabilitation. *Mental Health Special Interest Section Newsletter, 4*(3).

Llorens, L.A. (1981). Occupational therapy: State-of-the-art—potential for development. *Proceedings of the New Zealand Occupational Therapy Association.* Auckland, New Zealand.

Llorens, L.A. & Burris, B. (1981). Development of sensory integration in learning disabled children. In *Development theories and research in learning disabilities.* Baltimore: University Park Press.

1982

Llorens, L.A. (1982). *Occupational therapy sequential client care record.* Laurel, MD: Ramsco Publishing Company.

Llorens, L.A. (1982). Facilitating achievement of higher level behaviors. In J.H. Henry (Ed.), *Readings in clinical education: A resource manual for clinical instructors.* Augusta, GA: Medical College of Georgia.

Llorens, L.A. (1982). Continuing clinical competency for the occupational therapy educator. *Journal of the New Zealand Association of Occupational Therapists,* Summer.

1983

Llorens, L.A. (1983). The DSM III, sensory integration and child psychiatry: Implications for treatment and research. *Sensory Integration Special Interest Section Newsletter, 6*(1), 2.

Llorens, L.A. (1983). Educating for professional competence: Accountability theory in practice. *Journal of the New Zealand Association of Occupational Therapists,* Winter.

Llorens, L.A. & Donaldson, K. (1983). Documentation of occupational therapy: A process model. *Canadian Journal of Occupational Therapy, 50,* 171–175.

1984

Llorens, L.A. (1984). Changing balance: Environment and individual. *American Journal of Occupational Therapy, 38,* 29–34.

Llorens, L.A. (1984). Theoretical conceptualizations of occupational therapy: 1960–1982. *Occupational Therapy in Mental Health, 4,* 1–13.

Llorens, L.A. (1984). Semantic uses of "sensory integration" questioned. *Occupational Therapy Journal of Research, 4*(3), 244–245.

Llorens, L.A., Ward, J.M., Still, J.R., & Eyler, R.K. (1984). The role of professional education for occupational therapy. *Occupational Therapy Education Bulletin,* Spring, 6–9.

1985

Llorens, L.A., & Gillette, N.P. (1985). Nationally speaking—the challenge for research in a practice profession. *American Journal of Occupational Therapy, 39,* 143–146.

1986

Llorens, L.A. (1986). Activity analysis: Agreement among factors in a sensory processing model. *American Journal of Occupational Therapy, 40,* 103–110.

Llorens, L.A. (1986). An analysis of occupational therapy theoretical approaches for mental health: Are the profession's major treatment approaches truly occupational therapy?: A response. *Occupational Therapy Journal of Research, 5,* 25–26.

1987

Llorens, L.A., & Snyder, N.V. (1987). Nationally speaking: Research initiatives for occupational therapy. *American Journal of Occupational Therapy, 41,* 491–493.

Chapter Five

A. Jean Ayres

Kay W. Sieg

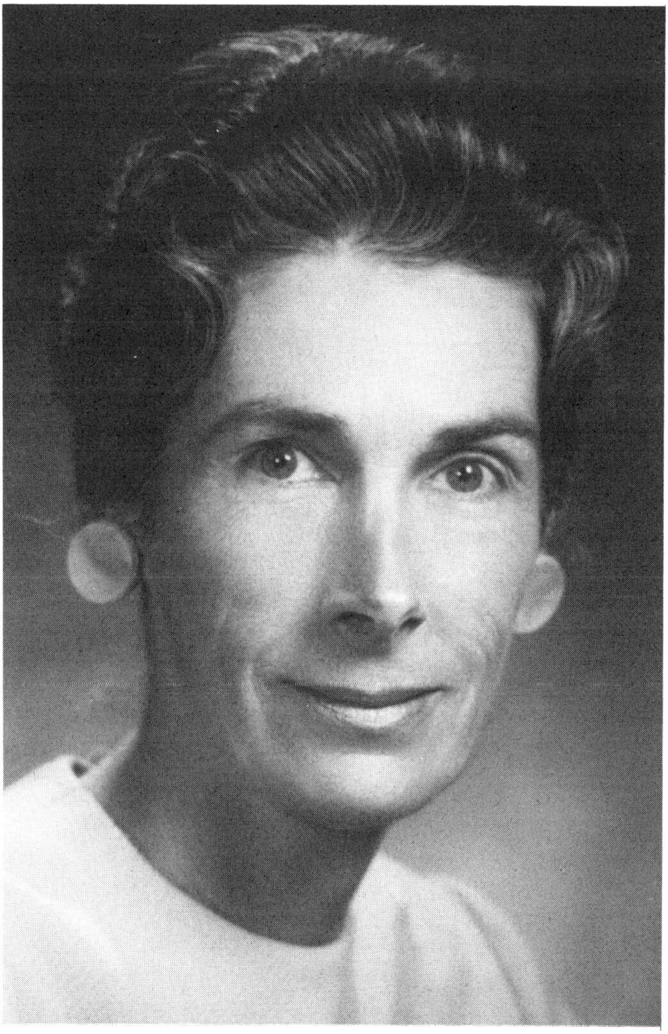

A. Jean Ayres

BIOGRAPHICAL SKETCH

Childhood

Anna Jean Ayres is a native Californian who was born in 1923 and grew up on a farm. Trees and the earth were friends, affording her comfort from the tensions of an unhappy relationship with her mother and older sister. Her brother and she found pleasure in creating recreational activities out of whatever was available on the farm. Later, a younger sister provided additional company in a socially deprived situation.

She suffered from "constitutional inadequacy." As a child she was never healthy and seldom happy. Her perception of herself as a bad, difficult child who should be ashamed of herself was reinforced by her mother who often complained of her daughter's "ugly disposition." Her father was a stern, distant, but loving man, who embodied the work ethic and who instilled in his children the principles of efficiency, economy, hard work, and responsibility for self and others. He valued education highly and was an educator himself until he could afford to farm. He made many sacrifices in order to send his children to college (A.J. Ayres, personal communication, June 29, 1981, June 3, 1987).

She coped with an emotionally deprived childhood and troubled adolescence by retreating into herself and following the advice of her mother to use her willpower to overcome unhappiness. A strong introversion trait developed in these early years. What others perceive as her fortitude in the face of rejection she sees simply as introversion. She states, "No, I don't think it's courage, I think it's being an introvert and being withdrawn . . . . I've just pulled into myself and I overreacted to the negativism, I just crawl even lower into myself and go my own way. I've had to do it. But I'm suited to doing it" (A.J. Ayres personal communication, June 29, 1981).

Although she lacked normal love relationships in childhood, she found it in her marriage. She dedicated her first book, *Sensory Integration and Learning Disabilities,* to her husband, Franklin. "I will say that I have a nearly perfect, just nearly perfect marriage. Just a real love relationship. A complete pair bond. That's where the love is" (A.J. Ayres, personal communication, June 29, 1981).

Schooling

For her early schooling, she walked a mile and a half to a country school that had no electric lights or running water. She did not perform well during the first 3 years of school. She had problems understanding others, especially anyone with an accent, and difficulty speaking. Learning to read brought her the first true understanding of how words sounded. She cites her "damaged left hemisphere" as the cause of her problems, and although she has gone on to disseminate her work through writing and presentations, writing and speaking remain difficult for her (A.J. Ayres, personal communication, June 29, 1981).

She obtained her bachelor's degree in occupational therapy in 1945, her master's degree in occupational therapy in 1954, and her doctorate degree in educational psychology in 1961, all from the University of Southern California (USC). In 1964–1966 she did postdoctoral work at the Brain Research Institute, at the University of California, Los Angeles (UCLA), which she says "was the most fortunate experience I ever had." Although her ideas were not popular at UCLA and she was "low man on the totem pole" during her 2 years there (A.J. Ayres, personal communication, June 29, 1981), her work there enabled her to study with neuroscientists and to gain knowledge of the brain.

Work

Ayres' first job was in a Veteran's Administration Hospital in 1946. Next she established an OT program at a private psychiatric hospital. From there she went to the Kabat Kaiser Institute where she worked from 1948–1953, serving as head occupational therapist. Her first journal article was written while working at the psychiatric hospital. While working toward her master's degree, she gained experience with cerebral palsy patients and with vocational training. She held various positions in the OT and special education programs at USC from 1955–1964 and from 1966 to the present.

She felt that her work after her doctorate was not generally supported in the field of occupational therapy. She speaks frankly of her experiences:

> It isn't so much to what group I give that which I develop, but what group will accept me. Initially, occupational therapy would not accept me. I could not cope with the resistance and hostility and other negative attitudes. I became so disgusted with occupational therapy in general because I kept wanting to push the field and the field pushed back. I finally became so disgusted and had such a hard time relating to occupational therapists, I said to hell with OT, I'm going to go my way and they can go their way. That's when I left the OT department because I just couldn't tolerate the negativism toward me. (A.J. Ayres, personal communication, June 29, 1981)

She sees such rejection of new ideas as not unusual in a university, which can be a "teeth and claws" place but as she stated "I don't cope well with teeth and claws." She came to learn that "I'd just have to be satisfied within myself. I cannot satisfy anyone else. I just wanted to satisfy myself and the committees that grant research funds in Washington, D.C." (A.J. Ayres, personal communication, June 29, 1981).

For 8 years after her postdoctoral work, Ayres had a faculty appointment in the special education department of USC. She was accepted there because she brought in research funds. She states, "If you bring in research funds and if you produce enough you can keep your desk. If you have a desk and you have an appointment and you have an account number you can make it at a university" (A.J. Ayres, personal communication, June 29, 1981).

Federal grants were not renewed after 1971 and there was no support of any type from the occupational therapy "establishment." At this time an event of great significance to the profession occurred. Two occupational therapists, Lawrence Kovalenko and Patricia Wilbarger, recognized the importance of Ayres' line of inquiry and established a nonprofit foundation (now Sensory Integration International) to serve as a receiving agency for donated funds. Research funds, raised mainly through lecturing, qualified Ayres for additional receipt of a grant from another private foundation. Lecturing widely throughout the United States and abroad for 2½ years also brought gradual grassroots acceptance and financial support for the theory and implementation of principles of sensory integration.

However, Ayres does not perceive these obstacles—lack of financial and professional support—as the greatest barriers she has had to overcome. Rather, "The major obstacle is my own brain—my left cerebral hemisphere, in particular. Sensory integrative dysfunction is so complex, so great, that I don't really have the neuronal capacity to handle it as well as I'd like to. That's the biggest obstacle. That, and the problems presented as sensory integrative dysfunction" (A.J. Ayres, personal communication, June 29, 1981, June 3, 1987).

Ayres has consistently disseminated her thinking through publications. Since her first professional journal article, which was published when she was 29 years of age, she has written 54 professional publications, including two books. In addition, she has prepared four films and numerous test manuals. She has continued to pose questions, report research findings, and offer theories, which have allowed her work to be utilized and examined.

In 1976, she was appointed as an adjunct faculty member to the Department of Occupational Therapy at USC. In 1977 she opened the Ayres Clinic, a private facility in Torrance, California. In this carefully designed environment for sensory integrative therapy, she provided therapy for children, conducted research, and developed test instruments and theory. Through her affiliation with USC she offered postbaccalaureate clinical residencies at the Ayres Clinic through which numerous master's students and therapists from throughout the nation and abroad were trained. In 1984, she retired from the Ayres Clinic and turned her energies to the Sensory Integration and Praxis Tests standardization project (AOTA, 1985). She continues her affiliation with USC in an emeritus status. She also serves in an advisory capacity at the Ayres Clinic and for Sensory Integration International.

Development of Theory

Dr. Ayres cites the problems of her clients as the central inspiration for her work. "They have certain conditions, responsibility for modification of which I assume; therefore, I must learn what I need to know to ameliorate their condition" (A.J. Ayres, personal communication, June 24, 1981). In the perceptual-motor era of the 1960s Ayres and such contemporaries as Newell Kephart and Marianne Frostig were exploring the possible perceptual and motor contributions to learning. Ayres realized the need to develop tests of these functions. "I needed to develop tests in order to really get at the problem, and in learning situations, problems are not easily measured, determined, even recognized. When I started out, there weren't any really good tests for looking at dysfunction in children." She developed the motor accuracy test before her doctoral work, but did not standardize it until after she received her degree. In her doctoral program she "wanted to have the kind of instruction, guidance and supervision of test construction that I could see I was going to need later in research" (A.J. Ayres, personal communication, June 29, 1981).

Initially, Ayres focused on developing visual perception tests. "I spent a lot of time and a lot of money developing visual perception tests that never reached the market." The obvious role of visual perception for reading and other academic tasks was pursued by Ayres and her contemporaries. "When Marianne Frostig found out I was developing a test of visual perception she called me on the telephone and asked me not to develop it because she was developing one and I told her I didn't think there would be much conflict" (A.J. Ayres, personal communication, June 29, 1981).

However, Ayres began to look beyond visual perception.

> It wasn't a good area to pursue but it took me a long time to figure out that it wasn't the best area to pursue. We could see that visual processing problems were central to learning disorders, but we needed to look beyond vision. If you just look at children

> from a behavioral standpoint and do behavioral type research and modeling, you'll never really discover that a main foundation to visual perception is the vestibular system, with proprioception and other senses also contributing. (A.J. Ayres, personal communication, June 29, 1981)

Ayres has consistently relied on the neuroscience literature in formulating her theory. Her background in neurophysiology and the influence of such clinical theorists as Margaret Rood prompted her to seek alternative answers. "You get that (contribution of vestibular and proprioceptive systems to visual perception) more from studying neurology, and even then you have to make a lot of inferences. You have to go well beyond the printed word to come up with that interpretation" (A.J. Ayres, personal communication, June 29, 1981). Rather than waiting for someone else to extract clinical applications from the literature, Ayres did so, explaining:

> Therapists dash in where scientists fear to tread. It's a dangerous thing to do but it's what builds theory. Theory is not the facts. Theory is putting the facts together so you can use them and in our case to enhance the development of children. This is always my end objective. (A.J. Ayres, personal communication, June 29, 1981)

Ayres has received some of the highest accolades in the profession of occupational therapy: the Eleanor Clarke Slagle Lectureship in 1963, the Award of Merit in 1965, and appointment as a charter member of the Academy of Research in 1983. Despite the controversy surrounding her work, she nonetheless made a great impact on occupational therapy theory. Yet, because of her childhood and the rejection of her work in the past, when told of the thousands who hold her in extremely high esteem, she states "And you know, it's hard for me to hear it, but I hear the pediatricians quite clearly when they declare, in print, that sensory integration therapy lacks value" (A.J. Ayres, personal communication, June 29, 1981, June 3, 1987).

THEORETICAL CONSTRUCTS

Sensory Integration—The Term

The term "sensory integration" (SI) was first used by Ayres to describe sensory integrative processes and neuropsychological learning disability. Although the terms "sensation" and "integration" appeared frequently in her early writings (Ayres, 1958, 1960, 1961b, 1963b), it was not until 1968 that she combined these terms into "sensory integration" (Ayres 1968a, b). She described learning as one of the functions of the brain's ability to "filter, organize and *integrate* the masses of *sensory* information" (Ayres, 1968a, p. 43). Reading is postulated as "the end product of a long evolutionary course in which the increased capacity of *sensory integration,* accompanied by the ability to emit an adaptive motor response, has furnished a critical foundation" (Ayres, 1968a, p. 170). She states that "certain types of learning disability may be interpreted partially in terms of dysfunction within the brain's *integrative* functions" (Ayres, 1968b, p. 43). She acknowledged that "exactly how *sensory integration* occurs in the brain remains elusive", but that lack of knowledge should "not be an excuse for avoiding an issue basic to all learning" (Ayres, 1968b, p. 43). She challenges that this lack of knowledge "must be faced and dealt with in as adequate manner as possible with full recognition of the limitations involved and with the realization that any conceptual framework is in some respects erroneous and will require constant modification as new knowledge unfolds" (Ayres, 1968b, p. 43). Auditory language functions are part of the total SI process, but she notes that these functions are not the focus of her investigations (Ayres, 1968a, b).

These 1968 articles (Ayres, 1968a, b) are important for they contain the elements of what will become SI theory. In these works she first uses the term "sensory integration" and introduces related phylogenetic and ontogenetic developmental principles. She links learning and sensory integration, poses dysfunction in SI as being related to learning disabilities, and identifies related evaluation and treatment strategies. She addresses the need for developing a conceptual framework for the brain's integrative processes. She selects neural integrative processes that are most useful in the therapeutic situation and provides an explanation of neural mechanisms as derived from the basic science literature. Auditory language functions are not emphasized. These articles outline the parameters of what is to become her life's work.

Developmental Bases

Sensory integration theory is a developmental theory that is based on principles of phylogenetic and ontogenetic development. The source of these principles is in the neuromuscular and neurodevelopmental theories of Fay, Kabat, Knott, the Bobaths, Rood, and Brunnstrom and the motor development theories of Gesell and others. Ayres' knowledge of and interest in these theories were shown in her comprehensive chapter in the 3rd edition of Willard and Spackman's *Occupational Therapy* (Ayres,

1963b). In several other writings, she discussed phylogenetic and ontogenetic principles related to hand function (Ayres, 1954), visual-motor function (Ayres, 1958, 1961a), treatment (Ayres, 1966a), and reading (Ayres, 1968a).

Phylogenetic Development

The application of phylogenetic principles to SI integration theory focuses on (1) the importance of sensation and (2) the interdependence of higher and lower central nervous system (CNS) structures and functions. The first phylogenetic principle states that vertebrate organisms survived over the course of millions of years because they evolved increasingly complex neural systems that enabled them to interact successfully with their environment. These neural changes either may have resulted by chance from genetic mutations or through the modification of the CNS via sensory input. SI theory emphasizes the latter belief, i.e., that "sensory input from the environment actually modified the nervous system because it called for new types of responses" (Ayres, 1963b, p. 364). The evolution of vertebrates coincided with the increase in numbers of sensory nerve fibers and the development of complex systems for processing sensory information. "Enlarging the scope of information supplied the brain enabled it, in turn, to develop increasingly complex adaptive response" (Ayres, 1972c, p. 23).

A second phylogenetic principle states that, as vertebrates evolved, the earlier, simple neural structures were retained and new structures were added. The functions ascribed to the earlier systems remained and were not replaced, but instead were modified and integrated as each new neural level evolved.

> Each structure remained capable of receiving information, integrating it, and organizing an appropriate motor response. While the highest or youngest structure present at any one time in evolution or in any one species today (in man it is the cerebral cortex) exerted critical influence over all lower structures, the higher centers still maintained a dependence upon lower structures. (Ayres, 1972c, p. 23).

Ontogenetic Development

The ontogenetic principle states that the development of the individual organism recapitulates the development of the species. For example, the motor development of human infants replays the evolutionary progression of vertebrates that were first capable of swimming movements, then quadrapedal ambulation, and finally bipedal ambulation and dexterous upper extremities. Similarly, motor control progresses from cephalad to caudal, proximal to distal, gross to fine, flexion to extension, adduction to abduction, ulnar to radial, movement in straight planes to rotational movement, and reflexive contraction to voluntary contraction (Ayres, 1963b).

Hypothesized Development of Sensory Integrative Processes

In 1964, Ayres presented a chart, "Hypothesized Sequences in Perceptual Motor Development," which summarized developmental concepts from several other writings (Ayres, 1964a, p. 18) (see Figure 5-1). This chart was expanded in her 1976 book, *Interpreting the Southern California Sensory Integration Tests* (Ayres, 1976b, p. 4), and was more recently updated in the 1979 book, *Sensory Integration and the Child* (Ayres, 1979, p. 60). These charts reflect the increasing refinement of Ayres' conceptualization of SI development.

In 1962 Ayres hypothesized that academic skills and ability to conceptualize in level IV are based on visual-spatial perception and motor skills (level III), which, in turn, evolved from body scheme and motor planning (level II), which began with tactile and visual perception and proprioception (level I). The concepts of body scheme from level II and visual-spatial perception from level III are important early concepts whereas the other elements of the chart underwent considerable revision.

Body scheme "is defined as the knowledge we have of the construction and spatial relationships of the different anatomical elements, such as fingers, legs, arms, that make up our body. It involves being able to visualize these elements in movement and in different positional relationships" (Ayres, 1960, p. 308). It provides a postural model (Ayres, 1961a) or postural frame of reference (Ayres, 1964a) for movement.

Body scheme develops from the integration of tactual, proprioceptive, and visual sensations. Just as it provides a basis for movement, the body scheme is also a result of processing of sensory impulses that are generated through movement. "Motor planning and body scheme are two sides of

I	II	III	IV
Tactual Perception Proprioception Visual Perception	Body Scheme Motor Planning	Visual-Spatial Perception Motor Skill	Reading, Writing, Numbers Skill Ability to Conceptualize

Figure 5-1 Hypothesized Sequences in Perceptual Motor Development—1962. *Source:* From *Approaches to the Treatment of Patients with Neuromuscular Dysfunction* (p. 18) by C. Sattley (Ed.), 1962, Dubuque, Iowa: William C. Brown, Publishers. Copyright 1962 by William C. Brown, Publishers.

the same coin. The development of each is dependent upon the other" (Ayres, 1964a, p. 19).

Visual-spatial perception, which refers to the perception of form, direction, or position in space and to space visualization, develops in concert with manual manipulation and body scheme. As the child handles, explores, and experiments with objects and moves through and experiences space, he or she formulates perceptions and concepts of form and space. The role of vision is to verify what is experienced tactually and kinesthetically. "Visual impressions reinforce and become associated with the manual impressions so that later visual cues can recall the cutaneous and proprioceptive, and the latter can recall the visual" (Ayres, 1958, p. 132). Likewise, the visual stimuli are essential for interpretation of the stimuli arising from manual manipulation. Thus, "the same activities which enhance efficiency of motor planning also provided the basis of visual space perception" (Ayres, 1964a, p. 20).

Body scheme is both a basis for movement and is derived through movement. Visual-spatial perception is both a guide for movement and is derived from the integration of vision, proprioception (including vestibular), and cutaneous sensations. Thus, several important ingredients of SI theory are contained in this schematic representation of perceptual motor development.

By 1976, SI theory was well developed, and Ayres developed a model (see Figure 5-2) of SI process to serve as an organizing framework for interpreting the Southern California Sensory Integration Tests (Ayres, 1976b). An expanded version of this model (Figure 5-3) that was published in 1979 provided a framework for explaining how problems in behavior, learning, attention, and motor coordination can be traced developmentally to SI dysfunction. Ayres' conceptualization of how SI contributes to normal

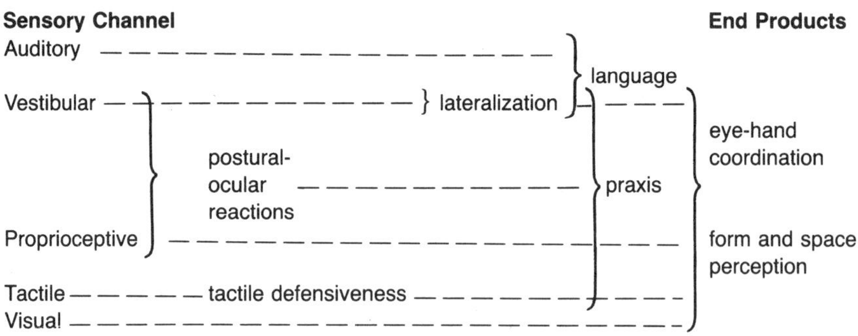

Figure 5-2 Sensory Integration Model—1976. *Source:* Copyright © 1976 by Western Psychological Services. Reprinted with permission of the publisher, Western Psychological Services, 12031 Wilshire Blvd., Los Angeles, CA 90025.

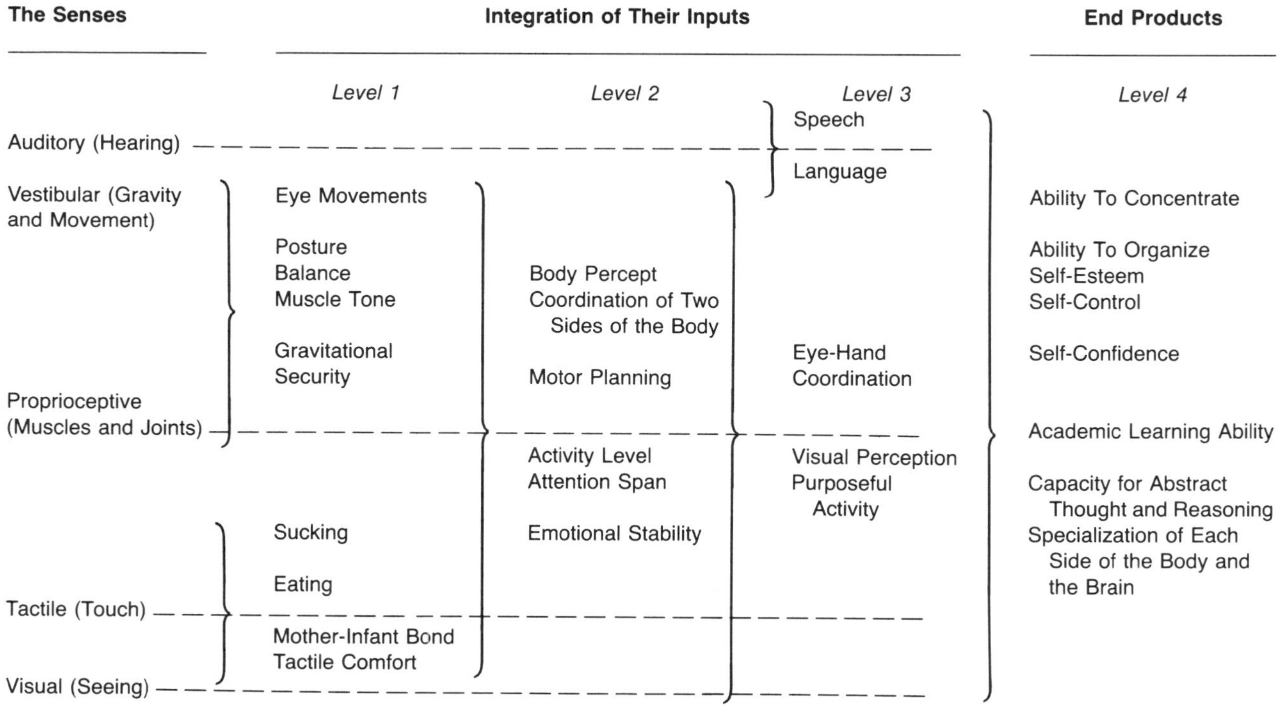

Figure 5-3 The Senses, Integration of Their Inputs, and Their End Products. *Source:* Copyright © 1979 by Western Psychological Services. Reprinted with permission of the publisher, Western Psychological Services, 12031 Wilshire Blvd., Los Angeles, CA 90025.

development is shown in four developmental levels that overlap considerably but are roughly equivalent to the first year of life, the toddler, preschooler and schoolager (Ayres, 1979).

Ayres hypothesizes that the end products (see Figure 5-3) necessary to perform in school and later on a job and to interact successfully with people develop as the result of many years of integration of the sensory systems: the auditory, vestibular, proprioceptive, tactile, and visual systems. In the early months of life, (level I) the tactile system contributes to the survival function of sucking and eating and the psychological function of mother-infant comfort and tactile comfort. Vestibular and proprioceptive sensations provide a basis for eye movements, posture, balance, muscle tone, and gravitational security. In toddlerhood, (level II) vestibular, proprioceptive, and tactile systems converge to contribute to the formation of a body percept and to the coordination of two sides of the body, motor planning, activity level, attention span, and emotional stability. By about age 3 (level III) the child works to refine skills in eye-hand coordination, visual perception, and speech and language and to engage in purposeful activity. At this level audition and vision join the three basic senses to bring about skill development. Although vision and audition are obviously very important senses, Ayres de-emphasizes their role in development and dramatizes the contribution of the less obvious senses: vestibular, tactile, and proprioceptive (Ayres, 1979).

The fourth level includes the end products of the integration of sensation occurring during the first 6 years of life. For formal schooling the child needs a foundation on which to develop the ability to concentrate, organize, and reason abstractly. Self-control, self-esteem, and self-confidence are important for human relationships in the classroom and at home. To provide a neurological basis for academic learning, the specialized functions of the cerebral hemispheres and body sides must be well lateralized. Ayres proposes that these abilities develop through the brain's ability to integrate sensory processes (Ayres, 1979).

Neurological Bases

SI theory is a neurologically based theory and, as such, is derived from concepts of neural functioning. Four predominant concepts are central to the theory: (1) the integrative process; (2) movement-generated sensation; (3) tactile, vestibular, and proprioceptive basis for visual and auditory functions; and (4) brainstem functions as the foundation for cortical functions.

Integrative Processes of the Central Nervous System

In order to function effectively the brain must be able to organize sensory input from many sources into a meaningful pattern that can be utilized for movement and learning. The brain must be able to take information received from an isolated sensory source and compare it to another sensory source for clarification and validation. Because the brain has five times as many afferents as efferents, it must be able to structure the massive sensory input it receives if it is to perform effectively. The brain's ability to organize, compare, and structure sensory information is referred to as its integrative function.

This integrative process occurs at and among all levels of the CNS—from the spinal cord to the cortex. Within each level, sensory processing from one side is integrated with sensory processing from the other side of the neuroaxis. Thus, integrative functions occur both vertically and horizontally in the CNS.

Intersensory or intermodality integration is that capacity of the CNS to associate information from two or more different sensory modalities. The brain gives meaning to the combined input from several sources and then information about another without direct stimulation (Ayres, 1968a). For example, the ability to identify an orange simply by its scent is possible after the integration of the sight, touch, taste, and smell of an orange from numerous previous sensory experiences with oranges. Future sensory encounters with an orange through one sense—for example, its scent—will produce associations with its appearance, texture, and taste. In this way, intersensory integration contributes to concept formation.

This ability to make sense of the environment is compatible with the human's adaptive powers. The development of this adaptive ability parallels the human's phylogenetic development. As the vertebrate nervous system evolved, neural structures developed that allowed for increased capacity for processing sensory information.

Convergent neurons provide the neuroanatomical basis for intersensory integration. These multisensory neurons receive input from several sensory modalities. "The most commonly reported modalities showing convergence are visual, auditory, olfactory, somesthetic, and vestibular" (Ayres, 1972c, p. 30). The spinal cord, brainstem, and cerebrum contain nuclei that are made up of convergent neurons that provide for intersensory integration throughout the neuroaxis (Ayres, 1958, 1968b, 1972c, 1975a).

Movement Processes

Movement has an organizing effect on the CNS, requiring it to integrate sensation. Thus, movement generates sensations that are essential to sensorimotor functions. These two observations are central themes in SI theory.

Sensation is one of the first components of a motor act. Motor acts are

> initiated, either directly or indirectly by some environmental factor which became known to the individual through sensory stimulation. The pencil is seen before it is grasped; the covers are thrown off because one felt too warm; one changes the direction of the car upon hearing a horn at the side; the bag of groceries is felt to be slipping before it is given a firmer hold. (Ayres, 1963b, p. 365)

To produce movement, the CNS must integrate sensation. Incoming sensations must be organized and combined with past sensory processes and used to formulate an anticipated motor response. Once underway, the movement must be monitored, evaluated, and altered as needed for future reference. Although movement is a product of CNS organization, the process of integrating sensation for movement imposes order on the CNS. Therefore, sensory integration for movement is both a result of and a prerequisite for CNS organization.

Movement, as it occurs, generates sensations that provide additional data for CNS processing. These include sensations arising from the body as it moves: tactile, kinesthetic, proprioceptive, and vestibular. These sensations inform the CNS about the movement as it is being produced, i.e., the stretch of the skin as it moves over a joint, joint motion and position, relative position of body parts, position of the head in relationship to the body and to the earth's gravitational force, speed, and duration and strength of muscle contraction. This sensory information must be integrated with that from other senses to determine whether the intended movement was executed. The analysis of sensory information enables the CNS to adjust the formulation of subsequent motor responses. The integration of the sensations that are generated through movement enables the development of sensorimotor abilities.

The integration of sensation for movement is important not only for sensorimotor functions but also for learning and cognition. Humans became intelligent creatures through the evolution of a motor system that afforded them the opportunity as sensorimotor beings to explore and learn about their environment. The sensory integrative aspects that enable one to become a competent sensorimotor being are believed to be related to competence in early academic skill. The brain's ability to integrate sensations for movement is believed to underlie the brain's ability to organize sensations for learning. In short, Ayres proposes that "sensory integrative processes subserve some aspects of cognition" (Ayres, 1975a, p. 304).

Tactile, Proprioceptive, and Vestibular Bases for Auditory and Visual Functions

The tactile, proprioceptive, and vestibular sensory systems are thought to be as important as the auditory and visual systems for learning and behavior. The contribution of vision and hearing to academic performance is readily apparent and has been widely studied by numerous researchers and theorists. Ayres' work has focused attention on the impact of tactile, proprioceptive, and vestibular systems on the neural processes that underlie the ability to learn.

Based on neuroscience literature, Ayres reports that the tactile, proprioceptive, and vestibular systems mature in utero earlier than the visual and auditory systems. "There is quite general agreement that the phyletically older systems (tactile, olfactory, gustatory, vestibular and proprioceptive) mature before the younger auditory and visual systems" (Ayres, 1975a, p. 314). During fetal life the stimulation of these older systems results in reflex movements of the neck and mouth and then the arms, legs, and trunk (tactile); eye movements (vestibular); and muscle contraction (proprioception). The functioning of these systems early in life makes possible the life-sustaining abilities to suck, swallow, breathe, and move.

The sensory systems develop in concert with one another and not independently of each other. Through sensory integration, each sensory system influences and is influenced by other sensory systems. Sensory systems that develop earlier have an impact on those that develop later. Likewise, the functioning of the earlier systems influences the functioning of the later developing systems: "the normal development of visual perception requires intersensory integration from other sources, especially somatosensory and vestibular" (Ayres, 1968b, p. 46). Ayres hypothesizes that auditory processing probably is enhanced through stimulation of other senses (e.g., vestibular) and visual perception and auditory processing are to a certain extent dependent upon processing of stimuli from the tactile and vestibular systems" (Ayres, 1972f, p. 83).

Dysfunction in development of the early systems may affect the development of the later systems. Thus, SI dysfunction involving tactile, proprioceptive, and/or vestibular systems may contribute to learning problems that are observed in the performance of auditory or visual tasks. The child's learning difficulties may be due not only to problems in auditory or visual processes but also the SI deficits caused by problems in tactile, proprioceptive, and vestibular processes. Enhancing the brain's ability to learn through auditory and visual modes by ameliorating SI dysfunction involving the tactile, proprioceptive and vestibular systems is the goal of SI therapy (Ayres, 1958, 1968b, 1972a,c, 1972f, 1975a).

Brainstem Functions

SI theory explains how the CNS integrates sensation for human learning and movement. Unlike theories and research that focus on cortical processes for learning and movement, this theory emphasizes the functions of subcortical structures for human performance.

The cerebral cortex, also called neo- (or new) cortex, developed last phylogenetically and is responsible for the complex cognitive abilities and skilled manipulation capabilities that characterize humans. However, the neocortex did not replace the earlier developing neural structures, nor did it eliminate the functioning of these structures. Instead, it was developed on these older structures and came to refine the functions of these early systems. That is, the nervous system developed phylogenetically in an additive fashion, not in a substitutive one. Functions became replicated with increasing complexity as the neuroaxis evolved from spinal cord to brainstem to cerebrum. "Cortical functions, then, are in some respects still dependent upon brainstem functions" (Ayres, 1975a, p. 318).

The brainstem is one of the major structures in which sensory integration occurs (Ayres, 1975a).

> At one time in the evolutionary process, the brainstem, as the highest neural structure, provided sufficient organization and direction to enable the organism to interact adaptively with its environment, albeit at a primitive level. Those functions, although greatly modified, still operate in man today. (Ayres, 1972c, p. 40)

The major nuclei and functions of the brainstem, including the thalamus, are:

- *sensory nuclei* for the vestibular, tactile, proprioceptive, auditory, visual, gustatory systems
- *motor nuclei* for eye, facial, and throat movements; eye and postural reflexes; and muscle tone
- *limbic nuclei* for mood and for stereotypical motions associated with survival functions

- *autonomic nuclei* for cardiovascular, gastrointestinal, and pulmonary functions
- *reticular nuclei* for arousal, alerting, and attentional functions.

The brainstem houses nuclei that mediate sensory, motor, limbic, autonomic, and arousal/attentional functions. It is in a position to perform major integrative functions and to influence the functioning of the neocortex. "Any major neural structure receiving sensory input from many sources is apt to have widespread influence over the rest of the brain. Multiplicity of input usually means convergence of input and where there is convergence of input there is integration of input" (Ayres, 1972f, p. 82). Ayres also writes, "The brainstem and thalamus are good examples of structures to which the principle is applicable" (Ayres, 1972c, p. 53).

In addition to the brainstem, the other subcortical structures also have important intersensory integration functions. The *cerebellum* "receives input from all sensory sources over the afferent neurons and from much but not all of the cerebral cortex, processes it, and then uses it to influence ongoing neuronal activity, especially down the spinal cord, to brainstem nuclei, the thalamus, basal ganglia and cortex" (Ayres, 1972c, p. 47). The cerebellum plays a role in the smoothness and timing of movements, muscle tone, vestibular functions, and limbic functions.

The *basal ganglia* plays a role in the "regulation of posture and movements of the body in space and the production of complex motor acts." The basal ganglia appear to be "involved in a type of sensory integration that allows one type of sensory input to influence the integration of another type and to utilize that input for moderately complex postural and other bodily movements" (Ayres, 1972c, p. 49).

The limbic system

> is concerned with primitive patterns of behavior necessary for individual and species survival, including vegetative functions, defending the body against attack, and the simple perceptual motor functions needed to fulfill these survival functions. Its function is clarified when it is considered the primary cortical structure in a large proportion of vertebrates. Fish have no neocortex; amphibians, reptiles, and birds have little, yet all of these animals show basic but well integrated behavior including perceptual, motor, and simple learning and memory. (Ayres, 1972c, p. 49)

In summary, SI for sensorimotor functions occurs in all subcortical levels and provides a foundation for cortical functions. SI dysfunction can contribute to difficulties in cognitive processes. Enhancement of cognitive processing by improving SI functions mediated in subcortical structures is the aim of SI therapy (Ayres, 1967, 1968b, 1972b,c, 1972f, 1975a).

Sensory Integrative Dysfunction

In her Eleanor Clarke Slagle lecture in 1963, Ayres proposed five major syndromes of perceptual-motor dysfunction: apraxia, perceptual dysfunction—form and position in space, integration of sides of the body, perceptual dysfunction—visual figure ground, and tactile defensiveness (Ayres, 1963a). This classification scheme was based on her factor analytic study of 100 children with learning or behavioral problems who were given a battery of tests of visual, tactile, proprioceptive, and motor functions.

These five syndromes have been revised and updated from knowledge generated through research. Major themes of dysfunction will be described, including: visual form and space dysfunction, developmental dyspraxia, tactile defensiveness, and vestibular dysfunction and related problems. In addition, auditory language dysfunction will be presented as it pertains to sensory integration theory.

Visual Form and Space Dysfunction

Visual form and space dysfunction refers to difficulty with form constancy (perceiving a form as being the same, regardless of changes in apparent size or color), spatial orientation (perceiving location and position of objects in space), spatial relationships (perceiving the relative position among objects), and visual figure-ground (distinguishing figure from opposing background). These problems are readily identified when the individual makes letter reversals in reading and writing activities.

Numerous tests have been developed in education and psychology to assess visual form and space dysfunction. Ayres also spent years developing visual-perceptual tests.

In contrast to the predominant viewpoint in education and psychology that visual form and space dysfunction was an isolated problem that needed to be identified and treated, Ayres found that it often accompanied postural, ocular, and somatosensory disabilities in children with learning and behavior problems. Elaborating on Trevarthen's hypothesized dual modes of vision, she describes focal vision as perceiving immediate, close visual stimuli and ambient vision as perceiving the surrounding environment. Ambient vision develops in concert with locomotion and postural abilities mediated at the brainstem level. Thus, the brainstem develops a spatial map of the environment. Focal vision, in contrast, requires precise attention to details of orientation and form in central vision and is a function of the cortex. The ability of the cortex to sort out the orientation of a letter on a page is believed to derive from the environmental spatial map provided by the brainstem. As stated above, the brainstem produces this map through postural-ocular experiences with gravity and space as locomotion develops through prone, sitting, quadraped, and bipedal planes. In summary, Ayres has consistently theorized that some visual form and space problems are related to inadequate postural and ocular reactions (Ayres, 1972c).

Developmental Dyspraxia

Developmental dyspraxia is "a disorder of sensory integration interfering with praxis, e.g., the ability to plan and execute skilled or non-habitual motor tasks" (Ayres, 1972c, p. 165). Sequencing of movements to produce a coordinated series of actions is faulty. Although the child can learn new tasks, doing so takes longer and is difficult. Everyday activities, such as fastening buttons and riding a bicycle, may be laborious and frustrating for the child and may be late to develop. Such problems are found in the absence of neurological problems of muscle weakness, tremors, spasticity, or sensory loss.

Having consistently found a relationship between low scores on praxis and tactile tests (Ayres, 1965, 1969a, 1977a), Ayres theorizes that the development of praxis is related to somatosensory processing. The somatosensory system is a major contributor to the formation of a body scheme; that is, the brain's concept of the body's parts and the relative location, position, and movement of those parts. This body scheme provides a dynamic map that the brain uses for organizing, ordering, and timing of movements. This neuronal model of the body is developed from, and is sustained by, the constant flow of somatosensory and proprioceptive sensory input to the CNS. Cutaneous, muscle, joint, tendon, and deep tissue receptors are constantly activated as the skin moves over a muscle that is contracting. Ayres postulates that the faulty integration of this somatosensory and proprioceptive input leads to the poor development of and, consequently, poor support of an adequate body scheme for motor planning (Ayres, 1972c).

In an address at the seminar, "Occupational Therapy for Sensory Integrative Dysfunction" held in Cincinnati, Ohio, in 1981, Ayres presented an expanded version of her 1972 theory of developmental dyspraxia. This 1980s view of developmental dyspraxia was based on recent investigations of clumsy children and research in adult dyspraxia, as well as her own insights from her clinical practice and research.

Three basic processes in praxis are ideation, planning, and execution of the action. Ideation is the conceptual process of imagining an interaction between one's body and an object through purposeful movement. Ayres refers to this cognitive process as a "concept of possible object-person interaction" (Ayres, 1985, p. 20). It is "believed to be largely dependent upon sensory integration and resultant knowledge of available body actions" (Ayres, 1985, p. 21). Such knowledge of available body actions is dependent on the tactile system.

Ayres goes on to question whether ideation is a "generalized neurophysiological function" (Ayres, 1985, p. 22) that serves various functions, including praxis, language, and organized behavior. Research is needed to verify the links among praxis and language and behaviors that have been observed clinically when therapy for dyspraxia results in improvements in praxis, language, and organizational abilities.

The motor planning process of praxis is "a consciously formulated internal plan of action that occurs before actual motor execution" (Ayres, 1985, p. 23). The planning process is an intermediate process between ideation and execution of a purposeful act. Thinking about one's actions characterizes the motor planning process and is requisite for learning motor tasks. When thinking and planning are not required, the movement has become automatic.

Two requisites for the motor planning process are somatosensory integration and sequencing ability. Somatosensory integration of tactile, kinesthetic, proprioceptive, and vestibular sensation provides the brain with information about "how the body is designed and how it functions as a mechanical being" (Ayres, 1985, p. 24). The sequencing aspect of motor planning orders a series of joint positions and movements and muscle tensions into an organized action. Providing a plan of transition from one component of the movement to the next is a sequencing function. Sequencing functions are generally thought to be mediated in the left hemisphere.

Execution of the action—that is, the observable motor act itself—is the culmination of ideation and planning. Through execution, one can infer the quality of ideation and planning. Problems in execution due to dyspraxia are distinguishable from those due to neuromotor problems. Neuromotor problems involve spasticity, fluctuating tone, and involuntary motion, whereas dyspraxia may (or may not) involve reduced muscle tone. Thus, in a child who has no neuromotor problems but does have motor execution problems, one could look for difficulty in ideation and planning.

In summary, Ayres' updated theory of praxis emphasizes conceptual processes that are dependent on somatosensory integration. She retains her emphasis on the importance of tactile, kinesthesic, proprioceptive, and vestibular system functioning as a basis for cortical processes of ideation, planning, and sequencing (Ayres, 1985). Manifestations of developmental dyspraxia include postural dyspraxia, oral dyspraxia, constructional dyspraxia, and dyspraxia of symbolic use of objects.

Tactile Defensiveness

Tactile defensiveness is characterized by expressions of "feeling of discomfort and a desire to escape the situation when certain types of tactile stimuli are experienced" (Ayres, 1964c, p. 8). During testing of tactile functions, negative reactions to tactile stimuli may be expressed by questions about when the test will end, comments about not liking the test, withdrawing the hand or moving the body away from the examiner, complaints of a painful stimulus, giggling, or angry comments (Ayres, 1964c). Other examples of tactile defensive behavior include avoidance of bathing, haircuts, being touched on the face, sand play, going barefoot, or wearing certain fabrics (Ayres, 1979).

The disinhibition syndrome of hyperactivity and distractibility has been long recognized as a major problem in many children with learning and behavioral deficits. Ayres expanded this syndrome in 1964 to include tactile defensiveness. She also referred to prolonged nystagmus (Ayres, 1975b) and to choreoathetosis (Ayres, 1977c) as forms of CNS disinhibition or hyperexcitability.

Excessive excitation of the reticular formation through the diffuse thalamic projection system is proposed as the neurological correlate for the syndrome of hyperactivity, distractibility, and tactile defensiveness. For unknown reasons, in some individuals the arousal functions of the reticular activating system predominate and interfere with cortical association and recruitment responses needed for perceptual, attentional, and cognitive processes. Sensory input is inadequately modulated, resulting in heightened responsivity to sensation and difficulty in controlling behavioral responses and focusing attention.

In 1964, (Ayres, 1964c) Ayres proposed that tactile defensiveness was a result of the predominant influence of the protective tactile system, which leads to diffuse, alerting, and warning reactions in response to tactile stimuli with concomitant fright, flight, or fight responses. The protective system is older phylogenetically, develops early ontogenetically, and must be inhibited in order for discriminative functions to develop. The discriminative tactile system provides for tactile discrimination of two- and three-dimensional objects and for tactile localization. Predominance of the protective system prevents optimal functioning of the discriminative system.

The presence of tactile defensiveness seems related to poor performance on tactile discrimination tests that are susceptible to distractibility or that include a light tactile stimulus. However, in general, tests of tactile discrimination have had stronger correlations with praxis tests, whereas somatosensory scores may or may not be depressed in the presence of tactile defensiveness. Thus, tactile defensiveness seems to be a problem of disinhibition involving the tactile system, rather than a product of a disordered tactile system itself (Ayres, 1976b). Although a hierarchy of protective and discriminative tactile system functioning has not been substantiated in Ayres' recent work, the concept remains useful for heuristic and clinical purposes.

Vestibular Dysfunction

In Ayres' 1963 Eleanor Clarke Slagle lecture, she described the rudiments of her theory of vestibular-based bilateral integration dysfunction: "The fact that diminished body balance is associated with poor integration of sides of the body leads to wondering whether there is a neurophysiological deficit basic to both balance and body side integration" (Ayres, 1963a, p. 224). Twelve years later, she expanded this premise to explain deficits in interhemispheral communication.

> Central to the theory and treatment of this syndrome is the postulate that the brainstem interhemispheral integrating mechanism is functionally associated with the brainstem postural reflexes and reactions and, furthermore, that inadequate maturation of the brainstem mediated postural reactions interferes with maturation of the interhemispheral integrative mechanisms at that level. The resultant dysfunction interferes with the development of specialization of function of the cerebral cortex. (Ayres, 1975a, p. 342)

Assuming that the vestibular system is a major contributor to brainstem postural reflexes and reactions, Ayres proposed a significant role for the vestibular system in interhemispheral communication and hemispheric specialization. Such speculation evolved over a period of several years and was based on several fruitful research studies.

Bilateral integration deficits were identified and linked to postural problems in studies of children with academic difficulties (Ayres, 1965, 1969a). Major symptoms of the syndrome of postural and bilateral integration include poorly integrated postural and ocular mechanisms, poor bilateral integration, and poor visual perception. Immature righting and equilibrium responses, poorly integrated primitive postural reflexes, lack of flexibility in rotation around the longitudinal axis of the body, reduced postural background movements to orient and adjust body posturing to a task, muscle hypotonicity, poor co-contraction, and poor ocular pursuits across the midline comprise the postural and ocular problems. Bilateral integration deficits include the tendency for each hand to be used independently of the other on its own body side, the tendency not to cross the body midline, poor coordination of hands in a bilateral task, poor discrimination of right and left body sides, and lack of strong hand preference. Although these studies did not identify any specific type of visual-perceptual problem, Ayres proposed a tendency for some form of visual-perceptual problem to accompany the postural and bilateral integration deficits (Ayres, 1972c).

The hypothesized syndrome of vestibular and bilateral integration dysfunction involves poor interhemispheral communication and inadequate cerebral specialization and deficits in the vestibular system (Ayres, 1976a). Inadequate integration of the two body sides, hyporesponsive nystagmus, and deficient postural responses describe its symptomatology. Criteria for including children in the vestibular bilateral integration group are: postrotary nystagmus score of −1.1 or more and at least three of the following: poor eye pursuits across the midline, lack of agreement of eye/hand preference, lack of agreement of ear-hand preference, lack of definite right ear superiority on the dichotic listening test, preferred hand scored lower on the Motor Accuracy test, deficit Space Visualization Contralateral Use score, and poor Bilateral Motor Coordination test score. Similar diagnostic guidelines are provided in the book, *Interpreting the Southern California Sensory Integration Tests* (Ayres, 1976b). Studies related to vestibular functions are reviewed in the next section of this chapter.

Auditory Language Dysfunction

Auditory language dysfunction is not considered an SI problem, yet it is appropriate to include some discussion of this area because much of Ayres' work was directed at identifying the relationship of SI processes to auditory language functions. As was discussed earlier, recent advances in praxis-related theory include references to programming functions of the cortex for language. Studies related to auditory language functions are discussed in the section on clinical practice and research.

Documentation

Ayres tested her theories through literature review, research studies, and clinical practice. Factor analytic studies were used in theory development and test construction. Clinical studies investigated the effectiveness of SI therapy for learning disabled and other patient groups.

Literature

Ayres consistently used neuroscience, neuropsychology, and neurophysiology literature sources to support her assumptions, pose questions, extrapolate findings, and interpret clinical problems. SI theory is a neurologically based theory that seeks to bridge the gap between basic science research and its application to human clinical problems. The neuroscience body of knowledge is a continuing resource for the development of new theory.

Although references to neuroscience literature are found in nearly all of Ayres' writings, her book, *Sensory Integration and Learning Disorders* (1972c), served as a forum for her to explore fully the conceptual neurological bases of her theory. This book includes a comprehensive review of principles of brain function, integrative processes, CNS levels, sensory modalities and factors, syndromes, and neural systems as they relate to SI theory. Chapters on specific disorders include sections on neurological, neuroanatomical, and neurophysiological considerations (Ayres, 1972c).

Factor Analytic and Related Studies

Factorial designs are useful for summarizing interrelationships among variables concisely and accurately. The R-technique and Q-technique are the most frequently used types of two- and three-mode analysis. The R-technique is used to factor variables (test scores) collected at the same time from a number of individuals. Computation of R involves correlations among various test scores from each subject, thus preserving information about tests but obscuring information about the individual, i.e., when pairs of a subject's score are summed, information about that subject is lost. The Q-technique is used to factor an individual's data collected at the same time from a number of variables (test scores). Computation of Q involves correlations among various subjects' scores on a given test, preserving information about subjects but obscuring information about tests. Thus, the R-technique is used when one wishes to know how test scores are grouped but is not concerned with the subjects' characteristics because R identifies traits among tests. Conversely, when groupings of subjects is desirable and one is not concerned with test characteristics, the Q-technique is useful in identifying types of individuals (Gorsuch, 1974).

In a 1965 study of 100 learning disabled children and 50 normal children Ayres used the R-technique for the two groups and the Q-technique for the dysfunction group. She identified five factors as behavioral correlates of patterns of neurological dysfunction: (1) developmental apraxia; (2) perceptual dysfunction, form, and position in two-dimensional space; (3) tactile defensiveness; (4) deficit of integration of function of the two sides of the body; and (5) perceptual dysfunction and visual figure-ground discrimination. These five discrete patterns of dysfunction provide a framework for test development and theory building in sensory integration (Ayres, 1965).

Because the five syndromes were not found in the normal subjects in the 1965 study, Ayres had indeed isolated areas of dysfunction that were not characteristic of normal development (Ayres, 1965). Support for the aberrant nature of these symptom complexes was gained in two studies in 1966 (Ayres, 1966b, c) of normal children in whom these factors were not clearly shown. In these studies, R-technique orthogonal rotation factor analysis of intercorrelated scores was used.

However, in one study, praxis (motor planning) and somatosensory scores accounted for most of the variance (Ayres 1966c), and in the other study, praxis accounted for least of the variance (Ayres, 1966b). In the first study, (Ayres, 1966b) 10 percent of the subjects had probable CNS dysfunction, and three children had mild cerebral palsy; in the other study, all subjects were normal. The children with CNS deficits in this study may have accounted for the praxis factor loadings and, if so, would support the apraxia syndrome as a developmental deviation.

Assuming that the Gesell Developmental Scales and perceptual motor tasks reflect CNS maturity, a correlation between Gesell Developmental Quotients and perceptual motor test scores should be found. This assumption was supported in Ayres' study of 92 children who had been given the Gesell Development Scales at a mean age of 57 months and the perceptual motor tests at a mean age of 70 months. A multiple R of .75 was obtained for intercorrelations of overall scores of the two testing procedures. In addition, group mean perceptual motor scores of children who had above average Developmental Quotients (DQ) were significantly higher than those with below average DQs. Thus, these two testing procedures seem to reflect aspects of CNS integrity and maturity (Ayres, 1969b).

In 1969, Ayres (1969a) compared one subject's pattern of dysfunction with each other subject's pattern in a group of 36 children with educational handicaps. The purpose of the study was to identify groups of low scores on 64 neurological, perceptual, and cognitive measures that were used for children with learning disorders. Identified factors included (1) auditory language, (2) tactile-motor planning, (3) poorer coordination on left than right side of the body, along with deficits in postural and bilateral integration, (4) postural and bilateral integration and academic achievement, and (5) auditory and visual cognitive associations and ability to perceive horizontal sequence of stimuli.

Auditory language problems in factor 1 were consistent with the population being sampled. Postural and bilateral integration test scores were associated with several factors, particularly with academic achievement. Left hemisphere dysfunction was suggested in factor 1 and right hemisphere dysfunction in factor 3. The developmental apraxia syndrome was identified in factor 2 (Ayres, 1969a).

Elucidation of types of SI dysfunction was the purpose of a 1971 (Ayres, 1971) study of 48 test scores of 148 learning disabled children. Criteria for the five hypothesized dysfunctional neural systems as factorially derived in the 1965 (Ayres, 1965) study were applied to these 48 test scores. Stepwise regression equations were used to identify the ten variables that best predicted disorders in each of five neural systems: postural and bilateral integration, praxis, functions of left side of body, form and space perception, and auditory language functions. This study (Ayres, 1971) provided specific guidelines for interpreting these five hypothesized syndromes. Similar constellations of scores were found when R-technique factor analysis was applied to the 48 intercorrelated test scores of 148 children (Ayres, 1972a).

A 1977 study further delineated the nature of various types of SI dysfunction among learning disabled children (Ayres, 1977b). One hundred and twenty-eight children were given tests of sensory integration, intelligence, language, and dichotic listening. A series of four R-technique factor analyses was used, with different variables included on the four analyses. The selection of variables for inclusion in the various analyses was based on prior factor analytic studies. In an attempt to simplify the various clusters, a final analysis eliminated variables that contributed least to the previous four analyses. Four identifying factors were found: auditory language, postural ocular reactions, eye-hand coordination, and somatosensory and praxis. These findings were consistent with previous studies.

Helpful additional guidelines for test interpretation were also derived from the 1977 study. Preference for the left hand tended to be associated with poor postural and somatosensory functions. The motor accuracy test loaded on a separate factor did not load more on one factor than another indicating that this score is sensitive to dysfunction and is influenced by various factors. Inadequate postural responses were inconsistently associated with dyspraxia. Disorder in postural and bilateral integration did not emerge as a discrete factor. Choreoathetosis shared variance with the effect of the asymmetrical tonic neck reflex on equilibrium, suggesting that choreoathetosis is a release phenomenon.

In defense of the weak statistical associations in this study, Ayres proposed that "the tendency toward weak or occasional associations may be due to the flexibility and plasticity of the brain, or it may be due to the presence of fairly strong relationship in only a few of the subjects whose scores were analyzed" (Ayres, 1977a, p. 365).

Clinical Practice and Research

Throughout her career, Dr. Ayres has been actively involved in clinical practice. In the therapy setting she has identified problems, formulated questions, and applied her theoretical approaches. The real world of clinical practice has consistently guided her research and theory development efforts.

Early in her career, Ayres investigated the relationship between work habits and workshop production (Ayres, 1955) and between manual dexterity and workshop wages in persons with cerebral palsy (Ayres, 1957). Results of her published study of 31 hemiplegic patients showed no significant difference between right and left hemiplegics on the Ayres Space Visualization Test, although both groups showed impaired performance (Ayres, 1962a). Other clinical research studies investigated perceptual-motor and then SI dysfunction, primarily in the learning disabled, and in autistic, aphasic, and deaf-blind subjects.

With William Reid she co-investigated the self-drawings of 100 children with suspected perceptual dysfunction and 50 normal children. Highest correlations were found between self-drawings and visual perception and use of a pencil. It was concluded that the self-drawing is a good index of visual perception and eye-hand drawing ability, but has limited value as an indicator of body scheme as derived from a sensorimotor-based neuronal model, i.e., from kinesthesia, tactile discrimination, and motor planning functions (Ayres & Reid, 1966).

In a 1972 study, (Ayres, 1972b) Ayres administered SI therapy to children in whom auditory language problems were identified as the cause of their academic difficulties. Five months after the termination of therapy, greater gains in academic scores were made by the experimental group that received SI therapy than by the control group. To explain how this nonacademic therapy improved academic performance, Ayres proposed that vestibular and somatosensory input, which were carefully controlled in therapy, enhance the brain's capacity for intersensory integration of visual, auditory, vestibular, and somatosensory processing, thereby enhancing the brain's capacity for learning. She also hypothesized that "normalization of postural mechanisms organized in the midbrain enable better cortical interhemispheral communication upon which reading must be quite dependent" (Ayres, 1972b, p. 342).

A study reported in 1976 (Ayres, 1976a) yielded significant additions to the theory of vestibular-based functions in learning disabled children. Ayres compared academic gains made by matched groups of children with hypoactive, normal, or prolonged postrotary nystagmus who did or did not receive SI therapy in addition to special education. She found that children with hyporesponsive nystagmus who received SI therapy made favorable academic gains, whereas those who only received special education showed a lack of academic achievement. Furthermore, the children with hyporesponsive nystagmus were less able to profit academically from special education only when compared to children with hyperreactive or normal nystagmatic responses. She concluded that hyporesponsive nystagmus identifies a type of vestibular disorder that interferes with academic learning. Therapy aimed at improving vestibular functioning results in improved academic achievement.

Learning disabled children with hyporesponsive nystagmus appeared less dysfunctional and more normal than children with normal or prolonged nystagmus. The hyporesponsive nystagmus group was more intelligent, in better physical condition, and had better academic and auditory language functions than the normal or prolonged nystagmus groups. Hyporesponsive nystagmus was found in one-half of the sample, whereas the normal incidence is 14%. Thus, the more capable learning disabled children appeared to suffer from a prevalent vestibular disorder.

Children with prolonged duration nystagmus seemed to have more neurological involvement, and some of them had signs of left cerebral hemisphere dysfunction. This group was less responsive to SI therapy.

As part of this 1976 study, Ayres investigated the predictability of the dichotic listening test for SI dysfunction in learning disabled children. Patterns of associated scores were identified, but were not statistically significant. Children who showed low right-left ear ratios (infrequent use of the left hemisphere) scored poorly on tests of auditory language function (Ayres, 1977b). Two explanations were offered: (1) poor interhemispheral communication leading to poor hemispheric specialization and (2) poor left hemisphere functioning. Because nearly one-half of the sample population had hyporeactive nystagmus, the involvement of the vestibular system was implicated (Ayres, 1976a).

In summary, this important 1976 study yielded many useful theoretical, diagnostic, and clinical results. Learning disabled children with vestibular sensory integrative dysfunction made academic as well as sensory integrative gains when sensory integration therapy was provided in addition to special education. The syndrome of vestibular and bilateral integration was described (Ayres, 1976a). Vestibular disorder as characterized by hyporesponsive nystagmus was linked to academic deficits, including auditory language dysfunction (Ayres, 1978).

The association between the vestibular and somatosensory systems and auditory language functions was further shown in a 1981 study (Ayres & Mailloux, 1981) of four aphasic children. Using a single case method, Ayres found that rate of growth in language comprehension increased in all of the children and expressive language improved in two of the children after they received SI therapy. Attenuated postrotary nystagmus was found in the pretesting of the two children who made the greatest gains in expressive language. The therapy emphasized, and all the children sought, experiences in vestibular stimulation.

These results led to the hypothesis that SI therapy promotes auditory processing in those neural systems that are dependent on vestibular and somatosensory processing. Further, the vestibular system was proposed as one of a complex of contributing mechanisms underlying expressive speech. She concluded that SI therapy was effective in facilitating language development in aphasic children with somatosensory and vestibular processing disorders (Ayres & Mailloux, 1981).

In a study of ten autistic children, Ayres and Tickle (1980) investigated sensory processing of auditory, visual, tactile, vestibular, proprioceptive, olfactory, and gustatory stimuli as a predictor of response to SI therapy. Responsivity to 14 sensory stimuli was classified as either hyporesponsive, normal, or hyperresponsive. After 1 year, the group was divided into the best and poorest respondents to therapy. Children with tactile defensiveness, avoidance of movements, gravitational insecurity, and an orienting response to an air puff were the best respondents. They concluded that those autistic children who were able to register sensory input but could not modulate it benefited more from the organizing effect of SI therapy than did those children who were hyporesponsive to or did not orient to sensory stimuli. Thus, the hyporesponsive nystagmus that predicted the best respondents to therapy in a group of learning disabled children was not a predictor of good respondents in a group of autistic children. Nonetheless, SI therapy was an effective treatment approach for both groups.

A case study of a 7-year-old schizophrenic child showed improvement on tests for intelligence, perceptual-motor, and language functioning following a 6-month daily treatment program that emphasized adaptive responses to somatosensory and vestibular input. Ayres hypothesized that the therapy provided affective stimulation and organization and that this allowed the "presence of an internal drive toward normality and self-actualization to operate" (Ayres & Heskett, 1972).

The effects of SI therapy on the reduction in constant self-stimulating behaviors in a deaf, partially sighted, severely retarded girl of 11 1/2 years did not endure at puberty. After the onset of menarche, 55 weeks of additional therapy did not reduce the self-stimulating behavior to previous levels. Other factors during the 2-year course of therapy included a 9-week absence, scoliosis surgery, immobilization in a body cast, and the initiation of medication for seizures. The results of this case and four others described in the 1983 report indicate that adolescence may not be the optimal time for initiating therapy directed at improving an autistic child's interaction with the environment. Further, steps are needed to address the relationship between the effects of puberty and therapeutic gains (Ayres & Mailloux, 1983).

Children with choreoathetoid movements made gains in eye-hand coordination after a year of SI therapy, although the gains were not statistically significant. Ayres compared eye-hand coordination scores of 31 learning disabled children who received SI therapy to 23 learning disabled children who did not receive therapy in addition to special education. Choreoathetosis was viewed as a problem of insufficient inhibition of motor responses. Whether the SI therapy affected the SI substrates of eye-motor coordination or the motor release problem itself was not clarified in this study (Ayres, 1977c).

APPLICATION TO OCCUPATIONAL THERAPY PRACTICE

The extent to which a theory is used by persons in the profession is an ultimate criterion for evaluating it. Meleis (1985, p. 158), in her model for theory critique, states, "The final test of any theory is whether or not it is adopted by others." A theory's "circle of contagiousness" indicates where the theory is used geographically; how the theory has been used for research, education, administration, and/or clinical practice; and whether the theory has been used cross-culturally (Meleis, 1985).

The literature on SI published by persons other than Ayres provides a means to assess the circle of contagiousness of SI therapy. This therapy has been applied in research and clinical practice and has influenced education in occupational therapy. Through the organization, Sensory Integration International (SII), and the efforts of interested therapists, SI theory courses have been taught by SII faculty in several countries, including Canada, Japan, and Israel. A review of this literature is beyond the scope of this chapter.

Evaluation and Assessment

Test construction has occupied much of Dr. Ayres' efforts. She has developed, revised, and reformulated tests for identifying what was termed perceptual-motor problems in the 1960s and later was referred to as SI dysfunction.

Ayres' first test, the Ayres Space Test, was published in 1962 (Ayres, 1962b). This test consisted of 60 egg and diamond formboard items. Other early tests included the Southern California Motor Accuracy Test (Ayres, 1964b), the Southern California Kinesthesia and Tactile Perception Tests (Ayres, 1966e), and the Southern California Figure-Ground Visual Perception Test (Ayres, 1966d). The Southern California Perceptual-Motor Tests (Ayres, 1968c) included tests for imitation of postures, bilateral motor coordination, crossing the body midline, standing balance, and right-left discrimination. These tests were compiled and republished as the Southern California Sensory Integration Tests in 1972 (Ayres, 1972d), which made testing materials for all 17 tests available in one test kit. Changes in the 1972 version included restandardization and reduction of the number of items of the Space Visualization Test (formerly Ayres Space Test), extension of norms for the Figure-Ground Visual Perception Test and the Motor Accuracy Test, and addition of the Position in Space Test and the Design Copying Test (Ayres, 1972d).

The Southern California Postrotary Nystagmus Test, which was published in 1975, is a procedure for testing the functioning of this vestibular-ocular reflex (Ayres, 1975b). This test, along with other observations of vestibular-related postural abilities, was important for the interpretation of syndromes related to vestibular functioning.

Revisions of the Southern California Motor Accuracy Test provided norms for three different speeds for right and left hand performance. This new procedure allowed children with dysfunction who tend to draw very quickly or very slowly to be more accurately compared to the normative sample (Ayres, 1980a). The Motor Accuracy Test-Revised was the major change in a 1980 edition of the Southern California Sensory Integration Test (Ayres, 1980b).

The Sensory Integration and Praxis Tests (SIPT) were developed in the early 1980s to provide a psychometrically sound test instrument that included tests not available in the Southern California Sensory Integration Tests (SCSIT) (Ayres, Mailloux, & McAtee, 1985). Several tests from the SCSIT were omitted or revised, and four new praxis tests were developed. The SIPT normative data were collected on 2,500 children in the United States and Canada, unlike the SCSIT, which was standardized with children from southern California and which included differing numbers of subjects for the various tests. Computer scoring and interpretation of the SIPT by the test publisher offer accurate, efficient test results for the test user and incorporate up-to-date research findings in the test interpretation (Ayres, Mailloux, & McAtee, 1985).

Treatment

Principles

Sensory integrative therapy focuses on control of sensory input that proceeds according to a developmental sequence and requires an adaptive response. The therapist carefully selects therapeutic equipment and activities for the desired somatosensory and vestibular sensation. Developmental sequences are used to recapitulate normal development. Somatosensory and vestibular system development enhances visual and auditory functions. Activities emphasize brainstem, postural responses, and subcortical intersensory integration as precursors of cortical functions. Adaptive responses require organized interaction between the child and the environment and are a natural outcome of accurate and precise sensory input. Thus, adaptive responding is the ability to integrate sensations for motor behavior for effective interaction with the environment. Adaptive responses may be as simple as figuring out how to get one's body in a prone position on a scooter board or as complex as writing one's name. A procedure is considered therapeutic if it helps the child make increasingly mature responses in the therapy environment (Ayres, 1979).

The child's responses are used to guide the treatment. The therapist closely observes the child's spontaneous movements, postural responses, and motor patterns and skills for the desired adaptive behavior. Responses to a given activity or piece of equipment indicate how the child's nervous system interprets the stimuli. Activities that the child enjoys and seeks are generally considered indicative of those things that are integrating to the child's nervous system. Self-initiated activity in a selected environment is thought to be more integrative than imposed activities or tasks. Such an approach offers pleasurable, playful experiences that tap into the child's innate drive toward sensory integration. This invitational approach to therapy is referred to as the "art" of therapy (Ayres, 1979).

The therapist uses activity analysis to analyze the sensations needed for and generated by the activity. The reaction being facilitated or inhibited and the SI requirements for the motor response are carefully observed as the child interacts with the activity (Ayres, 1979).

Movement is used for its sensory-producing effect. Movement generates vestibular, tactile, and proprioceptive sensation that is integrated with visual and auditory sensation. Movement imposes organization on sensation and is an indicator of the status of that organization. SI therapy is a movement-based therapy (Ayres, 1979).

The treatment sequence begins with improving SI in general through general stimulation of vestibular and tactile systems. It then proceeds with enhancement of the maturation of postural responses and the body's dynamic relationship with the earth's gravitational force. Development of the capacity to motor plan and encouraging interaction of two body sides are then emphasized. These steps provide the basis for development of form and space perception and related behavioral, perceptual, and cognitive functions that are important for learning (Ayres, 1975a).

Because of the powerful effects of vestibular and somatosensory stimulation, precautionary measures are mandatory, and therapists should observe for signs of nausea, hyperexcitability, sleepiness or sleeplessness, undesirable increases or decreases in muscle tone, and defensive responses. Adherence to safety factors such as well padded floors and durable suspension supports and equipment maintenance procedures is also very important in ensuring a safe therapy environment (Ayres, 1975a, 1979).

Equipment

Sensory integrative therapy equipment enables movement in a variety of planes and requires innumerable combinations of muscular, balance, and coordination responses. Equipment developed in the Ayres Clinic includes the suspended hammock, scooter board ramp, platform swing, carpeted barrel, quadraped balancing board, inner-tube barrel, "helicopter"-suspended apparatus and vibrating table. Scooter boards, large therapy balls, suspended bolsters, and T-stools developed in other sensory motor therapies are used in SI integrative therapy as well (Ayres, 1979).

Therapy Emphasis in Various Forms of Sensory Integrative Dysfunction

Therapy for developmental dyspraxia addresses ideation or the concept of the activity, planning a course of action, and executing the plan. For the child with ideational problems, the therapist selects the simplest activity that the child can perform using his or her whole body in relationship to the therapeutic equipment. For severe ideational problems, the therapist helps the child through the activity manually and verbally and through modeling. Because the typical therapy equipment may be too complicated for the child with these conceptual problems, the therapist may need to create simplified activities.

Activities eliciting strong motor responses provide massive sensory flow from somatosensory and proprioceptive systems. These activities emphasize total flexion, extension, rotary, and diagonal movements, which provide the postural basis for planning and executing movements. Planning and executing movements proceed from simple praxis activities, such as moving effectively from one place to another, to more complex praxis activities involving sequences of movement (Ayres, 1985).

Therapy for vestibular-based dysfunction emphasizes motion, rotation, and starting and stopping actions to activate the vestibular system. Extension postures and alternating flexion and extension for co-contraction and bilateral activities are incorporated into the treatment. Righting and equilibrium responses are facilitated in prone, supine, and upright positions. The rate of vestibular stimulation is varied to produce desired calming or excitatory effects. Because of the autonomic reactions associated with vestibular stimulation the therapist must observe for signs of autonomic distress such as sweating, pallor, respiratory changes, flushing, nausea, seizures, or dizziness.

CRITIQUE OF SENSORY INTEGRATION THEORY

Theory

Naming sensory integration among the controversial therapies for learning disabilities, Sieben (1977) criticized this approach for its faulty assumption that children with learning disabilities have something wrong with their brainstems. He also criticizes the assumptions that controlled stimulation of vestibular and somatosensory systems improves brainstem integration with vision and hearing and that there is carryover from mastery of postural skills to academic skills. In contrast, Lerer (1981) stated that the SI concepts were accurate and were based on 100 years of biomedical research efforts. He also noted that brainstem-related sensory motor dysfunction described in SI theory is "probably valid" and that medical and other professionals recognize similar symptomatology in which the brainstem may be important.

Ottenbacher and Short (1985) identify literature that supports the assumption that subcortical brain areas contribute to complex processes of learning and cognition. The emphasis in sensory integration on "active management of children in meaningful, challenging activities that provide a vast array of multisensory and motor stimulation and feedback" (Ottenbacher & Short, 1985, p. 304) is also well documented in the literature. Ayres' use of a hierarchical model of brain function is also acceptable for heuristic purposes, although holistic and systems approaches are increasingly preferred for conceptualizing brain function. However, they view Ayres' claim that therapy alters brainstem synaptic organization as controversial and perhaps an overuse of the hierarchical model of the CNS. Complex psychological and cognitive processes are believed to be dependent on an array of neurological, behavioral, maturational, sociocultural, and environmental variables and cannot be pinpointed to an area or level of the brain. "Thus, it may be that environmentally mediated brain changes, such as those proposed by sensory integration theory, result from whole-brain neurotransmitter, glial, arousal or other changes rather than from altered synaptic efficiency in the brainstem" (Ottenbacher & Short, 1985, p. 306). They also state:

> Thus, the more important task for sensory integration may not be to determine how therapy alters brain function, but instead, to determine just what range of outcome it remediates, what populations are most affected, what are the most effective, discrete clinical measures of sensory integrative dysfunction, and what combinations of stimuli (as well as their context) bring about the most durable, yet rapid remediation of the outcome measures. (Ottenbacher & Short, 1985, p. 307)

These critiques represent a spectrum of opinion about SI theory. Sieben's (1977) cursory review of SI theory was part of an overall attack on alternative approaches to learning disabilities. A note on Lerer's (1981) article advised readers of the availability of his computerized world bibliography on SI therapy. Thus, Lerer appears to have presented a well-informed critique. However, Lerer's methodology might be objectionable considering that his "Open Letter to Occupational Therapy" was based upon his referring normal children for SI testing for the purpose of exposing the limitations of this approach. Ottenbacher and Short (1985) reviewed Ayres' theory in terms of recent and historical neuroscience literature and as occupational therapists and researchers in sensory integration. They presented a well-studied review of the theory.

Testing

The Southern California Sensory Integration Tests (SCSIT) have been criticized for their incomplete standardization information, sample size variations of 13 to 70 subjects on the subtests, and the small sample size of fewer than 100 in each age group. Other concerns have included its use of scores and its reliability and validity. The Sensory Integration and Praxis Tests (SIPT) were developed to replace the SCSIT with a psychometrically sound instrument. For historical purposes, however, the problems with the SCSIT are reviewed below.

Use of Scores

Scores of the normative sample in the SCSIT were adjusted to correct for sampling error. The discrepancy in some of the adjusted scores and original scores reduces the credibility of the adjusted scores (Ayres, 1980b).

The appropriateness of considering a standard deviation (SD) score of −1.0 or greater has been questioned because the normative sample had scores of −1.0 and greater and were considered normal (Evan & Peham, 1981). However, assuming a normal distribution, the z score of −1.0 SD is equivalent to a T score of 4, a Weschler IQ score of 85, a stanine score of 3, or a percentile rank of 16 (Lyman, 1971). Thus, the cut-off of −1.0 SD for considering dysfunction is comparable to that of other derived scores. The problem is not in the type of score reported, but possibly the erroneous assumption of normal distribution in Ayres' samples.

SD scores of up to −5.0 are reported in the test manual tables causing some user confusion (Ayres, 1980b). SD scores greater than −3.0 represent minute portions of the sample data and provide little meaningful test information. Thus, in certification courses, therapists have been cautioned not to report scores of more than −3.0 SD.

Reliability

Test-retest reliability coefficients of the 17 SCSIT subtests ranged from .01 to .94, with a median of .53 (Ayres, 1980b). Reliability coefficients of below .70 were reported for 73 percent of the tests (Evan & Peham, 1981). Ayres (1980b) provides several explanations for the low test-retest reliability. Small variances in the normative sample at certain ages lead to low test-retest coefficients. Maturational factors may account for low reliability of tests for some ages. For some tests reliability was compromised for the sake of test brevity; in the interest of keeping the child's attention, the number of test items was reduced, which lowered test-retest reliability. Because of the novel nature of some tests, the ability of children to "utilize cognition in addition to perception to solve the problems varies considerably and tends to invalidate the second test situation with some but not other children" (Ayres, 1980b). Ayres hypothesizes that the neurophysiological processes being tested are unstable, difficult to measure, and yield varying responses, all of which contribute to low reliability. She advises that every score be considered in terms of its standard error of measurement and that tests be considered in relationship to one another.

Although there is no total score for the SCSIT, Ayres suggests the Spearman-Brown formula could be applied to estimate the SCSIT in its entirety. She states, "If it were to be assumed that all the SCSIT were of equal length, otherwise comparable, and had a reliability of only .35, the reliability of 17 tests as one intact battery would be higher than .90" (Ayres, 1980b). Several criteria would need to be met to ascertain reliability using this method, including equal test length, high intercorrelations among items and similar variances, level of item difficulty, and processes measured by the tests (Ottenbacher & Short, 1985). Because the actual implementation of this method was not reported by Ayres, it is difficult to ascertain grounds for this assumption of an overall SCSIT reliability.

Ayres acknowledged that "to obtain information of a potentially meaningful parameter, moderate accuracy of test scores had to be accepted at times" (Ayres, 1980b, p. 52). Thus, it could be said that she sacrificed psychometric properties of the test for clinical relevance.

Validity

The tests developed by Ayres have good face validity (Ottenbacher & Short, 1985). Some validity data are provided in the original versions of the tests (Ayres, 1962b, 1964b, 1966e) and include the ability of the test to discriminate between normal and dysfunctional groups. Concurrent validity was also shown through correlation with similar published tests. Manuals for the later versions of the test did not include validity information (Ayres, 1972d, 1980a).

Factor analysis has been suggested as the way to identify theoretical constructs in a developing theory, as well as the operational characteristics of those constructs. Thus, factor analysis can be used to test both construct validation of these instruments and the underlying theory (Gorsuch, 1974). Ayres' factor analytic studies did establish construct validity of her testing instruments, as well as the theorized syndromes of dysfunction (Clark, Mailloux, & Parham, 1985).

Research

Factor analytic studies were used to delineate syndromes or types of SI dysfunction. These studies have been criticized for methodological inadequacies (Clark, Mailloux, & Parham, 1985). A closer look at Ayres' studies in terms of factor analytic criteria does reveal some flaws.

Gorsuch (1974) recommends that factor analytic studies meet the following six conditions for generalizability of factor analysis:

1. Number of subjects should not be less than 100; and the absolute minimum ratio is five individuals to one variable.
2. Split sample analysis should be used, keeping those factors that match across the two samples; a large sample is also necessary.
3. Variables should have a history of good reliability estimates and good correlation with other variables in the analysis.
4. Factors should be highly significant based on the tests for this criterion, although significance tests in factor analysis are poor.
5. Minimum of five to six variable loadings should be used for each factor.

6. Data should be factored by several different analytical procedures, keeping only those factors that appear across the procedures used.

Gorsuch's criteria can be applied to Ayres' factor analytic studies. Most studies had 100 or more dysfunctional subjects (Ayres, 1965, 1971, 1972e, 1977a), although one study of dysfunctional children (Ayres, 1969a) and two of normal children (Ayres, 1966b, c) did not meet this criterion. Ayres' 1965 study (Ayres, 1965) with 25 children in each of four groups did not meet the criterion of a large split sample. The poor reliability of the SCSIT compromises criterion 3 (Ayres, 1980b). Significances of factors of .01 and .05 were reported (Ayres, 1965, 1966b, 1966c, 1971, 1972e); thus criterion 4 was met to some extent, assuming that .01 is considered highly significant. Ayres identified factors with six or more variables, thus meeting criterion 5. Finally, Ayres used Q and R techniques factor analyses to identify factors. She retained those factors that consistently reappeared; namely, developmental dyspraxia, deficit in form and space, dysfunction in bilateral integration, and tactile defensiveness. Thus, the sixth criterion is met if applied to several studies together and not to individual studies.

Bochner (1978), Posthuma (1983), and Lerer (1981) and the Committee on Children with Disabilities (1985) criticize SI research as being poorly controlled, having too few subjects, not accounting for the Hawthorne effect, and being interpretive and anecdotal. Yet, the empirical merit of Ayres' clinical research has been supported by others (Ottenbacher & Short, 1985). In a direct response to Lerer's critique, then AOTA President May Hightower-Van Damm (personal communication, March 12, 1981) said, "In many instances in medicine, psychology, and education, carefully documented behavioral changes are the most important data we have to evaluate a given approach to a presenting problem, i.e., drug therapies, psychotherapy, behavior modification and self-contained classroom instruction." She went on to state that funding is scarce for comprehensive research projects, that anecdotal and case study research are increasingly acceptable research formats, and that research efforts by clinicians and educators yield empirical data that are important educationally. Hightower-Van Damm indicated that SI research is no more deserving of criticism than any other research in the perplexing problems of learning disabilities.

The Committee on Children with Disabilities (1985) advised pediatricians to recommend occupational therapy for severe motor problems but not for the dyspraxic or clumsy child because these problems improve with age and the therapy programs have not been the subject of scientific research. The Committee cited a single study to document its conclusion that dyspraxia often eventually improves without therapy. The dyspraxia study cited by the Committee (1985) was subjected to rigorous analysis and discredited for its small sample size and methodological and reporting flaws (SII, personal communication, December 20, 1985). Responses to the Committee's criticisms were made by then AOTA President Robert Bing (personal communication, December 20, 1985) and by a Sensory Integration International committee (personal communication, December 20, 1985). These respondents eloquently differentiated SI therapy from the passive, patterning therapies and cited research that supports its effectiveness and that showed long-term effects of dyspraxia. It seems that the Committee's assumptions were not based on a thorough literature review of dyspraxia.

Ottenbacher (1982) reported a meta-analysis of SI efficacy studies. In this statistical procedure, a group of research studies was analyzed for generalized findings. Strict criteria were applied to research reports for inclusion in the analysis. From an analysis of eight studies, including three by Ayres, Ottenbacher concluded that the performance of subjects who received SI therapy was significantly better than that of subjects in the control groups.

Several researchers, in addition to Ayres, have established that a subgroup of learning disabled children have difficulty processing and integrating proprioceptive and vestibular sensation and that similar problems may be seen in children with emotional and behavioral problems (Ottenbacher & Short, 1985). SI therapy effectiveness studies have focused on improved academic functioning (Ayres, 1972b, 1978). However, in Ottenbacher's (1982) meta-analysis, the dependent variables most affected by SI therapy were motor or reflex variables. Thus, this meta-analysis does not identify academic improvement as being the primary benefit of SI therapy. Ottenbacher and Short (1985, p. 321) conclude:

> There undoubtedly is a relationship between motor control, reflex integration, and cognitive ability, although the exact nature of this relationship is complex and not clearly understood. It appears from the research currently available that it is more difficult, both empirically and conceptually, to demonstrate a relationship between sensory integration and academic performance than to demonstrate a connection between sensory integration treatment and improvement in motor skills or reflex integration.

That only 8 of the 49 reports reviewed met the criteria for the meta-analysis indicates a need for improved design of SI efficacy studies (Ottenbacher, 1982). Another limitation in SI research is the lack of longitudinal study of therapy effects. Future studies need to address the

Hawthorne effect by providing placebo "therapy" for the control group (Ottenbacher & Short, 1985).

Occupational therapists have been criticized for their overzealousness in promoting SI therapy for children and for overextension of research findings to other patient populations. Lerer (1981) suggests that SI therapy not be used outside the experimental research situation, and he criticized therapists for subjecting families, taxpayers, and third party payers to the expense of this experimental therapy. He remarks that "Ayres, in her carefully conducted inquiries, is cautious about drawing definite conclusions from her theories, concepts and hypotheses" (Lerer, 1981, p. 4). Posthuma (1983) questions the widespread use of SI therapy by occupational therapists in adult psychiatry and cites cost ineffectiveness, lack of standardized tests for adults, and confusion over SI versus other movement therapies as areas that need to be addressed. She urges the development of research and speciality training to enable SI therapy to be appropriately applied to adults. In Ottenbacher's (1982) review of SI studies he found no studies in psychiatry, geriatrics, or physical disabilities that met empirical standards of traditional behavioral science research. He cautions therapists not to apply SI therapy prematurely to populations for which the therapeutic effects have not been established.

Summary of Critiques

In summary, the theoretical assumptions of SI theory have a basis in the neurosciences. However, the highly selective interpretations of the neuroscience literature that support sensory integration theory are suspect. Certainly frequent updatings of neuroscience conceptual bases are requisite for future sensory integration theory development.

Psychometric inadequacies of the SCSIT have been corrected in the Southern California Sensory Integration and Praxis Test. The primary purpose of this standardization project is to develop a valid and reliable instrument for evaluation of SI dysfunction in children with learning disabilities. There continues to be a need to develop instruments for identifying SI dysfunction in other patient populations.

Research has shown extant SI dysfunction in some learning disabled children. There is some evidence that SI therapy enhances academic learning. Other gains include improvements in motor performance. Further well-designed research needs to be conducted to delineate the types of patient problems most benefited by sensory integration therapy.

The work of Ayres has had a large impact on the OT field. Although developed for a specific patient group, e.g., children with learning problems, the theory is one of, if not the most, complete of existing theories.

Its scope includes clinical problem identification, formulation of theoretical constructs, theory validation research, test instrument development, therapy approaches and equipment, and therapy efficacy studies. SI theory has spawned more research, publication, and educational efforts in occupational therapy than any other OT theory to date. SI theory has helped therapists to view patient problems in the context of sensory functioning and has provided another way of perceiving health and dysfunction.

REFERENCES

American Occupational Therapy Association. (1985). Jean Ayres retires from clinical practice. *Occupational Therapy News, 39,* 24.

Ayres, A.J. (1954). Ontogenetic principles in the development of arm and hand functions. *American Journal of Occupational Therapy, 3,* 95–99.

Ayres, A.J. (1955). A pilot study on the relationship between work habits and workshop production. *American Journal of Occupational Therapy, 9,* 264–276.

Ayres, A.J. (1957). A study of the manual dexterity and workshop wages of thirty-nine cerebral palsied trainees. *American Journal of Occupational Therapy, 36,* 6–10.

Ayres, A.J. (1958). The visual motor function. *American Journal of Occupational Therapy, 12,* 130–138.

Ayres, A.J. (1960). Occupational therapy for motor disorders resulting from impairment of the central nervous system. *Rehabilitation Literature, 21,* 302–310.

Ayres, A.J. (1961a). Development of the body scheme in children. *American Journal of Occupational Therapy, 15,* 99–102.

Ayres, A.J. (1961b). The role of gross motor activities in the training of children with visual motor retardation. *Journal of the American Optometric Association, 33,* 121–125.

Ayres, A.J. (1962a). Perception of space of adult hemiplegic patients. *Physical Medicine and Rehabilitation, 43,* 552–555.

Ayres, A.J (1962b). *Ayres Space Test.* Los Angeles: Western Psychological Services.

Ayres, A.J. (1963a). The development of perceptual motor abilities: A theoretical basis for treatment of dysfunction. *American Journal of Occupational Therapy, 6,* 221–225.

Ayres, A.J. (1963b). Occupational therapy directed toward neuromuscular integration. In H.S. Willard & C.S. Spackman, (Eds.), *Occupational therapy* (3rd ed.), (pp. 358–466). Philadelphia: J.B. Lippincott.

Ayres, A.J. (1964a). Perceptual motor training for children. In C. Slattery (Ed.), *Approaches to the treatment of patients with neuromuscular dysfunction* (pp. 17–22). Dubuque, Iowa: W.C. Brown.

Ayres, A.J. (1964b). *Southern California Motor-Accuracy Test.* Los Angeles: Western Psychological Services.

Ayres, A.J. (1964c). Tactile functions: Their relation to hyperactivity and perceptual-motor behavior. *American Journal of Occupational Therapy, 18,* 6–11.

Ayres, A.J. (1965). Patterns of perceptual-motor dysfunction in children: A factor analytic study. *Perceptual Motor Skills, 20,* 355–368.

Ayres, A.J. (1966a). Interrelation of perception, function, and treatment. *Journal of American Physical Therapy Association, 46,* 741–744.

Ayres, A.J. (1966b). Interrelations among perceptual-motor abilities in a group of normal children. *American Journal of Occupational Therapy, 20,* 288–292.

Ayres, A.J. (1966c). Interrelationships among perceptual-motor functions in children. *American Journal of Occupational Therapy, 20,* 68–71.

Ayres, A.J. (1966d). *Southern California Figure Ground Visual Perception Tests.* Los Angeles: Western Psychological Services.

Ayres, A.J. (1966e). *Southern California Kinesthesia and Tactile Perception Tests.* Los Angeles: Western Psychological Services.

Ayres, A.J. (1967). Remedial procedures based on neurobehavioral constructs. *Proceedings, 1967 International Convocation on Children and Young Adults with Learning Disabilities.* Pittsburgh.

Ayres, A.J. (1968a). Reading—A product of sensory integrative process. In A. Henderson et al. (Eds.), *The development of sensory integrative theory and practice* (pp. 167–175). Dubuque, IA: Kendall/Hunt Publishing Co.

Ayres, A.J. (1968b). Sensory integrative processes and neuropsychological learning disability. In *Learning Disorders. Vol. III,* (pp. 41–58). Seattle, WA: Special Child Publications.

Ayres, A.J. (1968c). *Southern California Perceptual-Motor Tests.* Los Angeles: Western Psychological Services.

Ayres, A.J. (1969a). Deficits in sensory integration in educationally handicapped children. *Journal of Learning Disabled, 2,* 160–168.

Ayres, A.J. (1969b). Relation between Gesell development quotients and later perceptual-motor performance. *American Journal of Occupational Therapy, 23,* 11–17.

Ayres, A.J. (1971). Characteristics of types of sensory integrative dysfunction. *American Journal of Occupational Therapy, 25,* 329–334.

Ayres, A.J. (1972a). Basic concepts of occupational therapy for children with perceptual-motor dysfunction. *Proceedings of the Twelfth World Congress of Rehabilitation International.* Sydney, Australia.

Ayres, A.J. (1972b). Improving academic scores through sensory integration. *Journal of Learning Disabled, 5,* 338–343.

Ayres, A.J. (1972c). *Sensory integration and learning disorders.* Los Angeles: Western Psychological Services.

Ayres, A.J. (1972d). *Southern California Sensory Integration Tests.* Los Angeles: Western Psychological Services.

Ayres, A.J. (1972e). Types of sensory integrative dysfunction among disabled learners. *American Journal of Occupational Therapy, 26,* 13–18.

Ayres, A.J. (1972f). An interpretation of the role of the brain stem in intersensory integration. In A. Henderson & J. Coryell (Eds.), *The Body Senses and Perceptual Deficit. Proceedings of the Occupational Therapy Symposium on Somatosensory Aspects of Perceptual Deficit* (pp. 81–89). Boston: Boston University.

Ayres, A.J. (1975a). Sensorimotor foundations of academic ability. In W.M. Cruickshank & D.P. Hallahan (Eds.), *Perceptual and learning disabilities in children, Vol. 2* (pp. 301–358). Syracuse: Syracuse University Press.

Ayres, A.J. (1975b). *Southern California Postrotary Nystagmus Test.* Los Angeles: Western Psychological Services.

Ayres, A.J. (1976a). *The effects of sensory integration therapy on learning disabled children.* Los Angeles: University of Southern California.

Ayres, A.J. (1976b). *Interpreting the Southern California Sensory Integration Tests.* Los Angeles: Western Psychological Services.

Ayres, A.J. (1977a). Cluster analyses of measures of sensory integration. *American Journal of Occupational Therapy, 31,* 362–366.

Ayres, A.J. (1977b). Dichotic listening performance in learning-disabled children. *American Journal of Occupational Therapy, 31,* 441–446.

Ayres, A.J. (1977c). Effect of sensory integrative therapy on the coordination of children with choreoathetoid movement. *American Journal of Occupational Therapy, 31,* 291–293.

Ayres, A.J. (1978). Learning disabilities and the vestibular system. *Journal of Learning Disabled, 11,* 18–29.

Ayres, A.J. (1979). *Sensory integration and the child.* Los Angeles: Western Psychological Services.

Ayres, A.J. (1980a). *Southern California Motor Accuracy Test—revised 1980.* Los Angeles: Western Psychological Services.

Ayres, A.J. (1980b). *Southern California Sensory Integration Tests—revised 1980.* Los Angeles: Western Psychological Services.

Ayres, A.J. (1985). *Developmental dyspraxia and adult onset dyspraxia.* Torrance, CA: Sensory Integration International.

Ayres, A.J., & Heskett, W.M. (1972). Sensory integrative dysfunction in a young schizophrenic girl. *Journal of Autism and Childhood Schizophrenia, 2,* 174–181.

Ayres, A.J., & Mailloux, Z. (1981). Influence of sensory integration procedures on language development. *American Journal of Occupational Therapy, 35,* 383–390.

Ayres, A.J., & Mailloux, Z. (1983). Possible pubertal effects on therapeutic gains in an autistic girl. *American Journal of Occupational Therapy, 37,* 535–540.

Ayres, A.J., & Reid, W. (1966). The self-drawing as an expression of perceptual-motor dysfunction. *Cortex, 2,* 254–265.

Ayres, A.J., & Tickle, L.S. (1980). Hyper-responsivity to touch and vestibular stimuli predict positive response to sensory integration procedures in autistic children. *American Journal of Occupational Therapy, 34,* 375–381.

Ayres, A.J., Mailloux, Z., & McAtee, S. (1985). An update of the Sensory Integration and Praxis Tests. *Sensory Integration Special Interest Section Newsletter, 8:* (3), September, 1985.

Bochner, S. (1978). Ayres, sensory integration and learning disorders: Question of theory and practice. *American Journal of Mental Retardation, 5,* 41–45.

Clark, E., Mailloux, Z., & Parham, D. (1985). Sensory integration and children with learning disabilities. In P.N. Clark & A.S. Allen (Eds.), *Occupational therapy for children.* St. Louis: C.V. Mosby, pp. 359–405.

Committee on Children with Disabilities. (1985). School aged children with motor disabilities, *Pediatrics, 76,* 648–649.

Evan, P.R., & Peham, M.A. (1981). *Testing and measurements in occupational therapy: A review of current practice with special emphasis on the Southern California Sensory Integration Tests.* Minneapolis: University of Minnesota.

Gorsuch, R.L. (1974). *Factor analysis.* Philadelphia: W.B. Saunders Co.

Lerer, R.J. (1981). An open letter to an occupational therapist. *Journal of Learning Disabled, 14,* 3–4.

Lyman, H.B. (1971). *Test scores and what they mean.* Englewood Cliffs, NJ: Prentice-Hall.

Meleis, A.I. (1985). *Theoretical nursing: Development and progress.* Philadelphia: J.B. Lippincott.

Ottenbacher, K. (1982). Sensory integration therapy: Affect or effect. *American Journal of Occupational Therapy, 36,* 571–578.

Ottenbacher, K., & Short, M.A. (1985). Sensory integrative dysfunction in children: A review of theory and treatment. *Advances in Developmental and Behavioral Pediatrics, 6,* 287–329.

Posthuma, B.W. (1983). Sensory integration: Fact or fad. *American Journal of Occupational Therapy, 37,* 343–345.

Reed, H.B.C. (1978). Review of the Southern California Sensory Integration Tests. In O.K. Buror (Ed.), *Eighth mental measurements yearbook.* Highland Park, NJ: Gryphon Press.

Sieben, R.I. (1977). Controversial medical treatments of learning disabilities. *Academic Therapy, 13,* 133–147.

BIBLIOGRAPHY

1949

Ayres, A.J. (1949). An analysis of crafts in the treatment of electroshock patients. *American Journal of Occupational Therapy, 3,* 195–198.

1954

Ayres, A.J. (1954). A form used to evaluate the work behavior of patients. *American Journal of Occupational Therapy, 8,* 73–74.

Ayres, A.J. (1954). Ontogenetic principles in the development of arm and hand functions. *American Journal of Occupational Therapy, 8,* 95–99.

1955

Ayres, A.J. (1955). Proprioceptive facilitation elicited through the upper extremities. *American Journal of Occupational Therapy, 9,* 1–9, 57–58, 121–126.

Ayres, A.J. (1955). A pilot study on the relationship between work habits and workshop production. *American Journal of Occupational Therapy, 9,* 264–276.

1957

Ayres, A.J. (1957). A study of the manual dexterity and workshop wages of thirty-nine cerebral palsied trainees. *American Journal of Physical Medicine, 36,* 6–10.

1958

Ayres, A.J. (1958). The visual-motor function. *American Journal of Occupational Therapy, 12,* 130–138.

Ayres, A.J. (1958). Basic concepts of clinical practice in physical disabilities. *American Journal of Occupational Therapy, 12,* 300–302.

1960

Ayres, A.J. (1960). Hemiplegia. In *Occupational Therapy Reference Manual for Physicians,* (pp. 38–42). Dubuque, IA: William C. Brown. 38–42.

Ayres, A.J. (1960). Occupational therapy for motor disorders resulting from impairment of the central nervous system. *Rehabilitation Literature, 21,* 302–310.

Ayres, A.J. (1960). Research for therapists. *Proceedings of the American Occupational Therapy Association 1960 Conference* (pp. 79–82). Rockville, MD: American Occupational Therapy Association.

1961

Ayres, A.J. (1961). Development of the body scheme in children. *American Journal of Occupational Therapy, 15,* 99–102.

Ayres, A.J. (1961). The role of gross motor activities in the training of children with visual motor retardation. *The Journal of American Optometric Association, 33,* 121–125.

1962

Ayres, A.J. (1962). Perception of space of adult hemiplegic patients. *Physical Medicine and Rehabilitation, 43,* 552–555.

1963

Ayres, A.J. (1963). Development of perceptual-motor abilities. A theoretical basis for treatment of dysfunction. *American Journal of Occupational Therapy, 17,* 221–225.

Ayres, A.J. (1963). Occupational therapy directed toward neuromuscular integration. In H.S. Willard and C.S. Spackman (Eds.), *Occupational therapy* (3rd ed.) (pp. 358–466). Philadelphia: J.B. Lippincott.

1964

Ayres, A.J. (1964). *Perceptual-motor dysfunction in children. Monograph from the Greater Cincinnati District*, Ohio Occupational Therapy Conference, Cincinnati.

Ayres, A.J. (1964). Perceptual-motor training for children. In *Approaches to the treatment of patients with neuromuscular dysfunction: Study Course VI, Third International Congress World Federation of Occupational Therapists, 1962* (pp. 17–22). Dubuque, IA: Wm. C. Brown.

Ayres, A.J. (1964). Integration of information. *Approaches to the treatment of patients with neuromuscular dysfunction: Study Course VI Third International Conference World Federation of Occupational Therapists* (pp. 49–57). Dubuque, IA: Wm. C. Brown.

Ayres, A.J. (1964). Perspectives on neurological bases of reading. In M.P. Douglass (Ed.), *Claremont Reading Conference, 28th yearbook* (pp. 113–118). Claremont, CA: Claremont Graduate School Curriculum Laboratory.

Ayres, A.J. (1964). Tactile functions: Their relation to hyperactivity and perceptual-motor behavior. *American Journal of Occupational Therapy, 18,* 6–11.

1965

Ayres, A.J. (1965). A method of measurement of degree of sensorimotor integration. *Archives of Physical Medicine and Rehabilitation, 46,* 433–435.

Ayres, A.J. (1965). Patterns of perceptual-motor dysfunction in children: A factor analytic study. *Perceptual and Motor Skills, 20,* 335–368.

1966

Ayres, A.J. (1966). Interrelation of perception, function, and treatment. *Journal of the American Physical Therapy Association, 46,* 741–744.

Ayres, A.J. (1966). Interrelations among perceptual-motor abilities in a group of normal children. *American Journal of Occupational Therapy, 20,* 288–292.

Ayres, A.J. (1966). Interrelations among perceptual-motor functions in children. *American Journal of Occupational Therapy, 20,* 68–71.

Ayres, A.J., & Reid, W. (1966). The self-drawing as an expression of perceptual-motor dysfunction. *Cortex, 2,* 254–265.

1967

Ayres, A.J. (1967). Remedial procedures based on neurobehavioral constructs. *Proceedings, 1967 International Convocation on Children and Young Adults with Learning Disabilities,* Pittsburgh.

1968

Ayres, A.J. (1968). Sensory integrative processes and neuropsychological learning disability. *In Learning Disorders, Vol. III* (pp. 41–58). Seattle, WA: Special Child Publications.

Ayres, A.J. (1968). Reading—A product of sensory integrative process. In H.K. Smith (Ed.), *Perception and Reading, Proceedings of the Twelfth Annual Convention International Reading Association,* (*12,* Part 4). Newark, DE.

1969

Ayres, A.J. (1969). Relation between Gesell development quotients and later perceptual-motor performance. *American Journal of Occupational Therapy, 23,* 11–17.

Ayres, A.J. (1969). Deficits in sensory integration in educationally handicapped children. *Journal of Learning Disabilities, 2,* 160–168.

1971

Ayres, A.J. (1971). Characteristics of types of sensory integrative dysfunction. *American Journal of Occupational Therapy, 25,* 329–334.

Ayres, A.J. (1971). The challenge of the brain. *Perceptual Motor Conference.* Sponsored by the Physical Education Division of the American Association for Health, Physical Education, and Recreation, Sparks, NV.

1972

Ayres, A.J. (1972). Types of sensory integrative dysfunction among disabled learners. *American Journal of Occupational Therapy, 26,* 13–18.

Ayres, A.J. (1972, August–September). Basic concepts of occupational therapy for children with perceptual-motor dysfunction. *Proceedings of the Twelfth World Congress of Rehabilitation International.* Sydney, Australia.

Ayres, A.J. (1972). *Sensory integration and learning disorders.* Los Angeles: Western Psychological Services.

Ayres, A.J. (1972). Sensory integration process: Implications of deaf-blind from learning disability children. In W.A. Blea (Ed.), *Proceedings of the National Symposium for Deaf-Blind* (pp. 81–89). Pacific Grove, CA.

Ayres, A.J. (1972). Improving academic scores through sensory integration. *Journal of Learning Disabilities, 5,* 338–343.

Ayres, A.J., & Heskett, W.M. (1972). Sensory integrative dysfunction in a young schizophrenic girl. *Journal of Autism and Childhood Schizophrenia, 2,* 174–181.

Ayres, A.J. (1972). An interpretation of the role of the brain stem in intersensory integration. In A. Henderson & J. Coryell (Eds.), *The Body Senses and Perceptual Deficit. Proceedings of the Occupational Therapy Symposium on Somatosensory Aspects of Perceptual Deficits* (pp. 81–89). Boston: Boston University.

1975

Ayres, A.J. (1975). Sensorimotor foundations of academic ability. In W.M. Cruickshank & D.P. Hallahan (Eds.), *Perceptual and Learning Disabilities in Children, Vol. 2* (pp. 301–358). Syracuse, NY: Syracuse University Press.

1977

Ayres, A.J. (1977). Effect of sensory integrative therapy on the coordination of children with choreoathetoid movements. *American Journal of Occupational Therapy, 31,* 291–293.

Ayres, A.J. (1977). Cluster analyses of measures of sensory integration. *American Journal of Occupational Therapy, 31,* 362–366.

Ayres, A.J. (1977). Dichotic listening performance in learning disabled children. *American Journal of Occupational Therapy, 31,* 441–446.

Ayres, A.J. (1977). A response of defensive medicine. *Academic Therapy, 13,* 149–152.

1978

Ayres, A.J. (1978). Learning disabilities and the vestibular system. *Journal of Learning Disabilities, 11,* 18–29.

1979

Ayres, A.J. (1979). The sensory registration function in autistic and aphasic/apraxic children. In *Piagetian theory and its implication for the helping professions: Proceedings of the Ninth Interdisciplinary Conference.* Los Angeles: University of Southern California.

Ayres, A.J. (1979). *Sensory integration and the child.* Los Angeles: Western Psychological Services.

1980

Ayres, A.J., & Tickle, L.S. (1980). Hyper-responsivity to touch and vestibular stimuli predict positive response to sensory integration procedures in autistic children. *American Journal of Occupational Therapy, 34,* 375–381.

1981

Ayres, A.J., & Mailloux, Z. (1981). Influence of sensory integration procedures on language development. *American Journal of Occupational Therapy, 35,* 383–390.

1983

Ayres, A.J., & Mailloux, Z. (1983). Possible pubertal effects on therapeutic gains in an autistic girl. *American Journal of Occupational Therapy, 37,* 535–540.

1984

Ayres, A.J., & Cermak, S.A. (1984). Crossing the body midline in learning-disabled and normal children. *American Journal of Occupational Therapy, 38,* 35–39.

Ayres, A.J., Slavik, B.A., Kitsuwa-Lowe, J., Danner, P.T., & Green, J. (1984). Vestibular stimulation and eye contact in autistic children. *Neuropediatrics, 15,* 33–36.

1987

Ayres, A.J., Mailloux, Z.K., & Wendler, C.L.W. (1987). Developmental dyspraxia: Is it a unitary function? *Occupational Therapy Journal of Research, 7,* 93–110.

PSYCHOLOGICAL TESTS

1972

Ayres, A.J. (1972). *Southern California Sensory Integration Tests.* Los Angeles: Western Psychological Services.

1975

Ayres, A.J. (1975). *Southern California Postrotary Nystagmus Test.* Los Angeles: Western Psychological Services.

1987

In Process: *Sensory Integration and Praxis Tests.*

REPUBLISHED ARTICLES

1959

Ayres, A.J. (1959). Proprioceptive erleichterungsmethoden. *Krankengymnastic, 11,* 191–195, 196–200, 220–225

1967

Ayres, A.J. (1967). Types of perceptual motor deficits in children with learning difficulties. In A. Bilovsky, Attwell, & Jamison (Eds.), *Readings in Learning Disability.* New York: Selected Academic Readings.

1971

Ayres, A.J. (1971). Interrelations among perceptual-motor abilities in a group of normal children. In C. Kopp (Ed.), *Readings in Early Development for Occupational and Physical Therapy Students.* Springfield, IL: Charles C Thomas.

1973

Ayres, A.J. (1973). The development of perceptual-motor abilities: A theoretical basis for treatment of dysfunction. In American Occupational Therapy Association, Inc. (Ed.), *The Eleanor Clarke Slagle Lectures, 1955–1972.* Dubuque, IA: Kendall/Hunt.

1974

The development of sensory integrative theory and practice: A collection of the works of A. Jean Ayres. Compiled by A. Henderson, L. Llorens, E. Gilfoyle, C. Myers, & S. Prevel. Dubuque, IA: Kendall/Hunt.

PROFESSIONAL FILMS

1966

Ayres, A.J. (1966). *Perceptual-motor evaluation of a perceptually normal child.* Los Angeles: UCLA.

Ayres, A.J. (1966). *Perceptual-motor evaluation of a child with dysfunction.* Los Angeles: UCLA.

1969

Ayres, A.J., & Heskett, W.M. (1969). *Clinical observations of dysfunctions in postural and bilateral integration.*

Ayres, A.J., & Heskett, W.M. (1969). *A therapeutic activity for perceptual-motor dysfunction.*

Chapter Six

Mary Reilly

Julia Van Deusen

Mary Reilly

Source: Courtesy of The American Occupational Therapy Association, Inc., Rockville, Maryland.

BIOGRAPHICAL SKETCH

Mary Reilly was born in Boston in 1916. A major early influence shaping Dr. Reilly's scholarly career was her experience at Girls' Latin High School (W. West, personal communication, July 7, 1987). She became interested in occupational therapy while working as a camp counselor earning money for college tuition. There she became fascinated by stories of patients related by a fellow employee, an occupational therapist. Somehow, arts and crafts as media were never mentioned, so that it was with much surprise, on beginning OT training, that Reilly encountered her first craft lessons. (W. West, personal communication, July 7, 1987). She did, however, obtain her certificate of occupational therapy from the Boston School of Occupational Therapy in 1940 and for her first job chose to work with cerebral palsied patients at a Crippled Children's Program in Michigan (Occupational Therapy Yearbook, 1957). Experience with these patients, as well as with the brain-injured soldiers at Letterman Army Hospital (Reilly 1956b), led to her early studies on the central nervous system's relevance to occupational therapy. It is indeed interesting to note the sophisticated knowledge of neurodevelopmental principles and their application to occupational therapy demonstrated by Reilly in an early *American Journal of Occupational Therapy* article (Reilly, 1956b).

During her years with the U.S. Army Medical Department (1941–1955), Reilly came to realize that a focus only on the CNS ignored the necessary emphasis on the development of patient skills and competence. Reilly's work with the army began as Chief Occupational Therapist at Lovell General and Convalescent Hospital, Fort Devens, Massachusetts. From 1944–1946, she was OT Consultant, Service Command Surgeon's Office, Fourth Service Command, Atlanta, Georgia. In this position, she supervised occupational therapy at two convalescent, eleven general, and six regional and station hospitals. At this time, she also provided technical assistance for a War Department Technical Manual, a medical supply catalogue, and an apprentice training course of study. For this "outstanding devotion to duty and superior achievement" she was granted the Meritorious Civilian Service Award (Meritorious, 1947).

In 1951 and 1955 Reilly obtained, respectively, a B.S. degree from the University of Southern California (USC) and an M.A. degree from San Francisco State College in California. In 1959 she earned her Ed.D. degree

---

Note: Several years ago Dr. Reilly, who was distressed over the direction in which the profession was moving, determined that she needed to take an ethical position of withdrawal from active involvement in occupational therapy. When the authors communicated with her about this book, she wished them success in the venture but she chose not to make any active contribution out of concern that to do so would be construed as capitulation.

from the University of California at Los Angeles (UCLA), where she wrote her dissertation on a theoretical basis of planned change in professional education. Following her doctoral work she was chief of the Rehabilitation Department of the Neuropsychiatric Institute, UCLA (Reilly, 1966b; Yearbook, 1972).

At UCLA she came into contact with a person who had a major influence on her scholarly work, the social scientist M. Brewster Smith. Basic ideas relevant to Reilly's work were Smith's views on intrinsic motivation and competence. He proposed that an attitude of self-respect and hopefulness are highly relevant to competence and that human beings are capable of actively constructing their lives in a dignified manner (Smith, 1974a).

In his foreword to Reilly's book, *Play As Exploratory Learning* (1974c), Smith concurs with her underlying premises and expresses hope that "the efforts of Dr. Reilly and her collaborators will turn out to be a part of a new stream of interest in play as a scientific problem, and as a therapeutic and educational strategy" (Smith, 1974a, p. 16).

Although claiming the social psychology perspective of Smith as her primary influence, Reilly readily credits the contributions of other psychologists, such as Bruner, White, and McClelland; vocational theorists, such as Super and Roe; and the founders of occupational therapy, such as Adolph Meyer (Reilly, comments on unpublished student paper, August 9, 1986).

Reilly began her association with USC students while she was still at UCLA. After she assumed a full-time position as director of graduate programs in the OT department at USC, she influenced the work of her graduate students, which was to have a major impact on the field of occupational therapy.

Over the years, Reilly received a number of honors for her creative scholarly activities. She is a fellow of the AOTA and was awarded the Eleanor Clarke Slagle Lectureship (Reilly, 1962). She was named a charter member of the Academy of Research of the AOTF in 1983, being cited for her exemplary contributions to the development of a generic paradigm for practice" (AOTF, 1983). When she retired in 1977 she became a professor emeritus of USC. She also found an intellectual "home" at Oxford University in England where she occasionally studied, lectured, and consulted (W. West, personal communication, July 7, 1987).

In her retirement years, Reilly has lost faith in the field of occupational therapy because she feels it has placed the interests of the profession over those of the chronic patient—that patient most in need of OT services (Reilly, 1984). Without benefit of the occupational behavior (OB) approach, the chronic patient is at high risk of becoming "a member of the hard core unemployable poor" (To Treat, 1968). In fact, although continuing her interest in scholarly activity, she has abandoned the field because she perceives the reductionistic point of view as still inappropriately dominating occupational therapy (W. West, personal communication, July 7, 1987).

Reilly has indeed been a colorful and creative figure in the field of occupational therapy. An early contributor to the professional literature (Licht & Reilly 1943; Reilly & Barton, 1944), her development of the paradigm of occupational behavior is one of the most significant influences on the evolution of the OT profession. When introducing a number of proposals for "modernizing" the field into congruence with OB thinking, Reilly stated: "To the rational who value the continuity of civilization, tradition means pouring the old wine of knowledge into the new bottles of contemporary issues and problems" (Reilly, 1971 p. 243). Reilly has succeeded in doing just that!

THEORETICAL CONSTRUCTS

Foundations

The "occupation" in occupational therapy has been emphasized by Reilly from the time of her earliest scholarly work. In 1943, she wrote that the essential difference between occupational therapy and physical therapy was not active (occupational) versus passive (physical) treatment, but rather that occupational therapy's purpose is to help the patient integrate the fundamental motions elicited by physical therapy into total activities (Licht & Reilly, 1943).

This core concept of occupational functioning as the goal of treatment underlies Reilly's unending quest for truth. Addressing the occupational therapists' use of splinting, she wrote, "I shall attempt to explore what I believe my role should be. This I shall do via a process of rational thinking based upon some soul searching" (Reilly, 1956a, p. 118). Drawing on occupational therapy's unique perspective based on observations of patient functioning, she then concluded that appropriate orthopedic devices enabled patients to assume "their rightful place in life" (Reilly, 1956a, p. 132), that is, their occupational roles.

In her early writings Reilly explored occupational therapy for the physically disabled (Licht & Reilly, 1943; Reilly, 1956a, 1956b). Her knowledge of neurophysiology made her realize that for the newly brain injured, patient participation in activities of daily living must be delayed. Yet, Reilly never abandoned the central concept that patients must eventually perform movements voluntarily in occupational behavior (Reilly, 1956b).

Believing that the domain of occupational therapy is promotion of life satisfaction through occupational (work) and recreational roles, Reilly proposed to OT educators criteria for a curriculum designed to foster practice in performance of these roles (Reilly, 1958). Disease and injury can profoundly disrupt the self-actualization that is ordinarily obtained as worker and recreator, and occupational therapy restores the patient to these roles (Reilly, 1958). A curriculum to support OT practice would use qualitative, quantitative, and historical perspectives to promote the critical thinking of students. Course content would include growth and development, neurophysiology, and psychology (Reilly, 1958).

Research as well as educational programming must address the central domain of occupational therapy. In 1960 when Reilly addressed the role of research, OT research was in its infancy. She argued that it should focus on such variables as achievement, creativity, and patterns of aptitudes, interests, and abilities relating to activities as a whole, rather than dealing with a specific modality, such as arts and crafts (Reilly, 1960).

Having long advocated the individual's need for productive and creative occupation as the core concept of occupational therapy, Reilly was presented the opportunity to refine this concept as the Eleanor Clarke Slagle lecturer at the 1961 AOTA conference. Drawing on historical literature in the field, she formulated the central founding belief of occupational therapy as the oft-quoted hypothesis: "that man [humans], through the use of [their] hands as they are energized by mind and will, can influence the state of [their] own health" (Reilly, 1962, p. 2). The major implication of this hypothesis is that the individual can manually and creatively "deploy his [or her] thinking, feelings, and purposes to make himself [or herself] at home in the world and to make the world his [or her] home" (Reilly, 1962, p. 2).

Reilly's lecture considered the value of this hypothesis and whether 20th-century America was the time and place for its testing through occupational therapy practice. She supported the notion that human beings have an intrinsic need to master and improve their environment through skills acquired in their various life roles. If this need is blocked by disease or injury, human beings suffer dysfunction and dissatisfaction (Reilly, 1962). Reilly proposed that the unique content of the OT body of knowledge was the nature of productive and creative occupation, particularly from a developmental perspective. The treatment process should focus on work satisfaction and "the ability to experience pleasure in achievement, to tolerate the frustrations of struggle, to sustain the burden of routine tasks, and to maintain the level of aspiration within the reality level of work skills" (Reilly, 1962, p. 7). The goal of the OT process is for patients to engage actively with their life role tasks. Treatment techniques should address the dysfunctions and difficulties people experience in coping with play, work, and school situations (Reilly, 1962). Reilly (1962) closed her Slagle lecture by reiterating the grand purpose of occupational therapy—to help patients influence the state of their own health—but she did not predict whether the field could or would be able to fulfill this mandate.

Published in the *American Journal of Occupational Therapy* (Reilly, 1962) and reprinted in Canada (Reilly, 1963), Reilly's Slagle lecture had a profound impact on the field. As her paradigm of occupational behavior evolved it was fleshed out by her graduate students and cited and used throughout the United States and Canada (Madigan & Parent, 1985; Matsutsuyu, 1983; Woodside, 1976). Because of her position at USC, Reilly was also able to develop an OT graduate curriculum based on her occupational behavior point of view (Reilly, 1969a; 1969b).

Parameters of the Paradigm

From review of Reilly's writings it is evident that she considers four concepts central to her paradigm (Reilly, 1969a):

1. the human need to be competent and to achieve
2. the developmental aspects of work and play
3. the nature of occupational role
4. the relationship of health and human adaptation

Although Reilly's work was not organized according to these concepts, they are clearly discernible in both her writings and those of her graduate students.

The basic premise underlying the OB paradigm is that human beings have a vital need to produce, to create, to master, and to improve their environment; that is, to be competent and to achieve in their daily occupation. Thus, it follows that, because human beings need to be competent, they also need to function in occupational roles, which are the vehicles for competency (Reilly, 1962).

In the process of meeting their need for achievement, human beings acquire interests, abilities, skills, and habits of cooperation or competition that support their various occupational roles throughout the life-span. Reilly broadly defined occupational roles to include preschooler, student, housewife, and retiree, as well as the paid worker (Reilly, 1969a). Occupational choice is a key point in the occupational role developmental process, providing a bridge between the skills and habits of the child and the mature roles of the adult (Matsutsuyu, 1983).

It was Reilly's plan in building the OB paradigm to describe the aptitudes, abilities, interests, and motivational states supporting occupational roles at each stage of the developmental process (Reilly, 1969a). Only when normal roles could be understood at each stage would it be possible to identify and address occupational role dysfunction (Reilly, 1969b).

Reilly views the health of human beings in terms of level of adaptation to their environment, rather than in freedom from pathology. If the vital need for human beings to master their environment is blocked by disease or injury, dysfunction results. Occupational role dysfunction is the domain of occupational therapy. It is the responsibility of the occupational therapist to evaluate and facilitate the adaptive skills of occupationally dysfunctional patients. This responsibility entails maximizing the healthy behaviors of patients (Reilly, 1966b). A major hypothesis of the OB paradigm is that children's play, social recreation, and even chores are critical to the development of the adaptive skills necessary for competence in the complex work and daily living roles of adults. Play is a safe area for the handicapped child or dysfunctional adult to accumulate successful graded experiences for adaptation to life roles (Reilly, 1966a; 1966b).

It is the goal of occupational therapy to assess the developmental level of the patients' occupational roles, whether the patient is an adult or child, and to foster appropriate growth. Emphasis is placed on environmental support for achievement and an appropriate balance of daily activity. The occupational therapist becomes the advocate for patients to practice a healthy balance of work, rest, and play within the OT clinic, the institution as a whole, and eventually within the larger community environment (Reilly, 1966a; 1966b).

Because of the interdisciplinary nature and complexity of the constructs of open systems theory and hierarchy Reilly has used them to guide her paradigm development (Reilly, 1969a; 1974b). Viewing occupational behavior from these perspectives allows for both longitudinal and cross-sectional approaches to investigation.

Florey (1981) succinctly reviewed the constructs of open systems theory and hierarchy as they relate to the OB paradigm. The human being can be conceived of as an open system that evolves and undergoes different forms of growth and development. As an open system, the human being maintains itself in relation to its environment via a process of input, throughput, and output of energy or matter. As applied to human skills, growth or change may occur in terms of amount of skill or in complexity of skill.

The concept of hierarchy relates to the processing of change over time. This process is orderly but dynamic as behavior changes from simple to complex and from less to more autonomous. Higher levels of behavior direct lower levels. However, these lower levels serve to constrain the higher ones such that a change at any level of the hierarchy will affect all levels. Thus, newer skills can emerge from the recombination, reorganization, and transformation of more primitive skills (Florey, 1981).

Work-Play Continuum

According to Reilly, "Play serves the function of adaptation by facilitating man's manipulatory and social skills and serves society by socializing the aggression of its members" (Reilly, 1974a, p. 113). An action and an attitude are both involved in play. The action must be voluntary, and the attitude is one of amusement, fun, and pleasure (Takata, 1969). The label given to play changes as the person ages: "play" becomes "recreation" for adults and "leisure" for the retired. Examples of activity that may be play are music, dramatics, games, and crafts (Reilly, 1974a, p. 60).

Because Reilly proposed play as the instrument by which dysfunctional patients could experience achievement and learn healthy adaptation to their environment, her major work concerned the investigation of play (Reilly, 1974a; 1974b). She analyzed play from the perspectives of the evolutionary biologists, psychologists, anthropologists, and sociologists, concluding that play is "a behavior in search of an explanation" (Reilly, 1974a, p. 115).

Reilly sees play as one of three subsystems of the imagination system of learning (see Figure 6-1). The other two subsystems are myth and dream. Although the other subsystems use words or visual images, play uses rules as symbols to represent reality. Through "doing" in play, human beings learn the rules of the hows and whys of objects in their environments. The result is the development of skills leading to competency and the mastery of the real world (Reilly, 1974b).

Within the play subsystem of the imagination Reilly posed a hierarchy of three subsystems: exploration, competency, and achievement. Intrinsically motivated, play that is undertaken for the pure pleasure of doing it is termed *exploratory*. It is associated with sensory, esthetic, and novel experiences. Developmentally, it is the early childhood stage of play. Initially describing the attitude developed by exploratory play as trust (Reilly, 1974b), her later studies led to her present position that this stage of play generates an attitude of curiosity (Reilly, comments on unpublished student paper, August 9, 1986).

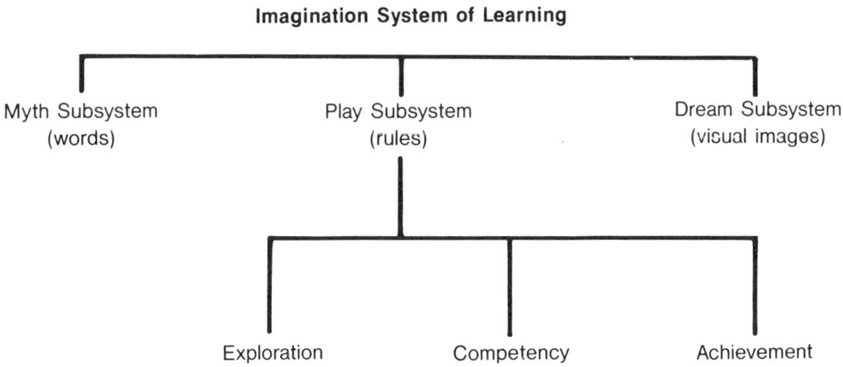

Figure 6-1 The Imagination System of Learning.

The *competency* stage of play comes developmentally later than exploration. It involves persistence and practice for task mastery. Originally believed to lead to an attitude of self-confidence (Really, 1974b), Reilly currently considers this stage to engender hope (Reilly, comments on unpublished student paper, August 9, 1986).

The third phase of play behavior is termed *achievement* because it focuses on competitive performance and has a standard of excellence. Competition may be with self or with others (Reilly, 1974b). Reilly presently believes that achievement behavior leads to an attitude of altruism (Reilly, comments on unpublished student paper, August 9, 1986). At this stage the human being has gained control over his or her environment. "[The individual] who has played his [or her] way gradually and safely towards the skillful mastery of his [or her] world" is now free to show concern for others (Reilly, 1974b, p. 148).

The results of Reilly's intensive interest in play were twofold: (1) she derived a number of "rules of thumb" about play to encourage others to pursue this line of investigation, and (2) a number of Reilly's graduate students chose to study play as their thesis projects. Before Reilly's major publication several students had already explored this area and thus contributed to the volume on play edited by her (Hurff, 1974; Knox, 1974; Michelman, 1974; Shannon, 1974; Takata, 1974).

Student Work

Because the OB paradigm was only in an early stage of development, the student studies of play were exploratory; they drew principles of relevance to occupational therapy from the literature, constructed assessment tools, and described clinical applications. Takata (1969; 1971; 1974; 1980) made contributions in all three areas. Of major importance were the six principles on play identified by Takata (Takata, 1971), which guided the studies of other graduate students working under the direction of Reilly (Florey, 1981).

1. Play is spontaneous, pleasurable, complex behavior.
2. Play involves sensory, motor, mental, or a combination of all three processes.
3. Play can involve exploration, experimentation, imitation, and repetition.
4. Play integrates the child's internal and external worlds.
5. Play has temporal and spatial limits.
6. Play follows a developmental sequence.

Robinson (1977) developed the concept of the construct of rule. Rules organize information from the environment. Play is the arena where this learning can occur—where information on space, time, and interpersonal relations can be processed for daily living skills. Concepts of curiosity and conflict are key to understanding rule learning through play.

Michelman (1969, 1971, 1974) was interested in the relationship between art experiences and symbolic and creative development. From an extensive review of the literature, Michelman identified a six-step symbolic developmental sequence starting with scribbling and culminating in representational works.

Zorn (1969) studied games as an arena for the development and practice of cognitive skills. DeRenne-Stephan (1980) used a systems approach to analyze imitation as a critical mechanism of play.

Florey (1969, 1971) identified four principles from her study of childhood play as the critical arena for the development of intrinsic motivation:

1. Play is spare-time learning.
2. Play involves action on human and nonhuman objects.
3. Environmental conditions affect play. For example, anxiety inhibits and novelty facilitates play.
4. Constitutional deficits may interfere with play satisfactions.

Congruent with Reilly's position on the developmental nature of work and play, Florey also discussed variables critical for fostering intrinsic motivation in the older child and adult.

Other major contributions to the OB literature by Florey were a review of Reilly's position on play for an OT textbook (Florey, 1985) and an analysis of the studies on play done under Reilly's guidance (Florey, 1981). Florey categorized these studies according to the principles identified by Takata and provided information on their relevance to OT practice.

Because play is the antecedent to work, occupational behavior addresses the entire developmental continuum of play and work (Reilly, 1969a). Reilly urged the study of work-play phenomena in their environmental context. Although Reilly herself did not investigate the work part of the continuum as intensely as she addressed play, several of her graduate students focused on the aspects of OB more directly related to work.

Shannon (1970, 1972b, 1977) and Matsutsuyu (1971) shared and disseminated Reilly's view of the importance of the work-play phenomena for occupational therapy. Occupational choice, occupational role, and also socialization are important concepts because human beings become socialized into their occupational roles (Matsutsuyu, 1971).

Shannon's work-play model (Shannon, 1970, 1972b) emphasized the kinds of work-play-social skills necessary for the adaptation of disabled persons to their environments. These work-play-social skills should be central to occupational therapy whether programming involves prevention, maintenance, or restoration. Shannon's model was based on six premises.

1. The human being is activity-oriented, and this activity consists of work and time free from work (maintenance activities and play).
2. A balance of rest, play, and work appropriate to each individual's needs is required for positive physical and mental health.
3. A deficiency in learning how to work or to play creates the potential for maladaptive behavior.
4. Inability to work or play leads to mental illness.
5. The hospital environment can contribute to the deterioration of work-play skills.
6. The primary objective for the hospitalized patient is restoration of function for resumption of daily living.

Although acknowledging the nature of the work-play continuum, Shannon showed particular interest in work adjustment programming for young men in the military (Shannon, 1970, 1972a, 1974). He identified the developmental tasks of adolescence, concluding that a common element was that of choice. Occupational choice involves a series of developmental stages spanning childhood play and adult work roles and ends in selection of an occupation. Shannon cited Ginzberg's stages of the development of occupational choice (Shannon, 1972a). Briefly, these stages are a pretend, fantasy period based only on interests, a tentative stage in which alternative vocational possibilities are weighed, and a final stage when a single, realistic choice is made.

True to the open systems perspective, Shannon also reviewed the environmental influences on occupational choice. Occupational therapy can facilitate the adolescent choice process by providing activities that foster self-discovery and decision making, that enable experimentation in work roles and the development of occupational skills, and that promote constructive use of time free from work.

Pezzuti (1979) centered her discussion of occupational choice on the female adolescent. She concurred with Shannon on the developmental nature of the process from the exploratory play of early childhood through the final phase of occupational choice. However, their dual role options—homemaker and paid worker—complicate the occupational choice process for women. The development of occupational choice includes these three elements:

1. opportunity for a genuine choice;
2. exposure to appropriate work role models and role playing; and
3. participation in play activity for development of skills, values, interests, and cognitive realization.

Pezzuti found that these attitudes and skills contribute to a sound occupational choice growth process at various life stages: trust (infancy), a sense of competence within immediate surroundings and motor development (early childhood), identification with role models and mastery of self-help skills (childhood), and rudiments of organizational, social, and work skill competencies (school age). By adolescence, a sense of competence in roles, independence from parents, and occupational choice should occur (Matsutsuyu, 1971).

A second work concept receiving the attention of Reilly's students was that of occupational role. Moorhead (1969) made a major contribution in this area, identifying the common elements among the various occupational roles, such as worker, homemaker, and retiree. These roles all serve as vehicles for self-identification and for identification within society. Early occupational roles—player, student and others—influence adult occupational behavior.

Moorhead (1969) provided a list of variables perceived as critical to occupational role performance. Autonomy and independence variables include a realistic perception of one's own strengths and weaknesses and an ability to make firm decisions and manage time. Motivation and orientation to one's interests and satisfactions and appreciation of alternatives are implementation variables. Maintenance variables include standards and stability of work task behavior, performance under stress, interpersonal competence, work-play-rest balance, and ability to handle role conflicts.

Moorhead (1969) also developed four categories for analyzing occupational role development: (1) learning and socialization in childhood roles, (2) issues around occupational choice, (3) influences of environment on patterns of achievement and failure, and (4) course of adult occupational mobility or solidification.

Matsutsuyu (1971) cited Schmaltz's thesis project on the place of the socialization process in learning occupational role. The OT setting should facilitate role maintenance, learning, and relearning. Maintenance focuses on keeping intact daily living skills active. If a patient is assessed as able to learn new roles, occupational role development is emphasized. If occupational role dysfunction is present, relearning may be the goal.

Motivation and Environment

A crucial concept of the OB paradigm is human motivation. Because of its importance this concept was addressed early by Reilly's students (Florey, 1969) and continues to be discussed (Bell, 1975; Burke, 1977; Sharrott & Cooper-Fraps 1986). Motivation cannot be understood apart from environment.

Florey (1969) proposed that intrinsic motivation was most relevant to occupational therapy. "Intrinsic motivation builds toward self-reward in independent action that underlies competent behavior" (Florey, 1969, p. 320). Satisfaction in completion of the activity itself is intrinsically motivating. Because competence breeds competence, Florey (1969) described in detail the environmental conditions that foster competence in children and adults.

Childhood play is vital to the development of intrinsic motivation. Environmental factors critical to play are the presence of humans and of novel nonhuman objects among familiar objects. The environment should allow for exploration, repetition, and for imitation of competent role models and should be free of such stresses as hunger, fear, and pain. For the older child the environment should provide tools, instruction for useful productivity, and opportunity to relate to peers and to adult models of sportsmanship and craftsmanship.

In adulthood, intrinsic motivation is related to achievement. Tasks should present challenges within the adult's range of abilities. The environment should foster responsibility for outcome and present feedback on results.

For some individuals when there is a standard for excellence competition fosters achievement (Bell, 1975). Therefore, competitive behavior needs a task-related, self-related, or other-related standard of excellence (Florey, 1969; Bell, 1975). Bell (1975) utilized the interrelationship between risk taking and competition to identify individuals for whom competition would be motivating.

Under Reilly's guidance, Burke's graduate thesis (Burke, 1977) elaborated the concept of personal causation—that human beings are motivated to interact effectively with their environment—as a means of understanding human motivation. This internal motivation is directed primarily toward producing environmental change. Feedback on the effectiveness of current behavior provides guidance for future behavior. Thus, adaptation to life's endless challenges can occur and humanity survives.

Four theoretical statements by Burke (1977) underlie the concept of personal causation:

1. Success leads to feelings of success, which lead to more success.
2. Individuals who perceive they have control over their environments show active behaviors.
3. A belief that one has skills to address obstacles generates a sense of control.
4. A feeling of worth accompanies use of one's own resources to change one's environment.

Sharrott and Cooper-Fraps (1986) associated lack of intrinsic motivation with dysfunction in occupational behavior and presented two criteria—lack of satisfaction to self and lack of satisfaction to society—for determining such dysfunction. Thus, people can become dysfunctional if they do not derive satisfaction from their occupational roles. Dysfunction can also occur if role performance does not meet society's standards.

Reilly (1966a) was probably the first vocal environmental manager in the field of occupational therapy. Addressing the 1965 AOTA conference, she stated, "We should be the first to realize that a hospital environment should be a place where the patient's daily living skill could be improved because of the environment and not despite it; and that the homes and the jobs or schools are progressive extensions of the same concepts" (1966a, p. 224). Although little of the work addressing the OB paradigm could avoid the environmental context, several of Reilly's students chose to address this topic directly.

Gray (1972) describes conditions or practices within a hospital environment that can negatively affect such daily living (work-play) skills as self-care, social, general or specific work skills. She also describes those practices affecting loss of time, leisure-time, and decision-making skills. Some practices cited are failure of staff to serve as appropriate role models, lack of patient evaluation in thc specified skill area, and lack of encouragement for patients to practice skills in the hospital setting.

Parent (1978) reviewed the literature on the effects of sensory and perceptual deprivation and of immobilization and social isolation. The demonstrated impact of deprivation and isolation on the hospitalized patient provides support for the OT position that meaningful occupation is essential to maintain hospitalized patients' functioning.

Klavins (1972) emphasized the importance of cultural influences on patient behaviors in occupational therapy. "As part of the human environment, culture is that special way of life which characterizes it" (Klavins, 1972, p. 176). Work-play behaviors are influenced by the values held by one's cultural group. Therapists must know, accept, and work within the value and belief structures of patients from a variety of cultural backgrounds.

Drawing on the research from the field of environmental psychology, Dunning (1972) developed a classification system for study of environments through analysis of their components—space, people, and tasks. Space is analyzed in terms of territoriality, privacy, and crowding and objects in the environment. Social role relationships and social distance are aspects of the people component. Task is analyzed through the potential use of objects and space in terms of their presence, availability, desirability, and feasibility. Dunning designed a grid showing the givens, possibility for change, and preference for change. She applied her analysis to psychiatric outpatients.

Temporal Adaptation

Although time is not a part of the physical environment, it is "the inescapable boundary for human existence and activity" (Kielhofner, 1977, p. 237) so that it is, in a sense, one's surroundings. Kielhofner (1977) treated the concept of temporal adaptation in depth as part of his master's work with Reilly. He derived seven propositions relevant to occupational therapy as a preliminary framework for the generation of treatment strategies and demonstrated their utility through discussion of case histories (1977).

The first proposition describes the cultural basis of every person's perspective toward time. In the second proposition he argues that the formal learning of the cultural notions of time is only part of the temporal training begun in childhood. There are three levels of learning—which also include formal, technical, and informal learning—through which each person acquires a unique temporal frame of reference.

The third proposition incorporates Reilly's notion of life spaces and a temporal order to daily living. Time is organized around the life spaces of existence (self-maintenance), subsistence (work), and discretionary time (recreation/leisure). Health in relation to this aspect of time means a balance of life spaces consistent with the values, interests, and goals of an individual and of his or her society.

Proposition four states that time for each individual is organized around his or her social roles, although these roles should not be considered as unchanging. Proposition five defines time use as a function of a person's internalized interests, values, and goals.

Habits are intimately linked with temporal functioning. According to proposition six, habits are the basic structures that order daily behavior in time.

Finally, in proposition seven, Kielhofner proposes that the temporal dysfunction of patients may be a more difficult problem to address than pathology per se. The goal of achieving temporal adaptation is applicable to all dysfunctional categories of patients.

APPLICATION TO OCCUPATIONAL THERAPY PRACTICE

Educational Needs

In order for occupational therapists to base service on the occupational behavior paradigm, their educational training must also be based on the OB perspective. The master's entry-level curriculum at USC, which Reilly developed, is based on that perspective (Reilly, 1969a).

The USC curriculum included content from the biological system of medical science, the personality system of the psychological sciences, and the social system of the social sciences. Because there is a fundamental difference between medicine's goal of reducing illness and occupational therapy's goal of reducing the incapacities resulting from illness, the medical sciences were part of the curriculum, but were not a major focus. However, emphasis was placed on the behavioral sciences because occupational therapy's major concern is the identification and treatment of occupational role dysfunction. The behavioral science content was made relevant by selecting from many disciplines—anthropology, psychology, sociology, social geography, psychiatry, economics, political science, and law—those portions dealing with human behavior (Reilly, 1969a). Social psychology, particularly the developmental aspects of human achievement, was a core curricular area because the development of healthy adaptive behavior is a basic part of the occupational behavior paradigm (Reilly, 1969b).

Clinical Application

Without clinical application a paradigm can have no value for a profession concerned with patient treatment. Reilly's OB paradigm has evolved along with OT service over the years. The best illustration of this symbiosis is Reilly's original psychiatric program at the Neuropsychiatric Institute (NPI) at UCLA (Reilly, 1966b).

The NPI program was designed both as a teaching model and to provide OT service to 100 psychiatric patients. "The NPI model assumed as its foundation and first specification the need (1) to examine the life roles of patients relative to community adaptation; (2) to identify the various skills which support them; and (3) to create an environment where the relevant rehabilitative behavior could be evoked and practiced" (Reilly, 1966b, p. 62). Occupational therapists functioned in clinician, administrator, and teacher roles. Evaluation of the NPI program showed that occupational therapy was an important service in the restoration of healthy adaptive behavior.

The NPI program was structured according to five principles.

1. Occupational behavior is developmentally acquired.
2. Patient programming should be graded from craft work in the OT clinic to work in the larger institutional environment to work in the community.
3. Occupational therapy must provide realistic decision-making arenas for the patients.
4. Because basic needs of patients in areas of food, shelter, and safety are met by other services in the hospital, occupational therapy should emphasize programming to meet cognitive, esthetic, and self-realization needs of patients.
5. Occupational therapy should engineer a normal daily pattern of work, play, and rest for the lives of the patients and tailor programs to their abilities, interests, ages, and occupational roles.

APPLICATION OF THE PARADIGM BY OTHERS

Assessment

From its inception the OB paradigm has been intimately linked to OT practice through the development of assessment tools for clinical use. The case method was the clinical problem-solving vehicle that was considered consistent with the OB paradigm (Line, 1969). Line evaluated the case methods of several disciplines and selected that of business administration as the model for occupational therapy. This method allows the professional to gain an understanding of the problem and develop a plan to solve it that maximizes patient assets and minimizes weaknesses. The case method as a problem-solving vehicle for OT was piloted by the OT graduate students at USC. The frame of reference was human adaptation to role expectations in work and play roles. Data were collected by direct observation, tests, interviews, and history taking and were classified according to structure, function, expectancies, patterns of success and failure, and prior learnings and learning style. The data thus collected were organized into social, ADL, and disease adaptation categories. Analysis of data led to problem definition and development of a plan of action. That plan seemed to be the weakest component in the pilot study for application of the OB method to occupational therapy.

The case method approach confirmed the need for assessment tools relevant to the OB point of view. Many of Reilly's graduate students conducted extensive literature searches to support the development of such tools. The purpose of their work was not to create rigorous psychometric instruments, but rather to develop tools to guide the data collection phase of clinical problem solving by a professional person knowledgeable about OB. Thus, the descriptions of the assessment tools were often illustrated with applications to patient case material. The flexibility of this approach to assessment allowed emphasis to be placed on the individual differences observable in human occupational behavioral dysfunction.

Fifteen approaches to assessment are briefly described below. The reader is referred to the references for the detailed information necessary for clinical application.

Takata (1969) developed the Play History to identify the quality and quantity of play in multihandicapped children. It can be used to obtain a play deficit diagnosis.

Matsutsuyu (1969) based her 80-item Interest Checklist on six propositions gleaned from a literature review. Interests:

1. are family influenced;
2. evoke affective responses;
3. are choice states;
4. can be manifested in effective action;
5. can sustain action; and
6. reflect self-perception.

Matsutsuyu's assessment tool also included a special interest section and a leisure-time history.

After an extensive review of the literature on interests, Borys (1974) investigated an indirect approach to interest study. She compared values of subjects showing a low interest in daily living (minimal activity participation, low curiosity, and low risk taking) to those with high interest. Low-interest subjects gave greater value to security, self-development, and contributing to others. Thus, one of the measures of values evaluated in this study (The Buhler Life Goals Inventory) had utility for occupational therapy in terms of daily living interests.

Michelman (1969) developed a sequential growth gradient as a means of evaluating symbolic and creative development. She developed a brief checklist for assessing creative growth.

Knox's Play Scale (1974), which was based on normal behaviors of the child from birth to 6 years, assessed the developmental level of space management, material management, imitation, and participation.

Hurff's Play Skills Inventory (Hurff, 1980) assessed the individual's readiness to move into adolescence in sensory, motor, perceptual, and intellectual areas. Pezzuti's self-evaluative tool (Pezzuti, 1979) provided information on the developmental task level of female adolescents.

Occupational choice and role were concerns of other assessments. Shannon designed the Inventory of Occupational Choice Skills (1974) with a companion rating scale. Black's Adolescent Role Assessment (Black, 1976) identified deficiencies in the occupational choice process by examining such issues as childhood-play, adolescence-socialization, school, peers, adolescence-occupational choice, and adulthood-work.

Moorhead (1969) developed an occupational history format centered around an analysis of childhood roles, the issue of occupational choice, patterns of achievement and failure, and occupational role mobility. Related to this assessment was a screening tool, the Occupational Role History (Florey & Michelman, 1982). This semistructured interview format contained questions about worker-homemaker roles and school. Role status could be classified as functional, temporarily impaired, or dysfunctional.

Zorn (1969) provided guidelines to determine cognitive level. Bell's five-question interview (1975) asked the participant to select low risk, intermediate risk, and high risk items. An intermediate risk score indicated that competition would motivate competent performance.

Dunning (1972) and Gray (1972) developed tools emphasizing the environment. Dunning's tool assessed the interaction between the patient and environment based on her environmental grid. Gray identified the presence of depersonalizing conditions in the hospital environment.

Treatment

The breadth of the clinical applicability of the OB paradigm has been demonstrated by its application to other cultures and to diagnostic groups other than psychiatric inpatients.

The Canadian inpatient psychiatric service at the McMaster University Medical Center organized its OT program to be consistent with Reilly's OB paradigm (Woodside 1976). Deficits in OB result from genetic or environmentally elicited gaps in occupational skill development and from the effects of illness or institutionalization. It is the task of occupational therapy to fill the gaps or counteract the effects of illness.

Treatment goals include maintenance, correction, or new learning of occupational behaviors. Through assessment, development, and patterns of work-play skills, OB strengths and weaknesses and current and potential environments can be identified. Therapist attitudes that foster occupational behaviors include respect for the patient and faith in the patient's ability to succeed and live his or her own life. The occupational therapist needs to be the patient's advocate in changing the environment to support OB.

Woodside (1976) suggested five treatment guidelines.

1. Select and use activities that are interesting and challenging for each patient.
2. Use activity that reflects the developmental stages from playing with the activity to learning under a teacher to independent performance.
3. Provide the patient with guidance and feedback.
4. Teach general, transferable work skills such as relating to authority figures, rather than specific work skills.
5. Make the OT clinic a laboratory for human productivity.

Although originating with psychiatric patients, the clinical application of the OB paradigm has been applied to several other occupationally dysfunctional populations. With young men considered to be juvenile delinquents (Paulson, 1980), occupational therapy focused on goal-oriented tasks in the problem areas of daily living skills, occupational social behaviors, and prevocational skills. The success rate as indicated by active participation in vocational training was 80%.

The OB approach also was found to be applicable to the young adult with mild mental retardation (Webster, 1980). Webster described a 20-year-old female who was assessed for her interests, abilities, skills, and values. Her assets and weaknesses were identified in terms of developmental level in the occupational choice process. In order to further development, treatment goals addressed her weaknesses, such as deficient money management skills.

Heard (1977) discussed the application of OB concepts to the chronically physically disabled adolescent. She identified three critical points for the use of concepts of role in treating OT patients in the clinic. Roles cannot be fulfilled without the skill mastery that leads to automatic routines or habits. Role progression organizes daily living, and the ease of occupational role acquisition depends on the adaptive nature of the individual. Heard's assessment of a 17-year-old female with cerebral palsy revealed her strengths and deficits. Through OT programming this patient was able to acquire the worker role of salesperson.

Research

Much research has been indirectly generated from Reilly's work as a result of Keilhofner's Model of Human Occupation (Kielhofner, 1985). A student of Reilly's late in her career at the University of Southern California, Kielhofner shaped a model that was immeasurably influenced by the work of Reilly and her previous students. The next chapter is devoted to this model.

REFERENCES

AOTF: From the Foundation (1983). Ayres, Reilly, Yerxa named to Academy of Research. *Occupational Therapy Journal of Research, 3,* 185–187.

Bell, C.H. (1975). Competition as a motivational incentive. *American Journal of Occupational Therapy, 29,* 277–279.

Black, M.M. (1976). Adolescent role assessment. *American Journal of Occupational Therapy, 30,* 73–79.

Borys, S.S. (1974). Implications of interest theory for occupational therapy. *American Journal of Occupational Therapy, 28,* 35–38.

Burke, J.P. (1977). A clinical perspective on motivation: Pawn versus origin. *American Journal of Occupational Therapy, 31,* 254–258.

Creighton, C. (1985). Three frames of reference in work-related occupational therapy programs. *American Journal of Occupational Therapy, 39,* 331–334.

DeRenne-Stephan, C. (1980). Imitation: A mechanism of play behavior. *American Journal of Occupational Therapy, 34,* 95 102.

Dunning, H. (1972). Environmental occupational therapy. *American Journal of Occupational Therapy, 26,* 292–298.

Florey, L.L. (1969). Intrinsic motivation: The dynamics of occupational therapy theory. *American Journal of Occupational Therapy, 23,* 319–322.

Florey, L.L. (1971). An approach to play and play development. *American Journal of Occupational Therapy, 25,* 275–280.

Florey, L.L. (1981). Studies of play: Implications for growth, development and for clinical practice. *American Journal of Occupational Therapy, 35,* 519–524.

Florey, L.L. (1985). Major theoretical approaches to pediatric occupational therapy—Reilly: An explanation of play. In P.N. Clark & A.S. Allen (Eds.), *Occupational therapy for children* (pp. 36–38). St. Louis: C.V. Mosby Co.

Florey, L.L., & Michelman, S.M. (1982). Occupational role history: A screening tool for psychiatric occupational therapy. *American Journal of Occupational Therapy, 36,* 301–308.

Gray, M. (1972). Effects of hospitalization on work-play behavior. *American Journal of Occupational Therapy, 26,* 180–185.

Heard, C. (1977). Occupational role acquisition: A perspective on the chronically disabled. *American Journal of Occupational Therapy, 31,* 243–247.

Hurff, J.M. (1974). A play skills inventory. In M. Reilly (Ed.), *Play as exploratory learning* (pp. 267–283). Beverly Hills, CA: Sage Publications.

Hurff, J.M. (1980). A play skills inventory: A competency monitoring tool for the 10 year old. *American Journal of Occupational Therapy, 34,* 651–656.

Kielhofner, G. (1977). Temporal adaptation: A conceptual framework for occupational therapy. *American Journal of Occupational Therapy, 31,* 235–242.

Kielhofner, G. (Ed.). (1985). *A model of human occupation: Theory and application.* Baltimore: Williams & Wilkins.

Kielhofner, G., & Burke, J.P. (1977). Occupational therapy after 60 years: An account of changing identity and knowledge. *American Journal of Occupational Therapy, 31,* 675–689.

Klavins, R. (1972). Work-play behavior: Cultural influences. *American Journal of Occupational Therapy, 26,* 176–179.

Knox, S.H. (1974). A play scale. In M. Reilly (Ed.), *Play as exploratory learning* (pp. 247–266). Beverly Hills, CA: Sage Publications.

Licht, S., & Reilly, M. (1943). The correlation of physical therapy and occupational therapy. *Occupational Therapy and Rehabilitation, 22,* 171–175.

Line, J. (1969). Case method as a scientific form of clinical thinking. *American Journal of Occupational Therapy, 23,* 308–313.

Madigan, M.J., & Parent, L.H. (1985). Preface. In G. Kielhofner (Ed.), *A model of human occupation* (pp. vii–x). Baltimore: Williams & Wilkins.

Matsutsuyu, J.S. (1969). The interest check list. *American Journal of Occupational Therapy, 23,* 323–328.

Matsutsuyu, J.S. (1971). Occupational behavior—A perspective on work and play. *American Journal of Occupational Therapy, 25,* 291–294.

Matsutsuyu, J.S. (1983). Occupational behavior approach. In H.L. Hopkins & H.D. Smith (Eds.), *Willard and Spackman's occupational therapy* (6th ed.) (pp. 129–134). New York: J.B. Lippincott.

Meritorious Civilian Service Awards (1947). *American Journal of Occupational Therapy, 1,* 33.

Michelman, S. (1969). Research in symbol formation and creative growth. In W.L. West (Ed.), *Occupational therapy functions in interdisciplinary programs for children. Proceedings of the Conference, The Training Function of Occupational Therapy in University-Affiliated Centers* (pp. 88–110). Rockville, MD: Department of Health, Education, and Welfare.

Michelman, S. (1971). The importance of creative play. *American Journal of Occupational Therapy, 25,* 285–290.

Michelman, S. (1974). Play and the deficit child. In M. Reilly (Ed.), *Play as exploratory learning* (pp. 157–207). Beverly Hills, CA: Sage Publications.

Moorhead, L. (1969). The occupational history. *American Journal of Occupational Therapy, 23,* 329–334.

Occupational therapy yearbook. (1957). New York: American Occupational Therapy Association.

Parent, L.H. (1978). Effects of a low-stimulus environment on behavior. *American Journal of Occupational Therapy, 32,* 19–25.

Paulson, C.P. (1980). Juvenile delinquency and occupational choice. *American Journal of Occupational Therapy, 34,* 565–581.

Pezzuti, L. (1979). An exploration of adolescent feminine and occupational behavior development. *American Journal of Occupational Therapy, 33,* 84–91.

Reilly, M. (1956a). The role of the therapist in protective and functional devices. *American Journal of Occupational Therapy, 10,* 118–132, 133.

Reilly, M. (1956b). Therapeutically influenced recovery. *American Journal of Occupational Therapy, 10,* 229–232.

Reilly, M. (1958). An occupational therapy curriculum for 1965. *American Journal of Occupational Therapy, 12,* 293–299.

Reilly, M. (1960). Research potentiality of occupational therapy. *American Journal of Occupational Therapy, 14,* 206–209.

Reilly, M. (1962). Occupational therapy can be one of the great ideas of 20th century medicine. *American Journal of Occupational Therapy, 16,* 1–9.

Reilly, M. (1963). The Eleanor Clarke Slagle lecture. *Canadian Journal of Occupational Therapy, 30,* 5–19.

Reilly, M. (1966a). The challenge of the future to an occupational therapist. *American Journal of Occupational Therapy, 20,* 221–225.

Reilly, M. (1966b). A psychiatric occupational therapy program as a teaching model. *American Journal of Occupational Therapy, 22,* 61–67.

Reilly, M. (1969a). The educational process. *American Journal of Occupational Therapy, 23,* 299–307.

Reilly, M. (1969b). Selecting human development knowledge for occupational therapy. In W.L. West (Ed.), *Occupational therapy functions in interdisciplinary programs for children, Proceedings of the Conference, The Training Function of Occupational Therapy in University-Affiliated Centers* (pp. 64–75). Rockville, MD: Department of Health, Education, and Welfare.

Reilly, M. (1971): The modernization of occupational therapy. *American Journal of Occupational Therapy, 25,* 243–246.

Reilly, M. (1974a). Defining a cobweb. In M. Reilly (Ed.), *Play as exploratory learning* (pp. 57–116). Beverly Hills, CA: Sage Publications

Reilly, M. (1974b). An explanation of play. In M. Reilly (Ed.). *Play as exploratory learning* (pp. 117–149). Beverly Hills, CA: Sage Publications.

Reilly, M. (Ed.) (1974c). *Play as exploratory learning.* Beverly Hills, CA: Sage Publications.

Reilly, M. (1977). A response to: Defining occupational therapy: The meaning of therapy and the virtues of occupation. *American Journal of Occupational Therapy, 31,* 673.

Reilly, M. (1984). The issue is—The importance of the client versus patient issue for occupational therapy. *American Journal of Occupational Therapy, 38,* 404–406.

Reilly, M., & Barton, W.E. (1944). Do's and don'ts in military occupational therapy. *Occupational Therapy and Rehabilitation, 23,* 121–123.

Robinson, A.L. (1977). Play: The arena for acquisition of rules for competent behavior. *American Journal of Occupational Therapy, 31,* 248–253.

Shannon, P.D. (1970). Work adjustment and the adolescent soldier. *American Journal of Occupational Therapy, 24,* 111–115.

Shannon, P.D. (1972a). The adolescent experience. *American Journal of Occupational Therapy, 26,* 284–287.

Shannon, P.D. (1972b). Work-play theory and the occupational therapy process. *American Journal of Occupational Therapy, 26,* 169–172.

Shannon, P.D. (1974). Occupational choice: Decision-making play. In M. Reilly (Ed.). *Play as exploratory learning* (pp. 285–314). Beverly Hills, CA: Sage Publications.

Shannon, P.D. (1977). The derailment of occupational therapy. *American Journal of Occupational Therapy, 31,* 229–234.

Sharrott, G.W., & Cooper-Fraps, C. (1986). Theories of motivation in occupational therapy: An overview. *American Journal of Occupational Therapy, 40,* 249–257.

Smith, M.B. (1974a). Foreword. In M. Reilly (Ed.). *Play as exploratory learning* (pp. 5–8). Beverly Hills, CA: Sage Publications.

Smith, M.B. (1974b). Competence and adaptation. *American Journal of Occupational Therapy, 28,* 11–15.

Takata, N. (1969). The play history. *American Journal of Occupational Therapy, 203,* 314–318.

Takata, N. (1971). The play milieu: a preliminary appraisal. *American Journal of Occupational Therapy, 25,* 281–284.

Takata, N. (1974). Play as a prescription. In M. Reilly (Ed.). *Play and exploratory learning* (pp. 209–246). Beverly Hills, CA: Sage Publications.

Takata, N. (1980). Introduction to a series: Occupational behavior research for pediatric practice. *American Journal of Occupational Therapy, 34,* 11–12.

"To treat not only the injury, but also the man . . . " (1968). *Tufts Alumni Review, 14,* 22–23.

Webster, P.S. (1980). Occupational role development in the young adult with mild mental retardation. *American Journal of Occupational Therapy, 34,* 13–18.

Woodside, H. (1976). Dimensions of the occupational behavior model. *Canadian Journal of Occupational Therapy, 43,* 11–14.

Yearbook. (1972). New York: American Occupational Therapy Association.

Zorn, J.A. (1969). Research in cognitive assessment. In W.L. West (Ed.), *Occupational therapy functions in interdisciplinary programs for children, Proceedings of the Conference. The Training Function of Occupational Therapy in University-Affiliated Centers* (pp. 111–120). Rockville, MD: Department of Health, Education, and Welfare.

BIBLIOGRAPHY

1943

Licht, S., & Reilly, M. (1943). The correlation of physical therapy and occupational therapy. *Occupational Therapy and Rehabilitation, 22,* 171–175.

1944

Reilly, M., & Barton, W.E. (1944). Do's and don'ts in military occupational therapy. *Occupational Therapy and Rehabilitation, 23,* 121–123.

1956

Reilly, M. (1956a). The role of the therapist in protective and functional devices. *American Journal of Occupational Therapy, 10,* 118–132, 133.

Reilly, M. (1956b). Therapeutically influenced recovery. *American Journal of Occupational Therapy, 10,* 229–232.

1958

Reilly, M. (1958). An occupational therapy curriculum for 1965. *American Journal of Occupational Therapy, 12,* 293–299.

1960

Reilly, M. (1960). Research potentiality of occupational therapy. *American Journal of Occupational Therapy, 14,* 206–209.

1962

Reilly, M. (1962). Occupational therapy can be one of the great ideas of 20th century medicine. *American Journal of Occupational Therapy, 16,* 1–9.

1963

Reilly, M. (1963). The Eleanor Clarke Slagle lecture. *Canadian Journal of Occupational Therapy, 30,* 5–19.

1966

Reilly, M. (1966). The challenge of the future to an occupational therapist. *American Journal of Occupational Therapy, 20,* 221–225.

Reilly, M. (1966). A psychiatric occupational therapy program as a teaching model. *American Journal of Occupational Therapy, 22,* 61–67.

1969

Reilly, M. (1969). The educational process. *American Journal of Occupational Therapy, 23,* 299–307.

Reilly, M. (1969). Selecting human development knowledge for occupational therapy. In W.L. West (Ed.). *Occupational therapy functions in interdisciplinary programs for children, Proceedings of the Conference, The Training Function of Occupational Therapy in University-Affiliated Centers* (pp. 64–75). Rockville, MD: Department of Health, Education and Welfare.

1971

Reilly, M. (1971): The modernization of occupational therapy. *American Journal of Occupational Therapy, 25,* 243–246.

1974

Reilly, M. (1974). Defining a cobweb. In M. Reilly (Ed.). *Play as exploratory learning* (pp. 57–116). Beverly Hills, CA: Sage Publications

Reilly, M. (1974). An explanation of play. In M. Reilly (Ed.). *Play as exploratory learning* (pp. 117–149). Beverly Hills, CA: Sage Publications

Reilly, M. (Ed.) (1974). *Play as exploratory learning*. Beverly Hills, CA: Sage Publications.

1977

Reilly, M. (1977). A response to: Defining occupational therapy: The meaning of therapy and the virtues of occupation. *American Journal of Occupational Therapy, 31,* 673.

1984

Reilly, M. (1984). The issue is—The importance of the client versus patient issue for occupational therapy. *American Journal of Occupational Therapy, 38,* 404–406.

Chapter Seven

Gary Kielhofner

Rosalie J. Miller

Gary Kielhofner

BIOGRAPHICAL SKETCH

Gary Kielhofner was born in 1949 in Oran, Missouri, a rural area on the northern edge of the Ozarks. He grew up on a 200-acre farm that his great-grandmother and great-grandfather (who came from Alsace-Lorraine) cleared from homestead woods. The local community was quite homogeneous and predominantly Catholic, with strong French and German ties. Kielhofner lived with his four sisters, paternal grandparents, mother and father, and an aunt. He worked on the farm before and after school, and as like his father and grandfather before him, was expected to take over the farm.

When he was about 10, an incident happened that had a significant influence on him and his choice of career. His grandparents were in a very serious automobile accident. His grandmother, a vibrant, active woman in her fifties, sustained multiple fractures in one leg. She was then in and out of the hospital for 27 months and stayed in a hospital bed in the family living room each time she was discharged. At the end of that long period, her leg was amputated, leaving about a 10-inch stump. She received only a few sessions of training with a prosthesis from a staff whose attitude was that "here was this mechanical thing she could try out. She fell a couple of times and that was it" (G. W. Kielhofner, personal communication, March 6, 1987). She spent the rest of her life in a wheelchair.

In addition to the impact of spending several years of his older childhood seeing a close relative in a hospital bed and wheelchair, this experience also influenced his later thinking about OT theory. He came to realize that the context of the prosthesis was not defined in meaningful terms for his grandmother, as in "You've got to struggle with this situation and if you hang in there, ultimately you will be able to walk and go back to a lifestyle you had before and do all the things you've always done" (G. W. Kielhofner, personal communication, March 6, 1987).

Also around the age of 10, Kielhofner felt a calling to become a Catholic priest. At 14 he went to live at St. Vincent's College, a high school seminary run by the Vincentian Order. He spent the next 4 years studying in the demanding classical tradition and living a very disciplined lifestyle. After graduating in 1967, he entered the novitiate in Santa Barbara, California. Two years later, after a long period of inner turmoil and searching, he left the seminary. He finished his college studies at St. Louis University in 1971 and graduated with a classical bachelor's degree in psychology. While in college at St. Louis, he was active in the peace movement and did volunteer work with rehabilitation patients at The Jewish Hospital. In his senior year he was drafted. He applied for and after considerable investment of time and effort was granted conscientious objector status (G. W. Kielhofner, personal communication, March 6, 1987). As his alternative service commitment, he arranged to work full-time for half-time pay as a director of recreation and aide in occupational therapy at Jewish Hospital in St. Louis. He describes this first job:

> Now, mind you, I had no idea of what occupational therapy was, and I still had plans to go on and be a clinical psychologist. What the occupational therapists learned quickly was that I was good with my hands, so they started having me do things such as cutting out splint materials and working with patients in woodworking and leatherwork. There was no other male in the department, and we had a lot of young male spinal cord injured patients from rural Missouri. They were farm kids. They related to me, and the occupational therapists had me do a lot of work with them. (G. W. Kielhofner, personal communication, March 6, 1987)

Kielhofner was excited about the combination of using his hands to do things and working with patients. Sandy Liemer (now Malone) was the head of that occupational therapy department, and she started encouraging him to become an occupational therapist. In 1972 he entered the OT program at Washington University in St. Louis while still working at the hospital on evenings and weekends. At the end of his first year of the program he went to the 1973 AOTA conference in Los Angeles. He was so impressed with Mary Reilly, the University of Southern California (USC) faculty and graduate students, and the USC philosophy that was a strong influence at that conference that he applied to the basic master's program at USC and began again his entire OT education.

> In the course of those 2 years Mary Reilly persuaded me to her essential theme, which was that occupational therapy needs to define what its business is, and that its business is dealing with people's everyday occupational problems and using occupation as a therapeutic media, and all that that means. (G. W. Kielhofner, personal communication, March 6, 1987).

Reilly had a tremendous influence on Kielhofner. She helped him identify his strengths and weaknesses, and she demanded more of him than anyone had before. While writing his thesis, Kielhofner felt pushed to his limits, doing seemingly endless rewrites.

> I remember times when I was so discouraged that I would think about "what else can I do besides being an occupational therapist because I am never going to make it, it's impossible." But all the time I really admired her. She probably is the most brilliant person

> with whom I have ever worked so closely. I lived and breathed her ideas. . . . In many ways I have often thought of myself as sort of an apologia for her because it was difficult to understand her, and she did not write a lot of what she said and what she taught. For a long time that is sort of how I perceived my work. Although now I think I am beginning to see that I am doing something unique and different. Obviously I stand on her shoulders as the foundation of what I believe, and I could not have ever thought or done anything that I did without her training me, although I think I can now say I disagree with her on some points. (G. W. Kielhofner, personal communication, March 6, 1987)

Kielhofner's master's thesis presented a history of occupational therapy and the beginnings of the model of human occupation, which he conceptualized as being in harmony with that history. Janice Burke was a post-professional master's student at USC while Kielhofner was a basic master's student there. They became friends and enjoyed lengthy discussions about Reilly's theories and ideas with which they were both working. After graduating in 1975, they worked together to rewrite the history section of Kielhofner's thesis for publication in the *American Journal of Occupational Therapy* (*AJOT*). It was published in 1977 as "Occupational Therapy After 60 Years: An Account of Changing Identity and Knowledge."

In practice at the NeuroPsychiatric Institute (NPI) in Los Angeles, Kielhofner found that he had to work very hard to find creative ways to apply the concepts of occupational behavior (OB). He and Burke "started moving to do this intermediate theory that was between Reilly's occupational behavior paradigm, and what we called a model of practice" (G. W. Kielhofner, personal communication, March 6, 1987). He feels that some people misunderstood their efforts and thought they were trying to *replace* Reilly's generic OB theoretical formula with this model. However, Kielhofner and Burke's "idea was that we were trying to find a way to translate occupational behavior for practice, . . . get something that you could use daily, and it would be more workable" (G. W. Kielhofner, personal communication, March 6, 1987). After rejections for both presentation and publication, the model was finally published in *AJOT* in a series of four articles in September, October, November, and December of 1978.

Kielhofner worked at the NeuroPsychiatric Institute of UCLA as a staff occupational therapist and coordinator of training from 1975–1979. From 1977–1979 he was also an assistant clinical professor in the Department of Occupational Therapy at USC. His last three years at NPI he worked on a doctorate in public health. The title of his dissertation was *Evaluating Deinstitutionalization: An Ethnographic Study of Social Policy.*

In July 1977, Kielhofner married Nancy Croatt who was head nurse on the adolescent psychiatry ward at NPI. According to Kielhofner, Nancy has influenced him more than anyone else. She has helped him be less concerned about appearances and more caring toward other people. "She is also a magnificent clinician and has an impressive ability to understand people. She is my constant teacher and mentor" (G. W. Kielhofner, personal communication, April 7, 1987). In 1979 they moved to Richmond, Virginia, where he took the position of associate professor and later director of graduate studies in the Department of Occupational Therapy at Virginia Commonwealth University (VCU). In 1982 the Kielhofner's daughter, Kimberly, was born, and in 1984, they had a son, Kristian.

Kielhofner worked at VCU for 5 years until 1984. During that time he gave over 40 scholarly presentations and workshops, edited one book and co-authored a second, and published over 15 articles on which he was author or co-author. In addition, in 1981 he received the National Merit Award for Outstanding Achievement from the American Public Health Association; in 1983 he was made a Fellow of the AOTA and received the OTR Award of Merit from the Virginia Occupational Therapy Association. In 1984 he was inducted as a charter member of the Academy of Research of the AOTF. During this time he also served on several national committees of the AOTA.

In 1984, the Kielhofner family moved to Boston, where Gary Kielhofner served for 2 years as Associate Professor in the Department of Occupational Therapy at Sargent College of Boston University. During that time he continued his extensive publications and workshop presentations.

Although he was not considering the position of chairperson of an academic department as a possible career move, he was approached by a trusted colleague about an opening at the University of Illinois at Chicago. The opportunity to work in a setting with unusually rich resources and to influence persons as a mentor was attractive. He also wanted the challenge of trying to provide leadership as a scholar, in addition to being a manager. Finally, the position offered the opportunity to be in charge of both an academic and clinical setting because as head of the department, he would also be responsible for OT clinical services in the University of Illinois Hospital. The challenge of bringing academic and clinical pursuits closer was very enticing, especially because they are often seen as incompatible or antagonistic in occupational therapy. So, in the fall of 1986, he became a tenured associate professor and head of the Department of Occupational Therapy, College of Associated Health Professions of the University of Illinois at Chicago.

Kielhofner sees his major scholarly work for the future as refining the model of human occupation.

> I think the model sort of evolved and matured the way a lot of deductive theories have. We started with a set of ideas that we inherited from a tradition and tried to put them into coherent statements of relationships. Now we're in the process of trying to link it to the empirical world . . . through research and testing. (G. W. Kielhofner, personal communication, March 6, 1987)

Kielhofner sees this work becoming a tradition of research that is responsible for revising, changing, and correcting the model. He hopes that by the time he leaves the field this tradition will have contributed an empirically sound practice model to the profession.

Kielhofner is a prolific writer who devotes much time to writing in addition to his 40-hour work week. He attributes his productivity to a passion for writing.

> I find it extremely exciting to formulate ideas and organize them into a written record. I also feel compelled to write because so much of occupational therapy wisdom exists in an oral tradition and has never been labeled and organized. (G. W. Kielhofner, personal communication, June 3, 1987)

From the beginning of his career, most of Kielhofner's publications have been written jointly with other authors. He states that he enjoys working with other people when he writes. To date, of the 48 articles in occupational therapy on which his name appears, 35 are co-authored. One of his books is co-authored with Barris and Watts, and Kielhofner was editor of the other two, each of which involved collaboration with many contributors.

Gerry Sharrot (recently deceased) was a friend and colleague who shared Kielhofner's strong sense of playfulness about ideas. Sharrot was important to Kielhofner because he analyzed Kielhofner's work critically, helping him become aware of subtle issues underlying his thinking. "I felt safer knowing he would help scout out flaws in my ideas, and he understood my insistence on the absolute right to disagree with myself after I had written something. His death is not only a loss to me personally but also to the profession " (G. W. Kielhofner, personal communication, June 3, 1987).

Kielhofner acknowledges that in his early years in the field he put forth his ideas fairly dogmatically. In recent years, however, he has sought to become more open and flexible in his thinking, based both on research findings and on dialogue and debate with others in the field, such as Sharrot. As he says, "I'm realizing more and more that there are very few black and white things in life" (G. W. Kielhofner, personal communication, March 6, 1987).

THEORETICAL CONSTRUCTS

Background

Kielhofner's theory, known as "A Model of Human Occupation," grew out of his work with Reilly at USC.

In 1977 Kielhofner won the Cordelia Meyers Award for "New Writer of the Year" from *AJOT* for his article "Temporal Adaptation: A Conceptual Framework for Occupational Therapy." In this article he described the concept of time and its meaning in organizing human activity. He presented a temporal frame of reference as a culturally determined perspective that is modified in action by each individual's own values, interests, and goals, which are naturally inclined toward a rhythm of self-maintenance, work, and play. Habits are the structures for organizing time in daily behavior, and social roles determine to a large degree what habits will be formed.

Kielhofner no longer sees temporal adaptation as a separate concept, but has incorporated it into his model of human occupation. He considers this concept to be a stepping stone in his own thinking and a part of the history and development of his model (G. W. Kielhofner, personal communication, March 6, 1987).

Kielhofner and Burke developed and refined the work on a model of human occupation, which they saw as providing a link between Reilly's theory of OB and daily practice in the OT clinic (G. W. Kielhofner, personal communication, March 6, 1987). In 1978, Kielhofner published an article in *AJOT*, "General Systems Theory: Implications for Theory and Action in Occupational Therapy," that laid out the foundation for this theory. As did Reilly before him, Kielhofner drew on the works of established theorists, such as von Bertelanffy, Boulding, and Feibleman, to explain the concept of systems theory and the laws governing it. In this article, Kielhofner describes the paradigm of general systems theory (GST) and compares and contrasts it with the paradigm of reductionism, which he considers to underlie much of current OT practice. He stresses the need to bring together the skills and techniques from the reductionist paradigm with the perspective of the GST paradigm.

Reductionism, a perspective popularized in science in the late 1700s, holds that one can reduce phenomena into units that can then be studied, measured, and looked at in relationship with other units through the concept of cause and effect. Its underlying assumption is that the parts can then be pulled together again to provide an understanding of the whole. The medical model is based on this paradigm.

However, reductionism has major flaws as a perspective for occupational therapy. First, putting the pieces together again does not give a complete picture and explanation of the whole. Second, when applied to humans, this view oversimplifies individual and social behavior:

> In occupational therapy, the various units of concern under the reductionist paradigm were joint range of motion, muscle strength, anxiety, reflex, defense mechanism, and others . . . . When all these disassembled components are combined in clinical thinking, the net result is less than the "gestalt" to which GST addresses itself. The larger units of reality for occupational therapy under a systems framework are the human career, the social role, and the ecology, competency, and fitness for social participation. (Kielhofner, 1978, p. 638)

To conceptualize according to a systems perspective is to look at patterns, rather than units. These patterns are governed by laws different from the laws of cause and effect. Rather than measures of central tendency and dispersion, which form the statistical method of description used in reductionist inquiry, GST uses model or network descriptions. Table 7-1 illustrates basic differences between the statistical questions asked in reductionist description and the systems model questions asked in GST descriptions. Kielhofner states:

> This is not to preclude the usefulness of statistical data, but to recognize their limitations. Qualitative data that focus on system and environmental conditions are more operational and more likely to yield effective intervention. For example, information about the degree of intelligence of a retarded patient is not nearly as useful as information about the person's interests, values, habits, skills, and the demands for performance under the larger spheres of human experience. Human mechanics, neurological circuitry, and affect are constructs of a lower order, about which decisions would be made in the larger context of patients' day-to-day and lifelong human experiences. This means that activities of daily living and the human career would become a central, rather than a peripheral, concern in occupational therapy.
>
> For instance, it is known that exercise can provide strength and that a dynamic splint provides increased function and that both

Table 7-1 Contrasting Statistical and System Descriptions

Statistical Questions	*Systems Models Questions*
Types of Data:	*Types of Data:*
Nominal. To what class of things does object belong?	*Network or Conditional.* What is the overall pattern of the system?
Ordinal. What is the rank order position of this object along a single dimension continuum?	*Historical.* How has the system performed over time and what have been its experiences?
Interval. How much of a given characteristic does this object have in relation to other objects? (e.g., 2 times or ½ time)	*Contextual.* What are conditions in the environment and how are they brought to bear on the system?
Ratio. How much of a given characteristic does this object have when zero equals none of the characteristic?	*Dynamic.* What is the status of this system's ongoing interaction with the environment?

Source: From "General Systems Theory: Implications for Theory and Action in Occupational Therapy" by G. Kielhofner, 1978, *American Journal of Occupational Therapy, 32,* p. 640. Copyright 1978 by American Occupational Therapy Association, Inc. Reprinted by permission.

> might contribute to increased capacity for self-care. However, self-care must be organized under a social role, a view of self, and a continuum of life experience. The contribution of increased physical function to overall adaptation depends on many higher-level functions within the patient. What is being suggested here is a hierarchy of function. The manner in which lower levels of functioning are related to higher levels is largely unconsidered in any theory of occupational therapy. (Kielhofner, 1978, p. 640)

Kielhofner acknowledges that much of the information learned under the reductionist paradigm in occupational therapy is useful and helpful. He recommends that occupational therapists use a process of critical analysis to discriminate the accurate information from the errors in reductionist theories and then that the accurate information be integrated and utilized within a GST perspective.

He concludes the 1978 article on general systems theory with a description of the laws and characteristics that govern GST. These are "hierarchical arrangement of subparts; openness or self-maintenance in the midst of an interchange of matter and information with an environment; and continuity in the midst of ongoing change" (Kielhofner, 1978, p. 644).

He draws on the work of Feibleman to describe further each of these characteristics of GST and the laws that govern them. A general understanding of GST is necessary to comprehend Kielhofner's model fully.

Examples from everyday experience are given to illustrate these concepts.

First, subsystems (gestalt wholes in themselves) are arranged hierarchically within an overall system. Feibleman delineates five laws, three of which govern the relationship between these subsystems and two of which concern change.

> 1. "Higher levels direct or organize lower levels."
>   Example: The goals one has set for the day can motivate the body to make the necessary movements to get up out of bed.
> 2. "Higher levels are dependent upon or constrained by the lower levels."
>   Example: If one has a bad case of the flu, one's body may strongly resist getting up out of bed, no matter how motivated one is by goals for accomplishment.
> 3. "At any level, the *mechanism* of the level can be found at the level *below,* and the *purpose* of the level, at the level *above.*
>   Example: The mechanism is moving the body; the purpose is to pursue the day's goals.
> 4. "Less time is required for change at higher levels than at lower levels."
>   Example: One can alter one's goals for the day more quickly than one can get over the flu.
> 5. "A disturbance or change at one level resonates throughout the other levels."
>   Example: Having the flu affects not only one's body but also one's ability to carry out habits and move toward goals. (Kielhofner, 1978, p. 644)

Second, systems are open and self-maintaining in dynamic interaction with the environment.

> This interaction involves: (1) the input of information and material from the environment, (2) a throughput process that transforms the input into some new project [sic] and (3) the output that acts on the environment (which then generates feedback). (Kielhofner, 1978, p. 644)

A third concept is that evolution and change in the system over time are guided by the feedback loop just described. The system begins as an undifferentiated, spontaneous whole that, through the process of interaction with the environment, becomes increasingly organized, skilled, and differentiated. In humans this process results in the development of habits and in the "establishment of leading parts that dominate the behavior of the system and centralize the system's function" (Kielhofner, 1978, p. 645). These processes enable the system to evolve and become increasingly complex.

It is within the context of these characteristics and laws of general systems theory that Kielhofner builds his theoretical framework—the model of human occupation.

Model of Human Occupation

In September 1980, the first of four consecutive articles describing the model of human occupation was published in *AJOT* co-authored by Kielhofner and Burke. At the outset they state:

> The model presented here is preliminary and exploratory and thus incomplete. It will require substantial empirical validation and conceptual refinement. It is presented to stimulate, rather than confine, thinking in OT. (Kielhofner & Burke, 1980, p. 573)

A basic assumption of this model, an assumption they attribute to Reilly and through her to such writers as Boulding, White, and Dewey, is that:

> all human occupation arises out of an innate, spontaneous tendency of the human system—the urge to explore and master the environment. The model is based on the assumption that occupation is a central aspect of the human experience. It is Man's innate urge toward exploration and mastery and his consequent ability to symbolize that makes him unique among animals. (Kielhofner & Burke, 1980, P. 573)

This interaction of the person with the environment is *occupational behavior.*

Arrangement in Subsystems

Kielhofner and Burke conceived the human occupation system as made up of three subsystems, which they called volitional, habituation, and performance. These subsystems are hierarchically arranged in accordance with GST laws, with volition the highest and performance the lowest. The *volitional* subsystem is motivated by the innate urge toward exploration and mastery. The function of this system is to initiate action (Kielhofner & Burke, 1980).

The volitional subsystem is made up of three aspects: (1) a sense of personal causation, which is the sense one has of one's ability to affect and influence one's environment; the inner symbolic model of the self as an actor in the world; and the degree to which one feels an ability to direct one's own life; (2) interests, which are those things one enjoys and prefers doing; and (3) values, which are those things one feels are important or right (Kielhofner & Burke, 1980, p. 576).

The *habituation* subsystem arranges behavior into patterns and roles. Its function is to organize patterns of action that are output by the system; "thus, it maintains order in the output" (Kielhofner & Burke, 1980, p. 574). This subsystem is governed by the volitional subsystem.

The habituation subsystem comprises habits, those activities that have become routine and automatic through practice and repetition, and roles, consisting of internalized expectations for the ways one will behave within certain relationships to people or situations.

The *performance* subsystem is made up of skills, which are the basic abilities for action. It is governed by the other two subsystems, and its function is to *enact* the behaviors that they call for (Kielhofner & Burke, 1980, p. 574). This subsystem is made up of motor, process, and communication skills. These skills have symbolic, neurological, and musculoskeletal components.

In Kielhofner's 1985 book, *A Model of Human Occupation: Theory and Application*, he and Burke elaborated on these subsystem components that they had defined earlier. Based on findings from research and observation done from 1980 to 1984, they described belief in skill, belief in efficacy of skill, expectancy of success/failure, and internal/external locus of control as aspects of the volitional component of sense of personal causation. They broke down the volitional component of values into temporal orientation, meaningfulness of activity, occupational goals, and personal standards. They defined interests in relation to discrimination, pattern, and potency (meaning frequency of interests being acted on).

They postulated that the habituation subsystem component of roles is influenced by perceived incumbency (meaning awareness of oneself as in a role); internalized expectations (one's image of others' expectations for oneself in that role); and role balance (a satisfactory integration of a number of roles). Habits are more or less adaptive and satisfying depending on the qualities of "degree of organization, social appropriateness, and flexibility/rigidity" (Kielhofner & Burke, 1985, p. 28).

Development of Subsystems

The human infant enters the world as a totally undifferentiated open system (except at the cellular level). The first activity of this new human system is exploration. As the baby explores it begins to develop skills. As these skills are repeated/practiced and the child develops competency and mastery (blocks on top of one another, ability to grasp spoon, etc.), combinations of skills are put together and routinized into habits (brushing teeth, feeding self, dressing, walking, riding a bicycle, etc.). The child begins to develop an understanding of expectations for his or her behavior in certain roles (family member, sibling, friend, student, etc.). Finally, as the child is exploring and developing skills and habits, things are discovered that he or she likes to do or does not enjoy, and so interests develop. Through the interaction that the child has with the environment (human and nonhuman) during exploration and development of competence and mastery, a sense of personal causation or a self-perception of how effective he or she is within the environment is developed. Through interaction with the environment—including family, community, and culture—the child develops values.

Once values, interests, and a sense of personal causation have developed, these qualities exert a controlling and motivating influence on habits, roles, and performance. Kielhofner maintains that occupational therapy's major focus has been on the lowest level in this hierarchy—on performance and its component skills. Although performance is a crucial aspect of function, Kielhofner suggests that occupational therapy needs to take what has been learned about the various performance components (much of that information coming from using a reductionist perspective) and to put it within the larger context of the system. Occupational therapists need to see those components of performance at the *lowest* level as they are motivated and directed by the higher levels of habits and roles (habituation) and by values, interests, and sense of personal causation (volition) (Kielhofner & Burke, 1980).

> These three subsystems organize and regulate the output of the system. Each contributes to the output in a different way. The volition subsystem has the greatest degree of freedom; it is the level at which action is freely and consciously chosen. The habituation subsystem represents automatic and routine behavior. It regulates the output of the system into regular and predictable patterns. The performance subsystem organizes output at the lowest level, governing small patterns of skilled action. (Kielhofner & Burke, 1980, p. 574)

Consistent with the rules of general systems, however, the lower levels *constrain* the higher ones. For instance, although one may be motivated to water ski (be interested in doing so, see that activity as fitting into one's value system, and feel that one *could* do so), if one had never skied before, one would not have developed the necessary skills and patterns of behavior and so would be unsuccessful. However, if one were to experiment, play, and practice, one would (hypothetically) eventually develop the skills and patterns of behavior necessary to ski successfully.

However, for the person who is a paraplegic, the lower subsystem would constrain the higher ones, no matter *how* motivated he or she was to practice and learn how to water ski. That is because, of course, the motor performance component would be *unable* to function in the necessary ways. However, because the higher subsystems direct and organize the lower ones and because change can happen more quickly at higher levels than at lower ones, he or she could decide to *adapt* the activity and learn to use a water *sled*.

SYSTEM INTERACTION WITH ENVIRONMENT

Kielhofner and Burke first presented their theory on the way the system interacts with the environment in 1980. In 1985, Kielhofner and others elaborated on this basic conceptualization. The environment consists of objects, people, and events with which the system (the person) interacts, influenced by the culture of which that person is a part. "The open system interacts with the environment by way of a process of input, output, throughput, and feedback. The system represents Man [Humans], and the interaction of the system with the environment is human occupation" (Kielhofner & Burke, 1980, pp. 573–574).

The system receives *input* from the environment. This input enters the system and is processed by each of the three subsystems—volitional, habituation, and performance—as appropriate. This process Kielhofner calls *throughput.* In this throughput stage, output is organized. The *output* comprises both information and action, which:

> are combined by the system to achieve results (in the use of skills), to meet expectations for performance (as organized by habits and roles), and to satisfy the system's own purposes (as contained in the volition subsystem). The output of information and action to achieve purposeful ends is occupational behavior. (Kielhofner & Burke, 1980, p. 580)

This behavior generates *feedback,* which is the last part of the loop. Feedback about the consequences of one's actions then joins with the *input* that begins a new cycle. "In the feedback process actual performance is compared to expected outcomes. This process allows the system to make adjustments in its performance that, in turn, influence the organization of the system itself" (Kielhofner & Burke, 1980, p. 580).

Input received directly from the environment also can reorganize the system. An example is the expectations for performance made by others—parents, teachers, and the larger culture. Because both feedback and input work to bring about change and adjustment in the system, the open system is said to be self-transforming.

> The system both changes and is changed by the environment; each shapes the other. [Humans] create [their] physical and symbolic environment at the time [they] learn to act competently in it. As the open system explores and masters the environment, it transforms both itself and the environment. (Kielhofner & Burke, 1980, p. 574)

Barris has elaborated on this system-environment interaction (Barris, 1982; Barris et al., 1985). Figure 7-1 illustrates the open system concept of the model of human occupation.

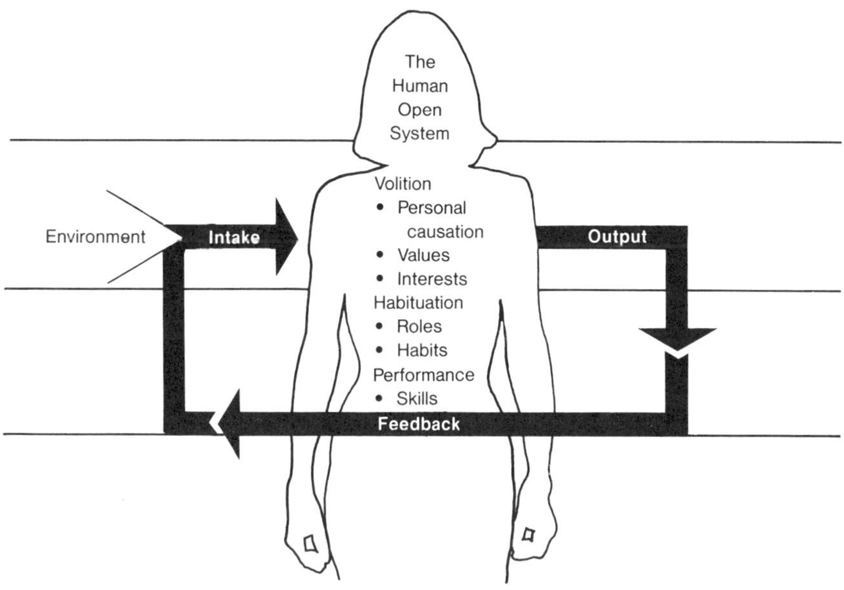

Figure 7-1 Open System Representing Human Occupation. *Source:* From *A Model of Human Occupation: Theory and Application* (p. 35) by G. Kielhofner (Ed.), 1985, Baltimore, Md.: Williams & Wilkins Company. Copyright 1985 by Williams & Wilkins Company. Adapted by permission.

Example of the Model of Human Occupation Applied to Normal Development

As a young girl learns to ride a bicycle, she gets *input* directly from the environment—the texture, temperature and color of the bicycle; the feel of it to her hands, feet, and buttocks; and the instructions of her mother who is standing beside her. As the child sits on the bicycle seat while her mom holds the bike, this input is processed (throughput). She is very motivated to learn to ride because it is a value, an interest, and she feels she can succeed (volition). She remembers being a whiz on her tricycle and has the clear motor pattern of peddling "down pat" (habituation). She has mastered a good degree of balance by walking on the curbstone, and she has developed normally in her motor skills (performance).

Now, her mother tells her to start peddling, assuring her that she will hold onto the bike. As the girl starts to propel the bike, she begins to get feedback from her vestibular system, from her eyes, and kinesthetically from her body. Meanwhile, her mother is giving her verbal input about how she is doing. This feedback and new input are processed in throughput by the volitional subsystem ("Oh, this isn't as easy as I thought, but Mom is encouraging me, bolstering my motivation"), the habituation subsystem ("It's like riding my tricycle only different"), and by the performance subsystem ("You're falling left"). This throughput is organized into output *action*—("Lean a bit right, turn the wheel slightly right, sit back"). As this process continues, the system is changed. Through practice the girl develops skill in performing the necessary actions. As she masters them they become *habits*. And once she can ride the bike successfully (once the basic performance requirements have become habits) her concept of herself is changed (increased sense of competence, increased self-esteem), she has a new role, (as bicycle rider), and her goals change. And so it goes. The environment is transformed also, by the addition of this girl as a bicycle rider.

Evolution and Change in the System

In "A Model of Human Occupation: Part Two," Kielhofner describes change and development, which he calls ontogenesis, from the perspective of temporal adaptation. Hierarchical change in an open system is influenced by the system's own internal tendencies and by the demands of the environment—two factors that come together in the throughput-output-input-feedback cycle (1980b).

> The central problem of change in occupation is to explain how a system with a global tendency toward exploring and mastering its environment is transformed into a socially functioning, pro-

> ductive and self-satisfying entity. The hierarchical change of occupation proceeds from this undifferentiated, innate tendency toward exploration and mastery to individual competence in occupational roles. (Kielhofner, 1980b, p. 657)

He presents Reilly's three stages of motivation—exploration to competency to achievement—as the aspects of the volitional subsystem that internally drive the other two subsystems to change. Through exploration one develops skills, through pursuing competence one organizes habits, and through striving for achievement, competent role behaviors emerge (Kielhofner, 1980b, p. 658).

So one explores and develops skills. Then, driven by the internal desire for competency that one measures to external standards, one develops habits. And finally, the internal desire to attain a role in the social group—to achieve—together with the external demands of that group for certain behavior, motivates role behavior.

He also suggests that, as the system changes and develops, these three motivations drive the balance of work and play through the lifetime. In his 1985 book, *A Model of Human Occupation*, Kielhofner states that this process is explained through "blending of the occupational behavior and development perspectives in occupational therapy" (Kielhofner, 1985, p. 77). He illustrates this concept in Figure 7-2 and calls it an "occupational life-span theory" (Kielhofner, 1980b).

Kielhofner devotes five chapters in his 1985 book to this concept of occupational development. Two principles affect the development of each subsystem and govern the interrelationship of the subsystems in development. First, development in one subsystem influences the others. (Developing the skills to ride a bicycle influences habits and sense of self.) Second:

> The period for development of each subsystem lengthens as one ascends the hierarchy. The child has mastered a wide range of perceptual motor skills before he or she takes on several differentiated roles and long before a personal system of complex values is shaped. (Kielhofner, 1985, p. 79)

In other words, the input-throughput-output-feedback cycle is functioning so as to propel the system toward greater achievement and satisfaction (Kielhofner, 1980c).

As the system matures in an adaptive way, through interaction with the environment and through the characteristics of the subsystems that influence its output, it becomes increasingly more complex and differentiated. This evolution in turn allows it to interact more and more flexibly with the environment. This adaptive development implies that the system is both

Levels of Organization of the Occupational Behavior Career

The Balance of Work and Play

	Childhood	Adolescence	Adulthood	Old Age
Waking Hours Occupied by Work and Play	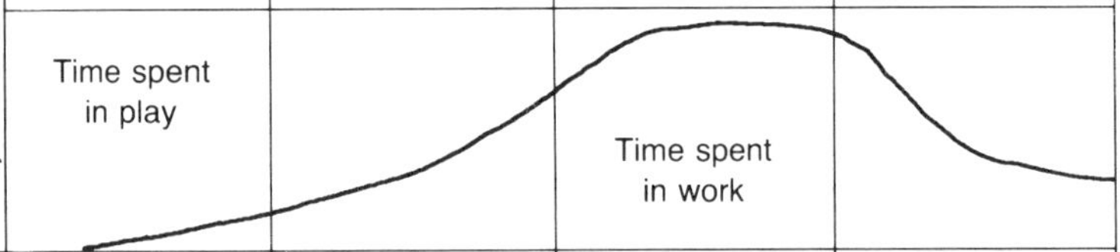 Time spent in play		Time spent in work	
Play Yields	Reality is explored via curiosity for rules of competent action.	Competent behavior is learned and experienced in games, personal hobbies, and social events.	Relaxation and recreation support the worker role. Exploration of novel situations allows new roles to be taken on.	Play allows the exploration of past achievements and the unknown future, and maintenance of competence through leisure pursuit of interests.
Relationship of Play and Work	*Exploration* Skills for productivity are acquired and work roles explored through imitation and imagination	*Competency* Personal and interpersonal competency are developed in a matrix of cooperation yielding habits of sportsmanship and craftsmanship.	*Achievement* Play supports the worker roles by providing an arena of retreat and rejuvenation. Exploration in novel situations allows the ongoing development of new competency for work.	*Exploration* Retirement leisure signals that the productive obligation to society has been fulfilled. Past work has earned for the person the right to leisure. Leisure replaces work as the major source of life satisfaction.
Work Yields	Productive behaviors are practiced through chores and in school.	The work role is practiced and the commitment process of occupational choice takes place.	There is entry into worker roles with the requirement of establishing and maintaining a productive and self-satisfying career.	Retirement brings reduced expectations for productivity and personal capacities for productive action are waning.

Figure 7-2 Balance and Interrelationship of Work and Play during the Life-Span. *Source*: From "A Model of Human Occupation, Part Two. Ontogenesis from the Perspective of Temporal Adaptation" by G. Kielhofner, 1980, *American Journal of Occupational Therapy, 34,* p. 661. Copyright 1980 by American Occupational Therapy Association, Inc. Reprinted by permission.

satisfying its own internal urge to explore and master and fulfilling the demands of the environment—not all the time, because failure is sometimes a consequence of action—but more often than not. This two steps forward and one step back progression toward increasing adaptation was originally called "a benign cycle" by Kielhofner (1980c). He currently uses the labels "adaptive" and maladaptive" cycles for what in 1980 he termed "benign" and "vicious" cycles. A maladaptive cycle develops when a pattern emerges in which either the system is unsatisfied, environmental demands are unmet, or both occur (Kielhofner, 1980c).

> [Maladaptive] cycles may begin from birth, precipitated by some incurred disability. These cycles may also develop slowly as a result of interactions with the environment. . . . They may be precipitated by interactions with the social environment that produce demands beyond the capacity of the system to adapt. They may also be the result of demands being decreased to such a degree that the system is no longer challenged to perform, and the volition subsystem's urge to mastery cannot find expression. Vicious cycles exist wherever the requirements of the system to fulfill the urge to explore and master the world cannot be fulfilled and/or where the environment's demands are not met. (Kielhofner, 1980c, p. 734)

Function/Dysfunction Continuum

Adaptive cycles result in a state of occupational function, whereas maladaptive cycles result in occupational dysfunction. Persons are occupationally functional when they meet both society's need for productive and playful participation and their own need for exploration and mastery, which in turn enhances volition, habituation, and performance. A person is occupationally dysfunctional when any of the above needs are not met (Kielhofner, 1985).

As occupation is enacted through the input-throughput-output-feedback cycle, any problems in function may have their origin at any part of the cycle. Occupational dysfunction is *recognized* at the interface of the person with the environment as a decrease, cessation, ineffectiveness, inappropriateness, or imbalance of output. Environmental factors must therefore be acknowledged in evaluating occupational dysfunction (Kielhofner, 1985).

The three levels of occupational function—exploration, competency, and mastery—are derived from Reilly's theory and "represent states of optimal arousal and involvement with the environment" (Kielhofner, 1985, p. 64). The states of occupational dysfunction, conceptualized by Kielhofner, represent stress and a lack of productive involvement with environment.

He conceptualizes states of increasing occupational dysfunction starting with inefficiency, which results "when there is an interference with performing meaningful activity accompanied by dissatisfaction with performance. Sources of inefficiency may be environmental constraints, disease processes, or imbalanced lifestyles" (Kielhofner, 1985, p. 69).

The second state of occupational dysfunction is incompetence, which is characterized by:

> a major loss or limitation of skills, a failure or disruption of self-confidence and satisfaction, and inability to routinely and adequately perform the tasks of everyday living associated with occupational roles. It may result from marginal learning due to poor environments, from disease or from a life-style which erodes system organization. (Kielhofner, 1985, p. 71)

Helplessness is the third stage of occupational dysfunction. Kielhofner describes this as:

> total or nearly total disruption of occupational performance coupled with extreme feelings of ineffectiveness, anxiety and/or depression. A state of helplessness may result from some traumatic episode which suddenly renders a healthy person totally dependent or from a lifelong series of negative experiences. (Kielhofner, 1985, p. 72)

The process of therapy is one of "providing opportunities for occupational function until individuals can maintain an adaptive open system cycle of their own" (Kielhofner, 1985, p. 74). In addressing how this goal can be achieved, he states:

> Any changes in the system must begin with the volition subsystem. This system, which enacts output, is critical for initiating cycles that can result in restoration of a positive trajectory. The environmental conditions are also of critical importance. The implications for occupational therapy at this point are twofold. The first is that *therapy should serve as an environment* that can begin to present demands for performance and elicit the enactment of responses that can result in positive feedback. The occupational therapy clinic is an important source of input to the system and

> a critical environment in which [adaptive] cycles can develop. (Kielhofner, 1980c, p. 736)

It is critical to determine at which level behaviors are disrupted and to begin with the lowest level of motivation. One must then manage the total environment of therapy so that the person is encouraged to explore.

> The patient or client is not only the focus but also the instrument of therapy. Through engaging in directed occupations, the person begins to change the entire cycle, to organize or reorganize the internal components of the system and to increase the potential for adaptive output in the future. (Kielhofner, 1985, p. 74)

Once the patient's curiosity has been engaged and exploration has begun, it is important to change the environment so that competence can be elicited. Then, once the patient has achieved a point of mastery the demands of the environment must be "integrated with existing skills and habits to reach achievement of valued goals" (Kielhofner, 1980c, p. 737).

APPLICATION TO OCCUPATIONAL THERAPY PRACTICE

Three assumptions underlie the application of this model in practice. As Kielhofner states:

> Reilly points out that occupational therapy is directed toward enabling [Humans] to fulfill [their] innate need for "occupation and . . . the rich and varied stimuli that solving life problems provides [them]." According to this primary assumption, humans are occupational creatures who cannot be healthy in the absence of meaningful occupation.
>
> Reilly has also stated the second assumption: "[Humans], through the use of [their] hands as they are energized by mind and will, can influence the state of [their] own health." According to this assertion, occupation can shape the health of a person, and can thus serve as a means to health. The first two assumptions assert that occupation is both a basic human activity essential to health and a healing process.
>
> A third assumption is that for occupational therapy to be instrumental as a means to an end, it must embody the characteristics of the end itself. This means that occupational therapy must

> be true "occupation." Therapy must embody the characteristics of purposefulness, challenge, accomplishment, and satisfaction that make up every occupation. Therefore, a theory of occupation is critical to practice.
>
> The idea that, by engaging in occupation designed as therapy, [Humans] can restore, increase, and maintain [their] ability as occupational creature[s] is the foundation of occupational therapy. A theory of human occupation serves to justify the field's commitment to occupation as a worthy goal for therapy. It also demonstrates how therapy should be organized and carried out. (Kielhofner, Burke, & Igi, 1980, pp. 777–778)

The model of human occupation helps the occupational therapist find an explanation for the pattern of occupational function and dysfunction presented by the patient by (1) indicating which variables one should gather information about, (2) pointing out the relationships among those variables through the schema of the subsystems and their hierarchical relationships, (3) indicating the relationship between subsystem components and the environment and the effect of this relationship on the whole system, (4) providing an outline of changes that can be expected at different levels of occupational development, and (5) presenting an occupational function-dysfunction continuum from which one can determine a patient's level of performance (Rogers & Kielhofner, 1985, p. 140).

Thus, in the model of human occupation, assessment is conducted to provide information about the status of the volitional, the habituation, and the performance subsystems; the feedback loop; the development of organization of occupation throughout the life cycle; and the environment. From this information the occupational therapist develops a picture of the patient's level of occupational function or dysfunction (degree of organization or disorganization) and a list of treatment options (Rogers & Kielhofner, 1985).

The choice of how one treats the various areas of dysfunction identified through this assessment is outside the domain of this model. Kielhofner sees evaluation, treatment planning, and treatment implementation as an hourglass (G. W. Kielhofner, personal communication, March 6, 1987). His model is the top half, which is used to conceptualize the individual in her or his occupational wholeness and to assess the level of occupational dysfunction. From this assessment is developed a treatment plan, with goals related to that person's occupational performance needs. Treatment must address all areas assessed—the three subsystems, age, the environment, and the feedback loop. The bottom half of the hourglass he sees as filled with whatever theories, modalities, and facilitative activities will best meet these treatment goals for that individual. In making these choices for treatment, the therapist is guided by her or his own training and personal frame of reference, and of course by the understanding of:

> the importance of making the patient's own concerns and values the guiding principle in clinical decision-making. It is the patient and not the therapist who is the agent of change. As open systems, patients organize or reorganize themselves through engagement in occupation. The choice to effectively occupy oneself comes from a sense of personal freedom. The patient must ultimately will the action which is undertaken as part of the clinical process or else true change cannot result. (Rogers & Kielhofner, 1985, p. 145)

The model of human occupation is being applied in practice settings throughout the United States and abroad. Application of the model to practice in psychosocial settings is described in Barris, Kielhofner, & Watts' book, *Psychosocial Occupational Therapy* (1983).

More than one-third of the 1985 book, *A Model of Human Occupation*, is devoted to applications of the model to evaluation and treatment in practice settings. This section of the book is divided into five chapters, each of which is concerned with a particular target population: the physically disabled, those with primary psychosocial dysfunction, children, elders, and the mentally retarded. In each chapter the general areas of dysfunction of the target group are reviewed according to the model of human occupation, with recommendations for assessment and intervention. Also included in each chapter are specific case examples illustrating use of the model to assess areas of function and dysfunction and develop treatment plans for individual patients. Much of this material was contributed by therapists who are currently working in direct practice with patients.

Several therapists have published articles describing their use of the model in clinical practice. In 1983, Salz wrote about her use of it as a theoretical framework for looking at and intervening in the occupational functioning of patients with a diagnosis of borderline personality disorder. Tigges and Sherman applied the model to treatment of hospice patients and published their experiences in 1983. And in 1984, Gusich reported on the application of the model with patients in chronic pain. Blakeney (1985) described adolescent development from the perspective of the model. And in 1987 Wieringa and McColl published a description of the model as they applied it to intervention with native Canadians.

An emphasis of Keilhofner and colleagues in recent years has been on the identification, development, and research of instruments that can be used to assess those elements needed to develop a picture of a person's level of occupational functioning (G. W. Kielhofner, personal communication, March 6, 1987). These instruments are discussed in a later section.

Documentation of Postulates through Research

In a 1984 article that appeared in the *Canadian Journal of Occupational Therapy* (*CJOT*), Kielhofner states:

> From the model there have been derived basic postulates which state relationships between variables. These have, in turn, been investigated through research. Four major postulates are as follows:
>
> 1. A disturbance of any part of the system reverberates throughout the system. Lower levels can constrain higher levels whereas higher levels can lead to disorganization of lower levels.
> 2. The output of the system (i.e., OB) and the status of the system's internal organization are interrelated.
> 3. Feedback to the system is influenced by the overall system dynamic including the relationship of volition or choice with output.
> 4. The output (i.e., OB) of the system is influenced by the environment of the system and its match to system's characteristics. (Kielhofner, 1984, p. 60)

Kielhofner has tested these postulates through reviews of the literature, research studies, and clinical practice.

> In addition to studies which are specifically designed to test propositions from the model and clinical research which has attempted to operationalize model concepts into assessment instruments of procedures, there has been descriptive research which elaborates the model. (Kielhofner, 1984, p. 60)

As Kielhofner himself has frequently stated, the development of this model has been influenced by many people. Most of the research has been done as a collaborative effort with colleagues or graduate students. Also a significant body of research has been conducted without Kielhofner's direct involvement.

Kielhofner sees the model as beginning with a set of ideas based in literature that are inherited from the tradition of occupational behavior. This literature is from sociology, including systems theory; from psychology, including the science of human adaptation; and from human development. Kielhofner and others have tried to frame these ideas into coherent statements of relationships. Presently they are working to link the model to the practical world through testing and research (G. W. Kielhofner, personal communication, March 6, 1987).

> A lot of my research has been, and continues to be, development of assessments. I like to do this because it has a strong clinical focus. Another source of research is descriptive research that asks whether relationships that we hypothesize or theorize are, in fact, borne out in the empirical world. And we are also doing qualitative research that asks what do we know about the volitional traits or the habituation traits or whatever, of people with different types of disabilities. Then the final piece of research is testing treatment based on the model. (G. W. Kielhofner, personal communication, March 6, 1987)

Kielhofner sees this research as his major work, and intends that through it, and the revising, changing and correcting of the model that will result, he will "leave the field with a practice model that it can use and for which there is empirical support" (G. W. Kielhofner, personal communication, March 6, 1987).

Development of Assessments

A vitally important area of research is determining the reliability and validity of tests or assessment instruments used to measure model variables. This determination is a long-term process as many studies need to be done with any one instrument before it can be used with confidence. The work has begun, and a number of such studies have been reported that have tested wholly new instruments and/or revised, adapted, and refined existing instruments to fit the needs of the model of human occupation. Kielhofner's edited book, *A Model of Human Occupation*, contains an appendix entitled "Instrument Library," which includes 64 assessment tools that have been used by the book's contributors to measure different aspects of the human occupation model. The majority of the tools listed were developed for other purposes and before the model of human occupation was formulated. Thus, although they can be used to assess various individual aspects of the model (i.e., self-esteem, interests) care must be taken in interpreting results in the context of model concepts until such time as extensive studies show their validity for those purposes. Therefore, instrument development studies are a critical part of the research effort for the model of human occupation.

The following assessment tools have been the focus of initial research concerning their validity and reliability for use with the model of human occupation: the Picture Interest Sort for Use with Retarded Adults (Shakun, 1982; Scott, 1982), the Role Checklist (Oakley, et al., 1986), the Occupational Role History (Kielhofner, et al., 1986), the Assessment of Occupational Functioning (Watts, et al., 1986), a Short-Term Psychiatric Interview and Rating Scale (Kaplan, 1984), the Bentz Measure of Personal Causation for Retarded Adults (Bentz, 1984), an Assessment of Process Skills (Doble, 1985), the Preschool Play Scale (Harrison & Kielhofner, 1986), and the Occupational Questionnaire (Smith, Kielhofner, & Watts, 1986).

Descriptive Research

Descriptive research on the model has been of two basic types: comparative and correlational. Each is used to test the reality of relationships hypothesized by the model. Comparative studies look at different groups of individuals to ascertain whether they really do differ on selected variables as the model would predict. Correlational studies look at different model variables and test whether they are indeed related in the way that the model suggests. Such studies test the relationship between the human system and the environment.

Comparative Studies

In 1980, Mailloux looked at children with visual-motor integration problems to see whether that disturbance in the performance subsystem would be reflected in a decreased sense of personal causation, a component of the higher-level volitional system. She also tested how self-esteem and visual-motor integration (i.e., aspects of two of the three throughput subsystems) would correlate with student role performance (output). She tested 40 children in a learning disabilities classroom in a public school and found no significant correlations.

In 1981, Scaff studied differences between 25 alcoholics and 25 nonalcoholics between 18 and 30 years of age to see whether behavioral output of the alcoholics would reflect disorganization in habituation and volitional subsystems. Based on her results, she was able to show significant differences in the habituation subsystem behaviors of the two groups and some meaningful differences in the volitional traits of interest.

In 1983 Lyons found no significant differences in selected volitional traits of 10 employed and 18 unemployed mentally retarded young adults.

In 1985 Lederer, Kielhofner, and Watts looked at 15 delinquent and 15 nondelinquent adolescents to see whether they differed on locus of control, values, and perceptual motor skills. Results showed no statistically significant difference between groups; however, the delinquents placed less value on the roles of student, volunteer, worker, homemaker, and caregiver.

Also in 1985, Smyntek, Barris, and Kielhofner compared volitional and habituation traits of 37 adolescents who were patients in several acute care psychiatric facilities and 36 adolescents who were high school students. Differences in locus of control and in self-esteem were significant, as were potency of interests and value placed on roles and number of present roles. Also, the hospitalized adolescents spent significantly less time in daily living tasks.

In 1986, a study compared personal causation, values, interests, roles and habitual use of time in three groups of adolescents: ten high school students, ten adolescents hospitalized for psychosocial problems in conjunction with a primary medical diagnosis, and ten hospitalized with a primary psychosocial diagnosis. Significant differences were found in locus of control and nearly significant differences were identified in a number of strong interests in the past 10 years. No other differences were found in occupational functioning (Barris et al., 1986).

Correlational Studies

In her research Mailloux (1980) also posed some correlational questions, such as whether there is a relationship among self-esteem and praxis, visual-motor integration, and student role performance. Although she did not find a relationship among these variables, she did find that the self-esteem of learning disabled children in her sample was significantly lower than that of a normative group.

In 1983, Gregory published the results of a study in which he looked at correlations between meaningfulness of activities and life satisfaction of 79 elder adults. He found that amount, enjoyability, meaningfulness, and autonomy of activity and occupational behavior were all correlated with life satisfaction. Age and length of retirement showed no significant correlation.

Knapp (1983) studied 129 elders living independently in Florida. She found no significant correlations between value, interest, and personal causation and life satisfaction for these people, although she did find that "valuing leisure" had some impact.

Also in 1983, Lyons studied the correlation between volitional traits and satisfaction in a group of retarded persons. He found a correlation only between locus of control and satisfaction.

Some correlation was found by Elliot and Barris (1987) between life satisfaction and number and value of roles performed by noninstitutionalized elders.

Kavanaugh, Barris, and Kielhofner found in 1985 that involvement in the environment correlated with number of interests and number of goals of a group of mentally retarded adults.

Oakley, Kielhofner, and Barris' 1985 study of adult hospitalized psychiatric patients was an effort to test assessment based on human occupation theory by determining the correlation between patients' adaptive functioning and their organizational status as measured by the individual's skills, habits, roles, interests, occupational values, and feelings of competence. Results were highly correlated and found to be significantly more predictive than was symptomatology or diagnosis.

Hand-injured adults were the subjects of Fronczek's 1985 study that considered the correlation between compliance and the composite of interests, locus of control, and roles. Some correlation was found between roles and compliance and between interests and compliance.

Duellman, Barris, and Kielhofner (1986) studied subjects from three nursing homes to assess the correlation between availability of activities and number of present and future roles. A positive correlation was found on both variables.

In 1986 Smith, Kielhofner, and Watts published a study that looked at the "relationships between the volition subsystem, activity pattern, and life satisfaction" of 60 older adults (p. 278). They found that in relationship to occupation and life satisfaction there were positive correlations among degree of interests, value, and personal causation. They also found that life satisfaction was more influenced by time spent in work and leisure than by time spent in activities of daily living and rest.

Critique of Descriptive Studies

The limited findings of the studies just cited can be attributed to several factors. First, and most important, the assessment tools used in most of those studies have not yet been proven to be valid and reliable. Indeed, a number of them were developed for the study in which they were used. Second, tools used that were developed outside the tradition of the model of human occupation may not measure the appropriate variables within the model. Third, a number of these studies were master's research projects in which the control for variables, the number of subjects, and subject selection process procedures may have been inadequate. Certainly there has been too little testing of postulates with too few subjects and with inadequately developed testing instruments to draw any conclusions about the efficacy of the model from the work done thus far.

Qualitative Research

In 1982, Kielhofner published two articles in which he described the process and importance of qualitative research in occupational therapy.

Work on qualitative research to test assumptions of the model of human occupation (i.e., does development of adjustment to disability actually occur the way the model would suggest?) and to look at interrelationships of variables has just begun.

FUTURE CHALLENGES FOR OCCUPATIONAL THERAPY

Kielhofner sees the biggest challenge to the profession today as the need to develop an academic discipline through research and theory development. He feels this needs to be done within the next 10 years if occupational therapy education is to continue to be offered at the college and university level.

> We've got to be able to argue to the academic community that we have an academic discipline or we will not remain in universities . . . we will only be in community colleges. To me, the survival of the occupational therapy university system is more critical right now than, for example, whether we survive in acute care practice or whether we survive in schools as practitioners. Those things will evolve and change over time. If we have an academic discipline and the professional status of being in the university we will always to able to go out and make our way in practice arenas. (G. W. Kielhofner, personal communication, March 6, 1987)

The other major challenge that Kielhofner feels strongly about is contributing to the building of a unified base for the profession. His work in this area has been an expansion on Reilly's solid foundation of a paradigm of occupational behavior.

Kielhofner's definition of a paradigm is taken from the work of the sociologist Kuhn. A paradigm of a field is a statement of the "consensus-determined definition of the phenomenon with which it is concerned" (Kielhofner & Burke, 1977, p. 676).

Because he has written about his concern for a unifying base and his recommendations regarding it at the same time as he has developed his model, there has been some confusion about the difference between the base and the model and some misunderstanding that he was suggesting his model as the unifying base for the profession. Adding to this confusion has been the fact that in his earlier work he sometimes used such labels as model, theory, and paradigm interchangeably or at least without clear definition and delineation. (This criticism can, of course, be applied to other writers as well).

Until recently, Kielhofner has asserted that this unifying base should be structured according to Kuhn's conceptualization of a paradigm. He and Burke first presented this idea in a 1977 *AJOT* article. In 1983, the book, *Health Through Occupation,* elaborated on the application of the Kuhnian paradigm to occupational therapy. And in 1986, he and Barris further spelled out how knowledge in the field would be organized using Kuhn's concepts as its base. This article in *OTJR* was followed by a critique by Labovitz and Miller (1986) in which they pointed out some of the inconsistencies and problems in Kielhofner's and Barris' proposals.

At this time, Kielhofner is less certain about how this unifying base should be structured. He acknowledges that, as a practice profession, OT's paradigm cannot be exactly what Kuhn conceptualized. He remains convinced, however, that the profession needs to arrive at some consensus about its foundational concepts and philosophical assumptions. As he says:

> I think there are two valid points about what the field needs; the field needs diversity in its views, and the field needs organization and consistency in its views. I think that the challenge for an occupational therapy paradigm is how to manage the tension between these two. (G.W. Kielhofner, personal communication, March 6, 1987)

REFERENCES

Barris, R. (1982). Environmental interactions: An extension of the model of human occupation. *American Journal of Occupational Therapy, 36,* 637–644.

Barris, R., Kielhofner, G., Levine, R.E., & Neville A. (1985). Occupation as interaction with the environment. In G. Kielhofner (Ed.), *A model of human occupation: Theory and application* (pp. 42–62). Baltimore: Williams & Wilkins.

Barris, R., Kielhofner, G., Burch-Martin, R., Gelinas, I., Kelment, M., Schultz, B. (1986). Occupational function and dysfunction in three groups of adolescents. *Occupational Therapy Journal of Research, 6,* 301–317.

Barris, R., Kielhofner, G., & Watts, J. (1983). *Psychosocial occupational therapy: Practice in a pluralistic arena.* Laurel, MD: RAM Associates.

Bentz, C. (1984). *A measure of personal causation for mildly and moderately retarded adults.* Unpublished master's project, Virginia Commonwealth University.

Blakeney, A.B. (1985). Adolescent development: An application to the model of human occupation. In Cromwell, F.S. (Ed.), *Occupational therapy and adolescents with disability* (pp. 19–40). New York: Haworth Press.

Doble, S. (1985). *Inter-rater reliability and concurrent validity of a process skills assessment.* Unpublished master's thesis, Boston University, Boston.

Duellman, M.K., Barris, R., & Kielhofner, G. (1986). Organized activity and the adaptive status of nursing home residents. *American Journal of Occupational Therapy, 40,* 618–622.

Elliott, M.S., & Barris, R. (1987). Occupational role performance and life satisfaction in elderly persons. *Occupational Therapy Journal of Research, 7,* 215–224.

Feibleman, J.K. (1969). Theory of integrative levels. In Coleman, J.C. (Ed.), *Psychology and Effective Behavior.* Glenview, IL: Scott Foresman and Co.

Fronczek, Y. (1985). *A study of the compliance and roles, locus of control, and interests of the acute hand injured patient.* Unpublished master's thesis, Virginia Commonwealth University.

Gregory, M. (1983). Occupational behavior and life satisfaction among retirees. *American Journal of Occupational Therapy, 37,* 548–553.

Gusich, R.L. (1984). Occupational therapy for chronic pain: A clinical application of the model of human occupation. *Occupational Therapy in Mental Health, 4,* 59–74.

Harrison, H., & Kielhofner, G. (1986). Examining reliability and validity of the preschool play scale with handicapped children. *American Journal of Occupational Therapy, 40,* 167–173.

Kaplan, K. (1984). Short term assessment: The need and a response. *Occupational Therapy in Mental Health, 4,* 29–45.

Kavanaugh, M., Barris, R., & Kielhofner, G. (in press). A study of mentally retarded adults' occupational behavior. *American Journal of Occupational Therapy.*

Kielhofner, G. (1975). *The evolution of knowledge in occupational therapy: Understanding adaptation of the chronically disabled.* Unpublished master's thesis, University of Southern California, Los Angeles.

Kielhofner, G. (1977). Temporal adaptation: A conceptual framework for occupational therapy. *American Journal of Occupational Therapy, 31,* 235–242.

Kielhofner, G. (1978). General systems theory: Implications for theory and action in occupational therapy. *American Journal of Occupational Therapy, 32,* 637–645.

Kielhofner, G. (1980a). *Evaluating deinstitutionalization: An ethnographic study of social policy.* Unpublished doctoral dissertation, University of Southern California, Los Angeles.

Kielhofner, G. (1980b). A model of human occupation, Part two. Ontogenesis from the perspective of temporal adaptation. *American Journal of Occupational Therapy, 34,* 657–663.

Kielhofner, G. (1980c). A model of human occupation, Part three. Benign and vicious cycles. *American Journal of Occupational Therapy, 34,* 731–737.

Kielhofner, G. (1982a). Qualitative research: Part one—Paradigmatic grounds and issues of reliability and validity. *Occupational Therapy Journal of Research, 2,* 67–79.

Kielhofner, G. (1982b). Qualitative research: Part two—Methodological approaches and relevance to occupational therapy. *Occupational Therapy Journal of Research, 2,* 150–164.

Kielhofner, G. (1983). *Health through occupation: Theory and practice in occupational therapy.* Philadelphia: F.A. Davis.

Kielhofner, G. (1984). An overview of research on the model of human occupation. *Canadian Journal of Occupational Therapy, 51,* 59–67.

Kielhofner, G. (1985). *A model of human occupation: Theory and application.* Baltimore: Williams & Wilkins.

Kielhofner, G., & Burke, J.P. (1977). Occupational therapy after 60 years: An account of changing identity and knowledge. *American Journal of Occupational Therapy, 31,* 675–689.

Kielhofner, G., & Burke, J.P. (1980). A model of human occupation. Part one, conceptual framework and content. *American Journal of Occupational Therapy, 34,* 572–581.

Kielhofner, G., and Burke, J.P. (1985). Components and determinants of human occupation. In G. Kielhofner (Ed.), *A model of human occupation: Theory and application* (pp. 12–41). Baltimore: Williams & Wilkins.

Kielhofner, G., Burke, J., & Heard Igi, C. (1980). A model of human occupation, Part four. Assessment and intervention. *American Journal of Occupational Therapy, 34,* 777–788.

Kielhofner, G., Harlan, B., Bauer, D., & Maurer, P. (1986). An exploratory investigation of the reliability of a historical interview when given to physically disabled respondents. *American Journal of Occupational Therapy, 40,* 551–556.

Knapp, J. (1983). *A study of leisure values and life satisfaction among retirees.* Unpublished master's project, Virginia Commonwealth University.

Labovitz, D.R. & Miller, R.J. (1986). Commentary: Organization of knowledge in occupational therapy: A proposal and a survey of the literature. *Occupational Therapy Journal of Research, 6,* 85–92.

Lederer, J., Kielhofner, G., & Watts, J. (1985). Values, personal causation and skills of delinquents and non-delinquents. *Occupational Therapy in Mental Health, 5,* 59–78.

Lyons, M. (1983). *Employment and personal adjustment of mentally retarded persons: Towards an emic perspective of the relationship.* Unpublished master's thesis, Virginia Commonwealth University.

Mailloux, Z. (1980). *The relationship between self-esteem and visual motor integration praxis and student role performance in children with learning disabilities.* Unpublished master's thesis, University of Southern California, Los Angeles.

Oakley, F., Kielhofner, G., & Barris, R. (1985). An occupational therapy approach to assessing psychiatric patients' adaptive functioning. *American Journal of Occupational Therapy, 39,* 147–154.

Oakley, F., Kielhofner, G., Barris, R., & Reichler, R. (1986). Reliability of the role checklist. *Occupational Therapy Journal of Research, 6,* 157–170.

Rogers, J.C., & Kielhofner, G. (1985). Treatment planning. In G. Kielhofner (Ed.) *A model of human occupation: Theory and application.* (p. 140). Baltimore: Williams & Wilkins.

Salz, C. (1983). A theoretical approach to the treatment of work difficulties in borderline personalities. *Occupational Therapy in Mental Health, 3,* 33–46.

Scaff, M. (1981). *Temporal adaptation and alcoholism.* Unpublished master's project, Virginia Commonwealth University.

Scott, M.B. (1982). *The validity of an occupational picture interest sort for mentally retarded adults.* Unpublished master's project, Virginia Commonwealth University.

Shakun, R. (1982). *The assessment of the reliability of the occupational picture interest sort for mentally retarded adults.* Unpublished master's project, Virginia Commonwealth University.

Smith, N.R., Kielhofner, G., & Watts, J.H. (1986). The relationships between volition, activity pattern, and life satisfaction in the elderly. *American Journal of Occupational Therapy, 40,* 278–283.

Smyntek, L., Barris, R., & Kielhofner, G. (1985). The model of human occupation applied to psychosocially functional and dysfunctional adolescents. *Occupational Therapy in Mental Health, 5,* 21–38.

Tigges, K.N., & Sherman, L.M. (1983). The treatment of the hospice patient: From occupational history to occupational role. *American Journal of Occupational Therapy, 37,* 235–238.

Watts, J.H., Kielhofner, G., Bauer, D., Gregory, M., & Valentine, D. (1986). The assessment of occupational functioning: A screening tool for use in long-term care. *American Journal of Occupational Therapy, 40,* 231–240.

Wieringa, N., & McColl, M. (1987). Implications of the model of human occupation for intervention with native Canadians. In Cromwell, F.S. (Ed.) *Sociocultural Implications in Treatment Planning in Occupational Therapy.* New York: Haworth Press.

BIBLIOGRAPHY

1975

Kielhofner, G. (1975). *The evolution of knowledge in occupational therapy: Understanding adaptation of the chronically disabled.* Unpublished master's thesis, University of Southern California, Los Angeles.

1976

Cromwell, F.S., & Kielhofner, G. (1976). An educational strategy for occupational therapy community service. *American Journal of Occupational Therapy, 30,* 629–633.

1977

Kielhofner, G. (1977). Temporal adaptation: A conceptual framework for occupational therapy. *American Journal of Occupational Therapy, 31,* 235–242.

Kielhofner, G., & Burke, J.P. (1977). Occupational therapy after 60 years: An account of changing identity and knowledge. *American Journal of Occupational Therapy, 31,* 675–689.

1978

Kielhofner, G. (1978). General systems theory: Implications for theory and action in occupational therapy. *American Journal of Occupational Therapy, 32,* 637–645.

1979

Kielhofner, G. (1979). The temporal dimension in the lives of retarded adults: A problem of interaction and intervention. *American Journal of Occupational Therapy,* 33, 161–168.

Kielhofner, G. (1979). Temporal adaptation: A conceptual framework for occupational therapy. In Payton, O. (Ed.), *Research: The validation of clinical practice.* Philadelphia: F.A. Davis (Reprinted from *American Journal of Occupational Therapy*).

Gillette N., Kielhofner, G. (1979). The impact of specialization on the professionalization and survival of occupational therapy. *American Journal of Occupational Therapy, 33,* 20–28.

1980

Kielhofner, G. (1980). *Evaluating deinstitutionalization: An ethnographic study of social policy.* Unpublished doctoral dissertation, University of Southern California, Los Angeles.

Kielhofner, G. (1980). A model of human occupation, Part two. Ontogenesis from the perspective of temporal adaptation. *American Journal of Occupational Therapy, 34,* 657–663.

Kielhofner, G. (1980). A model of human occupation, Part three. Benign and vicious cycles. *American Journal of Occupational Therapy, 34,* 731–737.

Kielhofner, G., & Burke, J.P. (1980). A model of human occupation. Part one, conceptual framework and content. *American Journal of Occupational Therapy, 34,* 572–581.

Kielhofner, G., & Takata, N. (1980). A study of mentally retarded persons: Applied research in occupational therapy. *American Journal of Occupational Therapy, 34,* 252–258.

Kielhofner, G., Burke, J., & Heard Igi, C. (1980). A model of human occupation, Part four. Assessment and intervention. *American Journal of Occupational Therapy, 34,* 777–788.

1981

Kielhofner, G. (1981). An ethnographic study of deinstitutionalized adults: Their community settings and daily life experiences. *Occupational Therapy Journal of Research, 1,* 125–142.

Kielhofner, G., & Miyake, S. (1981). The therapeutic use of games with mentally retarded adults. *American Journal of Occupational Therapy, 35,* 375–382.

1982

Vandenberg, B., & Kielhofner, G. (1982). Play in evolution, culture, and individual adaptation: Implications for therapy. *American Journal of Occupational Therapy, 36,* 20–28.

Kielhofner, G. (1982). Theory development in occupational therapy, in *Proceedings of the World Federation of Occupational Therapy,* Germany, 1982.

Chao, R., Clark, F., & Kielhofner, G. (1982). Development of time concepts in mentally retarded adults and its relationship to mental age. *Proceedings of the Annual Piagetian Conference,* Los Angeles, California, 1982.

Kielhofner, G. (1982). Qualitative research: Part one—Paradigmatic grounds and issues of reliability and validity. *Occupational Therapy Journal of Research, 2,* 67–79.

Kielhofner, G. (1982). Qualitative research: Part two—Methodological approaches and relevance to occupational therapy. *Occupational Therapy Journal of Research, 2,* 150–164.

Kielhofner, G., Barris, R., & Watts, J. (1982). Habits and habit dysfunction: A clinical perspective for psychosocial occupational therapy. *Occupational Therapy in Mental Health, 2,* 1–22.

Kielhofner, G. (1982). A heritage of activity: Development of theory. *American Journal of Occupational Therapy, 36,* 723–730.

1983

Kielhofner, G. (1983). "Teaching" retarded adults: Paradoxical effects of a pedagogical enterprise. *Urban Life, 12,* 307–326.

Kielhofner, G. (1983), Occupation. In H. Hopkins & H. Smith (Eds.), *Willard and Spackman's Occupational Therapy,* (6th ed.). Philadelphia: J.P. Lippincott.

Kielhofner, G. (Ed.) (1983). *Health through occupation: Theory & practice in occupational therapy.* Philadelphia: F.A. Davis.

Kielhofner, G., & Nelson, C. (1983). A study of patient motivation and cooperation/participation in occupational therapy. *Occupational Therapy Journal of Research, 3,* 35–46.

Kielhofner, G., Barris, R., Bauer, D., Shoestock, B., & Walker, L. (1983). A comparison of play behavior in nonhospitalized and hospitalized children. *American Journal of Occupational Therapy, 37,* 305–312.

Barris, R., Kielhofner, G., & Watts, J. (1983). *Psychosocial occupational therapy: Practice in a pluralistic arena.* Laurel, MD: RAM Associates.

1984

Kielhofner, G. (1984). An overview of research on the model of human occupation. *Canadian Journal of Occupational Therapy, 51,* 59–67.

Kielhofner, G. (1984). A paradigmatic view of rehabilitation. *Proceedings of the Second International Conference on Rehabilitation Engineering,* Ottowa, Canada.

Kielhofner, G., & Barris, R. (1984). Mental health occupational therapy: Trends in literature and practice. *Occupational Therapy in Mental Health, 4,* 35–50.

1985

Kielhofner, G. (Ed.) (1985). *A model of human occupation: Theory and application.* Baltimore: Williams & Wilkins.

Kielhofner, G. (1985). The demise of diffidence: An agenda for occupational therapy. *Canadian Journal of Occupational Therapy, 52,* 165–171.

Kielhofner, G., & Henriksson, C. (translator). (1985). The model of human occupation: ett hjalpmedel for kliniskt uerksamma arbetsterapeuter. *Arbetsterapeuten* (Swedish Journal of Occupation Therapy), *17,* 18–23.

Barris, R., & Kielhofner, G. (1985). Generating and using knowledge in occupational therapy: Implications for professional education. *Occupational Therapy Journal of Research, 5,* 113–124.

Barris, R., Kielhofner, G., & Bauer, D. (1985). Educational experience and changes in learning and value preferences. *Occupational Therapy Journal of Research, 5,* 243–256.

Barris, R., Kielhofner, G., & Bauer, D. (1985). Learning preferences, values, and student satisfaction. *Journal of Allied Health, 14,* 13–23.

Lederer, J., Kielhofner, G., & Watts, J. (1985). Values, personal causation and skills of delinquents and non-delinquents. *Occupational Therapy in Mental Health, 5,* 59–77.

Neville, A., Kriesberg, A., & Kielhofner, G. (1985). Temporal dysfunction in schizophrenia. *Occupational Therapy in Mental Health, 5,* (1), 1–20.

Oakley, F., Kielhofner, G., & Barris, R. (1985). An occupational therapy approach to assessing psychiatric patients' adaptive functioning. *American Journal of Occupational Therapy, 39,* 147–154.

Smyntek, L., Barris, R., & Kielhofner, G. (1985). The model of human occupation applied to psychosocially functional and dysfunctional adolescents. *Occupational Therapy in Mental Health, 5,* 21–40.

1986

Kielhofner, G. (1986). A review of research on the model of human occupation: Part one. *Canadian Journal of Occupational Therapy, 53,* 69–74.

Kielhofner, G. (1986). A review of research on the model of human occupation: Part two. *Canadian Journal of Occupational Therapy, 53,* 129–134.

Kielhofner, G. (1986). A response to Sharrott's "An analysis of occupational therapy theoretical approaches for mental health." *Occupational Therapy in Mental Health, 5,* 17–23.

Kielhofner, G., & Barris, R. (1986). Organization of knowledge in occupational therapy: A proposal and a survey of the literature. *Occupational Therapy Journal of Research, 5,* 67–84.

Kielhofner, G., & Barris, R. (1986). Response to commentary: Organization of knowledge in occupational therapy: A proposal and a survey of the literature. *Occupational Therapy Journal of Research, 6,* 183–190.

Kielhofner, G., & Nelson, C. (1986). The nature and implications of shifting patterns of practice in physical disabilities occupational therapy. *Occupational Therapy in Health Care, 3,* 187–198.

Kielhofner, G., Harlan, B., Bauer, D., & Maurer, P. (1986). The reliability of an historical interview with physically disabled respondents. *American Journal of Occupational Therapy, 40,* 551–556.

Barris, R., & Kielhofner, G. (1986). Beliefs, perspectives, and activities of psychosocial occupational therapy educators. *American Journal of Occupational Therapy, 40,* 535–541.

Barris, R., Kielhofner, G., Burch, R.M., Gelinas, I., Klement, M., & Schultz, B. (1986). Occupational function and dysfunction in three groups of adolescents. *Occupational Therapy Journal of Research, 6,* 301–317.

Duellman, M.K., Barris, R., & Kielhofner, G. (1986). Organized activity and the adoptive status of nursing home residents. *American Journal of Occupational Therapy, 40,* 618–622.

Harrison, H., & Kielhofner, G. (1986). Examining reliability and validity of the preschool play scale with handicapped children. *American Journal of Occupational Therapy, 40,* 167–173.

Oakley, F., Kielhofner, G., Barris, R., & Reichler, R. K. (1986). The role checklist: Development and empirical assessment of reliability. *Occupational Therapy Journal of Research, 6,* 157–170.

Riopel Smith, N., Kielhofner, G., & Watts, J. (1986). The relationships between volition, activity pattern, and life satisfaction in the elderly. *American Journal of Occupational Therapy, 40,* 278–284.

Watts, J.H., Kielhofner, G., Bauer, D., Gregory, M., & Valentine, D. (1986). The assessment of occupational functioning: A screening tool for use in long-term care. *American Journal of Occupational Therapy, 40,* 231–240.

PAPERS IN PRESS OR ACCEPTED FOR PUBLICATION

Kielhofner, G., & Henry, A. (in press). Use of an occupational history interview in occupational therapy. In B. Hempill (Ed.), *Evaluation Processes in Mental Health Occupational Therapy* (2nd ed.).

Barris, R., Oakley F., & Kielhofner, G. (in press). The role checklist. In B. Hempill (Ed.), *Evaluation Processes in Mental Health Occupational Therapy* (2nd ed.).

Kavanaugh, M., Barris, R., & Kielhofner, G. A study of mentally retarded adults' occupational behavior. *American Journal of Occupational Therapy* (accepted for publication).

Chapter Eight

Theory Analysis

Kay W. Sieg

Theory analysis provides a means to examine the unique features of a theory and, when applied to several theories in a field, can be used to identify major theoretical endeavors of that field. Because a theory is an attempt to explain, predict, or clarify phenomena, analysis of several theories in a profession serves to illuminate the field's major theoretical efforts.

In this chapter, the works of Gail Fidler, Anne Mosey, Lela Llorens, Jean Ayres, Mary Reilly, and Gary Kielhofner are analyzed in terms of (a) the theorists' backgrounds, (b) the processes of theory development, (c) the major premises posited by the theorists, (d) their clinical application, (e) the scope and complexity of the theories, and (f) the theorists' efforts to validate and disseminate the theory. Finally, the progress that has been made by these theorists in the development of theory for occupational therapy is explored through the identification of areas of theoretical agreement and areas where theory development is needed.

Theory assessment, the evaluation of theory through the use of checklists (Chinn & Jacobs, 1983), models (Meleis, 1985), or frameworks (Duldt & Griffin, 1985), may be a part of theory analysis. Theory evaluation can be a useful process to the practicing therapist for theory selection, to the student for heuristic purposes or, as was done in the preceding chapters, to be part of the synthesis of a theory. However, even the use of rigorous assessment tools to evaluate the strengths and weaknesses of a theory is idiosyncratic to the perspective of the analyzer. To one person a theory may be judged as parsimonious and clinically useful, whereas to another, that same theory seems vague and of little value.

Therefore, in this chapter, which compares six OT theories, the relative merits and flaws of the six theories are not discussed. The purpose of this final chapter is not to *assess* the theories, but rather to *review and compare* them for their contribution to the contemporary status of theory in occupational therapy.

BACKGROUND OF THEORISTS

A theorist's background influences her or his career development and, hence, theory development. Statements of theoretical positions reflect very individualized perceptions that have been shaped by the person's life experiences and the historical and professional events of the time in which the person lives. Examination of a theory against a backdrop of the theorist's life reveals important influences that contributed to the person the theorist became and, therefore, to the theory that was developed. The backgrounds of the six theorists included in this book are reviewed from a historical perspective (see Table 8-1).

Table 8-1 Historical Perspectives 1910–1950

	National and OT events		*Theorists*
National events	World War I (1914–1918) 19th Amendment ratified (1920) Stock market crash (1929) Great Depression (1930–1939) World War II (1939–1945) Polio epidemic (1947)	**Fidler**	Born 1916, Spencer, Iowa Oldest of 4 children Debating team, sports in high school BA education and psychology (1938) Aide in state mental hospital U Penn OT certificate (1942), White Inst. of Psychi & Psych (1947–1951) First publication *AJOT* (1948)
Occupational therapy events	National Society for Promotion of Occupational Therapy formed (1917) Reconstruction aides trained for WW I *Archives of OT* (1922). Later, *OT and Rehabilitation* (1925) and finally *American Journal of OT* (1947) War emergency courses for WW II Educational standards (1923) More OTs in psychiatry in 1937 but increase in physical disabilities OT with WW II Registration examination (1939)	**Reilly**	Born 1916, Boston, MA Strict girls' school Boston U OT certificate (1940) U.S. Army Medical Dept. (1941–1955) First paper, *OT & REHAB* 1943
		Ayres	Born 1923, California Farm life Childhood illnesses First publication *AJOT* (1949)
		Llorens	Born 1933, Shreveport, LA Pre-civil rights era
		Mosey	Born 1938 3rd of 7 children
		Kielhofner	Born 1949, Oran, Missouri Extended family Farm life

1910–1950

1910 to 1950—National Events

During the years 1910 to 1950, the United States was involved in World War I (1917–1918) and World War II (1939–1945), ratified the 19th amendment to the Constitution ensuring women's voting rights (1920), suffered through the stock market crash (1929) and the "Great Depression" (1930–1939) and in 1947 experienced the polio epidemic (Hopkins, 1983; Reed & Sanderson, 1980).

1910 to 1950—Occupational Therapy

The OT profession was established and its growth was influenced by the two world wars. During this period, educational training developed from nondegree training courses to master's degree programs, a journal was established, the populations treated in OT changed, and individuals who would go on to make major theoretical contributions to OT were born.

By the time the United States entered WW I, the National Society for the Promotion of Occupational Therapy had been organized (1917), its membership numbering 47 physicians, social workers, nurses, artists, and teachers. The United States' involvement in WW I provided an impetus for expansion of occupational therapy as OT Reconstruction Aides were trained to work with the wounded soldiers. In the next 5 years, training programs were designed, training manuals written, and a journal, *Archives of Occupational Therapy,* published (1922). With the increase in the number of training programs for occupational therapists came the establishment of educational standards (1923) and, by 1939, the registration examination.

World War II greatly stimulated the growth of the field and influenced the direction of OT treatment. In 1937, there were twice as many occupational therapists in psychiatric settings as in general hospital and orthopedic facilities, but the wartime need for occupational therapy in the treatment of the injured soldier resulted in increased development of treatment techniques in physical disabilities. The number of OT programs increased from 5 to 18 during the period 1940–1945, and the population of therapists nearly doubled between 1941 and 1946. OT graduate education began with the establishment of the first OT master's degree program in 1947 at the University of Southern California (Hopkins, 1983; Reed & Sanderson, 1980).

1910 to 1950—The Theorists

Both Fidler and Reilly were born in 1916, one year before the United States entered WW I and before occupational therapy was organized as a profession. The independent and goal-oriented nature of the careers of these two women was becoming more socially acceptable by the time Fidler and Reilly were growing up. Women had secured the right to vote and, because of the wars, had been initiated into previously male vocations, such as military nursing and civilian assembly line work. In addition, early school experiences seem to have fostered the independence of both Fidler and Reilly. Fidler's high school sports and debating team activities provided outlets for independent expression, and Reilly's early schooling in a strict scholastic girl's school contributed to her lifelong interest in scholarly pursuits. As college graduates in the late 1930s, OT training was available to Fidler and Reilly through the established 1-year certificate programs.

Early employment experiences influenced the directions of Fidler's and Reilly's careers. Fidler's first job was in psychiatry, setting her lifelong focus on mental health occupational therapy. Her first publication in 1948 concerned psychological evaluation of OT activities. After one year of working with children, Reilly worked for 14 years in the U.S. Army Medical Department in physical disabilities where she co-authored her first publication in 1943. Her enduring concern with the nature of the profession was evidenced in this first publication in which she addressed the relationship of occupational to physical therapy.

Ayres was born in 1923 and thus was influenced by national and professional forces similar to those affecting Fidler and Reilly. However, Ayres' childhood on a farm in California during the Depression years, her battles with childhood illnesses, and her struggles with family issues seem to have been key elements in the development of her characteristic determination and independence. She obtained her OT training from the University of Southern California (USC) in 1945 at the time when the country's first OT master's degree was being devised by Margaret Rood. This academic climate that promoted the obtaining of advanced degrees may have influenced Ayres' use of scientific research methodology for theory development; too, Rood's neurophysiologic theories may have promoted Ayres' use of neuroscience in her theory. Ayres' first OT job was in a psychiatric setting where she published her first journal article in 1949 on the use of crafts with electroshock patients.

Born in 1933, Llorens' grew up in the South before the Civil Rights movement at a time when racial segregation was the norm. Llorens' personal situation seems to have been a major contributing factor to her ambitions to surpass the usual limited expectations for black females in the South and to achieve independent career success.

Mosey was born in 1938 and grew up in a large Irish family where she was the third of seven children. Kielhofner, the youngest of the six theorists, was born in 1949 into an extended farm family. By the time Kielhofner was born, Fidler and Reilly were experienced therapists, Reilly and Ayres

Table 8-2 Continued Historical Perspective 1950–1980s

	1950–1960	1960–1970	1970–1980	1980s
National Events	Korean War begins (1951) VR Act of 1954 Fed $ Health Professions training	Civil Rights Movement Kennedy, Johnson administrations Vietnam War Medicare	Watergate Women's Movement Ecology issues P.L. 94-142 Education of All Handicapped Children's Act	Corporate health care Inflation Federal $ cutbacks Information age
Occupational Therapy Events	Shift from acute to chronic care as medicine controls polio, TB, etc. WFOT formed (1952) Therapeutic use of self in OT psychiatry Improved rehab techniques	OT shortages–roles absorbed by other professions OT in the community Group techniques and object relations in OT psychiatry Entry master's at USC (1964) AOTA-Business; AOTF-Research Theory: Reilly—Occupational behavior, Ayres—Sensory integration, Llorens—Developmental	Accountability in health care AOTA practice standards OT licensure Specialty sections Mosey's frames of reference for OT practice	Research emphasis OT doctoral degrees Training programs: TOTEMS: SCOPE: ROTE: PIVOT Governmental representation Role delineation Kielhofner's human occupation model
Fidler	*Intro to Psychiatric OT* (1954) Coordinator AOTA Mental Health Institute (1952–1955) Instructor Penn Dept Mental Health (1955–1957) Supervision workshops, Columbia University	ECS lecture (1965) *OT A Communication Process in Psychiatry* (1963) Directorships: NY Neuropsych. Inst., Activities Therapy NYU OT master's in psychiatry	Director AOTA 1971–1975 Adjunct appts. several universities Consultant to hospitals Administrator—state mental health	AOTA Award of Merit Consultancies NYU, NY Mental Health Hospital Chief Executive Officer
Reilly	UCLA Neuropsychiatric Institute (1959–1968) Intrinsic motivation of B. Smith	ECS lecture (1962) USC OT faculty, graduate director, and program chair	*Play as Exploratory Learning* (1974) Retired 1977	Charter member AOTF Academy of Research (1983) Article on client vs patient (1984)

Ayres	MA OT, USC (1954) USC faculty 1954–1968	ECS lecture (1963) AOTA Award of Merit (1965) PhD USC (1961) Postdoctoral work Brain Research Institute 1964–1966 USC Special Ed. faculty, 1966–1977	*Sensory Integration and Learning Disabilities* (1972) Sensory integration tests USC OT faculty 1976– Private foundation research $ Ayres Clinic opened	Charter member AOTF Academy of Research (1983) Retired from Ayres Clinic (1984) *Developmental Dyspraxia and Adult Onset Apraxia* (1985)
Llorens	BS OT W. Michigan U (1954) Lafayette Clinic Pediatric Psychiatry, influence of research team 1958–1968	First publication *AJOT* (1960) Instructor Wayne State 1960–1968 MA Wayne State (1962) Developing Ego Functions in Disturbed Children OT in Milieu OT Consultant 1968–1971 ECS lecture 1969	U FL faculty 1971–1976 U FL Chair 1976–1982 PhD Walden U (1976) *Consultation in the Community* (1973) *Application of Developmental Theory* (1976)	San Jose ST. OT Chair 1982– *OT Sequential Client Care Record* AOTA Award of Merit (1986)
Mosey		BS OT U Minn (1960) MA OT NYU (1965) PhD NYU (1968) NY Neuropsychiatric Institute 1962–1966 Instr OT Columbia U 1966–1968 First publication: *AJOT* (1968) *OT Theory and Practice* (1968)	NYU OT Chair 1972–1980 *3 Frames of Reference for Mental Health* (1970) *Activities Therapy* (1974)	*OT: Configuration of a Profession* (1981) ECS lecture (1985) *Psychosocial Components of OT* (1986)
Kielhofner	Seminary high school	Monastic college for 2 years Vietnam conscientious objector Hospital recreation job	BA Psychology, St. Louis U 1971 MS OT USC 1975 PhD USC 1979 First publication: *AJOT* 1976 Neuropsychiatric Institute, Los Angeles 1975–1979 USC OT faculty 1977–1979 VCU OT faculty 1979–1984	Charter member AOTA Academy of Research (1984) Boston U OT faculty 1984–1986 Univ. of Ill OT Chair 1986— *Health through Occupation* (1983) *Psychosocial OT* (1983) *Model of Human Occupation* (1985)

had each published an article in OT journals, Llorens was beginning college, and Mosey was in high school. While Kielhofner was still a youngster, these other authors would go on to develop theories that he would later study before developing his own theory. These events occur in the next period to be discussed, 1950–1987 (see Table 8-2).

1950–1987

1950–1987—National Events

Major events in the United States during this period included involvement in the Korean war in the early 1950s and, in the 1960s, the Civil Rights movement, protests of U.S. involvement in the Vietnam war, the "Great Society" of the Johnson administration that provided federal funding for social and health programs, the establishment of Medicare, and the first walk on the moon. The 1970s saw the Watergate scandal, the modern-day women's movement, concern with ecology, and the passage of the Education for all Handicapped Children's Act of 1974. Inflation, cutbacks in federal spending, the "information age," and corporate health care characterized the 1980s.

1950s—OT Events and the Theorists

During the 1950s, improved OT techniques for physical disabilities were developed through federally funded rehabilitation programs. The focus shifted from acute care, such as bedside therapy for the injured solider, to more chronic care as the war ended and medical science conquered such diseases as tuberculosis and polio. The World Federation of Occupational Therapists was formed. Occupational therapy in psychiatry focused on the therapeutic use of self, and Fidler's psychodynamic and psychoanalytic theories for the field in psychiatry were developed. She and her husband (a psychiatrist) co-authored the book, *Introduction to Psychiatric Occupational Therapy,* published in 1954. Her leadership in mental health occupational therapy was recognized in her appointment as coordinator of AOTA's Psychiatric Study Project 1955–57 (Hopkins, 1983).

During the 1950s the other theorists were involved in formative experiences that influenced the direction of their careers and theory development. Reilly was at the University of California at Los Angeles Neuropsychiatric Institute from 1959 to the mid-1960s where her mentor, B. Smith, influenced her thinking on intrinsic motivation. Ayres completed her master's degree in occupational therapy in 1954, worked with children with cerebral palsy, and was appointed to the USC faculty. Completing her OT training in 1953, Llorens worked in pediatric psychiatry at the

Lafayette Clinic where, over the course of the next 10 years, she was involved in teaching, research, and clinical roles with colleagues and mentors who were influential in her career development. In the late 1950s, Mosey was in college, where she was influenced by Marvin Lepley, an early mentor; and Keilhofner was in grade school.

1960s—OT Events and the Theorists

In the 1960s, the number of occupational therapists did not keep up with the demands for OT services, and other disciplines absorbed roles created by the shortage of occupational therapists. Group techniques and object relationships were developed for mental health OT, occupational therapy in community-based settings was emphasized, and the American Occupational Therapy Foundation (AOTF) was established in 1965 to promote research.

OT theory developed further with the emergence of Reilly's occupational behavior theory, Ayres' sensory integration theory, and Llorens' developmental theory (Hopkins, 1983). Their contributions to theory development were recognized as each, including Fidler as well, was awarded Eleanor Clarke Slagle Lectureships in the 1960s. Reilly was honored as the Eleanor Clarke Slagle lecturer in 1962 during which she stated her often-quoted OT premise: "Man, through the use of his hands, as they are energized by mind and will, can influence the state of his own health" (Reilly, 1962, p. 2). In 1963, Ayres lectured on perceptual motor development. Fidler's lecture in 1965 was on the teaching-learning process. In 1969, Llorens presented her developmental framework of occupational therapy in her Slagle lecture.

Fidler was professionally productive during the 1960s, publishing a book, *Occupational Therapy: A Communication Process,* in 1963 and directing both professional education at New York State Neuropsychiatric Institute and the master's program in mental health occupational therapy at NYU. Mosey was in school during the 1960s, completing her undergraduate OT degree in 1961, her OT master's degree in 1965, and her doctorate degree in 1968. She was influenced by Fidler who was OT director during the 4 years Mosey worked at the Neuropsychiatric Institute. Fidler was also director of the OT master's program in psychiatry when Mosey was a student in the program.

In the 1960s Llorens published her first article, in 1962 she completed her master's work, and in 1967 she co-authored the book, *Developing Ego Functions*. During this time, Ayres completed her doctoral work and engaged in postdoctoral studies at the Brain Research Institute, confirming her interest in the neurosciences. In the mid-1960s Reilly served as chairperson and graduate faculty member at USC. Kielhofner's classical and rigorous scholarly background in a Catholic seminary high school fueled his ability and interest in writing. He completed high school and began college during the 1960s.

1970s—OT Events and the Theorists

In the 1970s, accountability was the watchword in health care, and the AOTA adopted several documents that addressed quality care in occupational therapy: (1) standards for practice in mental health, developmental disabilities, physical disabilities, and home health; (2) guidelines for administration and supervision; (3) a statement on referral; (4) revised essentials for accredited curricula; (5) code of professional ethics; (6) an official definition of occupational therapy; and (7) uniform terminology guidelines. Occupational therapists were licensed in New York in 1976, and other states soon developed licensure laws. Specialization was recognized with the adoption of special interest sections in mental health, physical disabilities, developmental disabilities, sensory integration, and geriatrics. In OT theory, Mosey's emphasis on frames of reference for OT practice gained national recognition (Hopkins, 1983).

Two of Mosey's major works, *Three Frames of Reference for Mental Health* (1970) and *Activities Therapy* (1974), addressed the need for a frame of reference to guide practice, a need in keeping with the widespread concern that the field have standards, ethics, and defined practice guidelines. She taught her theories to OT graduate and undergraduate students at NYU, where she also chaired the OT program for 8 years during the 1970s.

In the 1970s, Fidler's publications addressed broad professional issues and reflected the concerns encountered in her work experiences as director of AOTA for 5 years, adjunct faculty to several universities, and consultant to hospitals and a state mental health agency.

The establishment of sensory integration as one of AOTA's specialty sections reflected the impact that Ayres' work was having on the field in the 1970s. During this decade, she served as an OT faculty member at USC and established the Ayres Clinic, training and teaching students in sensory integration therapy. Her research efforts were funded through grants from a private foundation. She authored two books during the 1970s, *Sensory Integration and Learning Disabilities* (1972a) and *Sensory Integration and the Child* (1979).

Llorens continued the development of her framework for OT practice in her book, *Application of a Developmental Theory for Health and Rehabilitation* (1976), and, reflecting the national trend for developing OT consultancy roles, edited a book, *Consultation in the Community* (1973).

She completed her doctoral degree during this decade and served as OT faculty member and then chairperson at the University of Florida.

In 1974, Reilly's book, *Play as Exploratory Learning,* was published; it was the culmination of her work-play theory of occupational behavior that she and her students had been developing for the three previous decades. Before her retirement from her faculty position at USC in 1977, she influenced the thinking of her many students over the years, most notably Gary Kielhofner. Kielhofner completed his bachelor's degree in psychology in 1971; in 1975, he received his master's degree in occupational therapy at USC where the mentoring relationship he enjoyed with Mary Reilly was a major determining factor in the development of his theoretical formulations. Kielhofner went on to publish several papers, earn his doctorate degree, and serve as OT faculty member in two universities in the 1970s.

1980s—OT Events and the Theorists

The 1980s have been characterized by an increased emphasis on research, study of OT personnel shortages (AOTA, 1985a), national training initiatives, increases in graduate education, entry-level role delineation concerns, political action, and human occupation theory. The AOTF's research initiatives include grants for OT research and sponsorship of (1) the research forum at the AOTA national conferences, (2) the publication, *Occupational Therapy Journal of Research,* and (3) the honorary Academy of Research. The AOTA has initiated continuing education courses in several areas: TOTEMS, Training: Occupational Therapy Management in Schools (1979); PIVOT, Planning and Implementing Vocational Readiness in Occupational Therapy (1985b); ROTE, the Role of Occupational Therapy with the Elderly (1986a); and SCOPE, Strategies, Concepts, and Opportunities for Program Development and Evaluation (1986b). In 1987, PATRA, Professional and Technical Role Analysis, was begun as a follow-up to the 1981 role delineation study. The number of master's programs slowly but steadily increased in the 1980s (AOTA, 1985c), and the field continues to debate the issue of master's level entry into occupational therapy. Two students were graduated from the occupational therapy doctoral program at New York University in 1984, initiating the doctoral degree as the terminal degree in occupational therapy (AOTA, 1985c). The AOTA Government and Legal Affairs Division has successfully lobbied the passage of legislation affecting occupational therapy, such as Medicare amendments to provide increased funding for OT services.

In 1980, occupation was officially adopted as the major concern of occupational therapy (Hopkins, 1983). This event coincided with increasing interest in the human occupation model of Kielhofner, who emerged as a leader in theory development for occupational therapy. Having completed his doctorate degree in 1979, he assumed faculty positions at Virginia Commonwealth University and Boston University and the chairpersonship at the University of Illinois. In addition to journal publications, his three books describe the human occupation model. In 1983, Kielhofner edited *Health Through Occupation* and co-authored with Barris and Watts *Psychosocial Occupational Therapy;* in 1985 he edited *A Model of Human Occupation.* Kielhofner's contributions to the field were recognized by his appointment for charter membership in the AOTF Academy of Research in 1984.

During the 1980s the other theorists continued to be recognized nationally for their contributions to the field. They were productive in various ways, continuing to develop their theories, to pursue work activities, and, in some cases, to begin to gear down or refocus their pursuits as they approached retirement age. Fidler served as consultant and administrator to mental health facilities and, in 1980, received the AOTA Award of Merit. Ayres retired from the Ayres Clinic in 1984 to devote time to the development of the Sensory Integration and Praxis Test. Both Ayres and Reilly were named to the Academy of Research in 1984. Reilly, although withdrawn from the field, expressed her opinions about the use of the terms "client" versus "patient" in a 1984 article.

Mosey and Llorens continue their careers in academia. Mosey published *Occupational Therapy: Configuration of a Profession* in 1981 and *Psychosocial Components of Occupational Therapy* in 1986 and was named the 1985 Eleanor Clarke Slagle Lecturer. Llorens became chairperson at San Jose State University in 1982, the same year that her book, *The Occupational Therapy Sequential Client Care Record,* was published.

DEVELOPMENT OF THEORY

The relationship of theory to practice and research can be examined by reviewing how the theory was developed. First, how does the theory begin? What is the impetus for the theorist to formulate the theory? What is the driving force that motivates the individual to assume the arduous task of committing formulations to writing? Is it derived from clinical questions, research findings, or identification of lack of theory in an area or the profession as a whole? Second, what focus does the theory take? Is it specific to one clinical area, or does it address the entire field? Last, what is the role of research in the theory's development? Is the theory validated through research? These questions can be addressed by examining three processes of theory development adapted from Meleis (1985): the *theory-practice-theory process,* the *practice-research-theory process* and the *theory-theory-research/practice process* (see Figure 8-1).

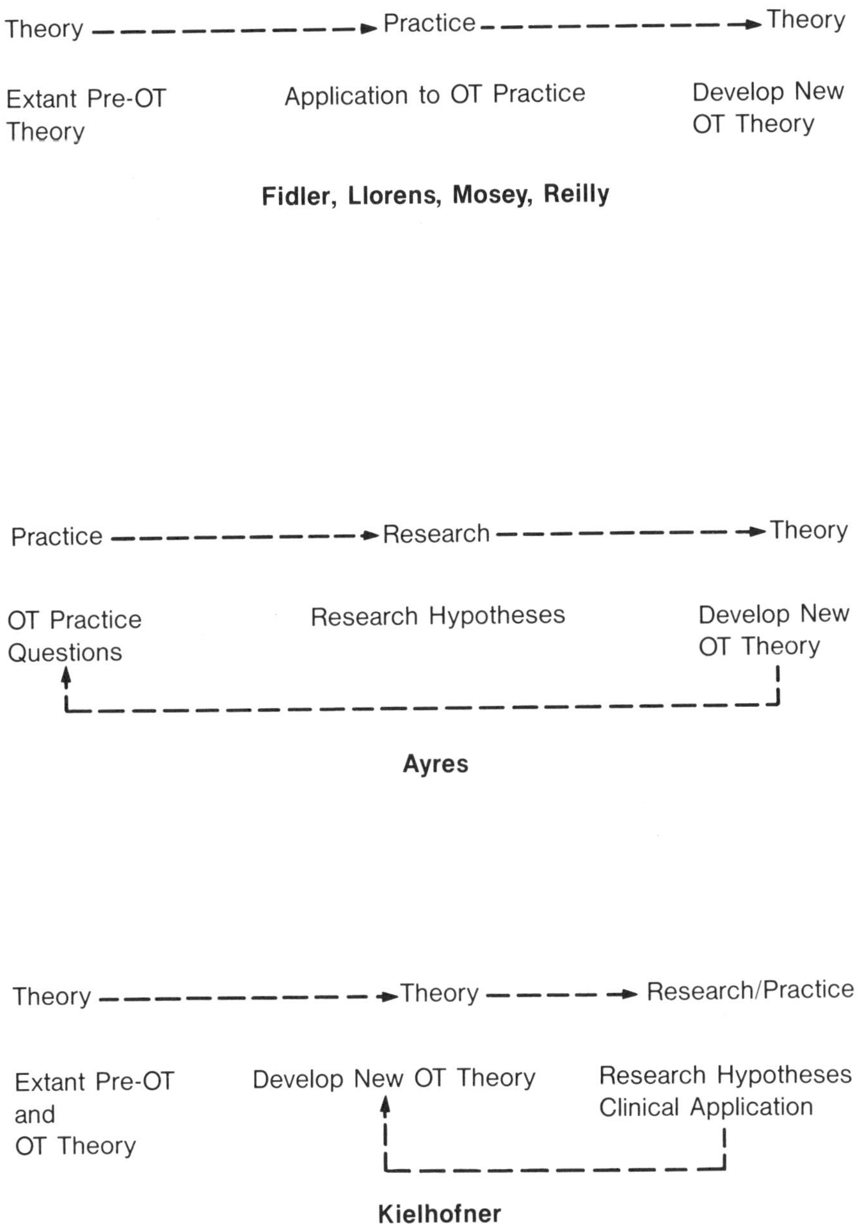

Figure 8-1 Three Theory Development Processes

Theory-Practice-Theory Process

In this process, the theorist selects pre-OT *theory* (i.e., theory from other fields) and systematically applies it to OT *practice* to evolve primary OT *theory,* i.e., new theoretical formulations for occupational therapy. The theory-practice-theory process is used when clinical questions pose problems for which the answers are not apparent in existing theoretical formulations. This process is identified in Fidler's, Mosey's, Llorens', and Reilly's work.

Fidler sought to develop a rationale for what her patients were doing in occupational therapy and whether or not it was helpful. Mosey, who was a student of Fidler, was inspired by Fidler's questioning of clinical practice theory definitions. Llorens realized early in her clinical career that therapists could readily demonstrate the value of occupational therapy, but could not explain its value. She selected pre-OT theorists including Gesell, Piaget, Havighurst, Ericson, and Freud and systematically applied their theories to OT practice in formulating her developmental frame of reference. Reilly came to realize that the reductionist emphasis that she saw as a clinician ignored the importance of patient skills and competence.

These theorists were all troubled by the lack of sound explanations for OT, and they looked to other theoretical bases for relevant principles. Fidler embraced a psychoanalytic theory base; Mosey, a combination of pre-OT theories; Llorens, developmental theories; and Reilly, a social psychology orientation. These OT theorists all identified a need to clarify therapy rationale, and because OT theory was yet to be articulated, they looked beyond the field for relevant theory. They found new ways to apply existing theory from other fields in order to explain and conceptualize the rationale for OT practice.

Practice-Research-Theory Process

In this process, the theorist identifies clinical *practice* questions and formulates theoretical hypotheses, conducts *research* aimed at answering questions and refuting or validating hypotheses, and uses research findings to develop and modify *theory*. This is the process used by Ayres in the development of her sensory integration theory.

In her efforts to formulate explanations and pose testable hypotheses about sensory integrative dysfunction, Ayres identified patient problems as the most challenging and motivating factor. She formulated her own ideas and consulted the neuroscience and neurobehavioral literature, designed and implemented research projects, and used the results of these studies to examine and modify her theory.

Theory-Theory-Research/Practice Process

This process uses existing pre-OT and primary OT *theory* to build new OT *theory,* which is then tested through *research* and clinical *practice*. This process is available to theorists when the field has developed sufficient primary theory—that is, theory developed by and for the field—so that the theorist can incorporate it in constructing new theory. Occupational therapy is just entering an era when this is possible because theory groundbreaking has been done by such theorists as Fidler, Mosey, Llorens, Reilly, and Ayres.

Kielhofner's work is an example of the theory-theory-practice/research process. He used Reilly's occupational behavior paradigm (primary OT theory) and systems theory (pre-OT theory) to develop the model of human occupation (new OT theory). The recent work of Kielhofner and colleagues applies and tests his model through clinical practice and research.

Common Elements of Theory Development

Although this schema of theory development processes is very simplified, it does reveal several important common elements. It is evident that such theorizing emanates from a concern for OT practice. As a practice profession, occupational therapy has an urgent need to identify the unique theoretical underpinnings of what it offers in service to patients and clients. Second, the pioneering efforts of Reilly, Fidler, Llorens, and Mosey bridged pre-OT and OT theory, making it possible for a second generation of OT theory to evolve, beginning with Kielhofner. Third, research to test and validate OT practice and to build a body of knowledge for the profession is underway. The incorporation of research in theory building that is characteristic of Ayres' work is being increasingly emphasized in the work of Kielhofner and colleagues. Thus, the diagramming of theory-building processes illustrates common clinical practice concerns, the evolution of theories building on theories, and the relationship of research in contemporary OT theory development.

PREMISES

A review of the premises of the six theorists is first needed in order to understand the theories' similarities and to examine their scope and clinical application and validation attempts of the theorists. This review attempts to answer these questions: What is the primary idea, conjecture, supposition, or position proffered by the theory and what are the key terms used

Table 8-3 Premises and Terminology

Theorist	Premises	Terminology
Fidler	Purposeful activity and "doing" is the core of OT. Activity is a communication process for nonverbal communication and expression. Object relationships are used for exploration and mastery of the environment.	Object relationships OT—a communication process Doing and becoming
Mosey	OT treatment process recapitulates ontogenesis of development. Three frames of reference are useful in mental health OT: analytic; acquisitional; and developmental. Activities therapies use action-oriented interaction to promote mental health. Therapists should have a frame of reference for practice.	Recapitulation of ontogenesis Biopsychosocial model Activities therapy
Llorens	Humans develop chronologically and simultaneously in all areas of development. OT is a facilitation process for achievement and mastery of life tasks at various life stages. OT activities and interpersonal relationships are used to facilitate development.	OT—a developmental process Sequential Client Care Record (SCCR)
Ayres	Learning occurs in the brain and learning disabilities reflect neural dysfunction. Sensory integration supports neural functioning and sensory integration dysfunction reflects neural dysfunction. Body senses and subcortical functions are important for visual, auditory, and cortical functions. Sensory integration therapy employs movement for its sensory-generating effects.	Sensory integration Tactile defensiveness Developmental dyspraxia Vestibular and bilateral integration dysfunction
Reilly	Humans are occupational beings who have an intrinsic need to act upon and master their environment. Occupational roles provide social meaning and belonging. Play is a precursor to occupational role and is important throughout life. OT uses occupations to restore abilities for role performance.	Occupational behavior Work-play continuum Occupational roles

Table 8-3 (*continued*)

Theorist	Premises	Terminology
Kielhofner	Humans are occupational beings who interact as open systems with the environment through the subsystems: volitional (personal causation, values and interests), habituation (roles and habits), performance (motor, process and communication/interpersonal skills). Humans interact with the environment in input-throughput-feedback processes. OT identifies and remedies problems in performance, habituation, and volitional subsystems to enhance occupational role functioning.	Human occupation Occupational function/ dysfunction continuum Volitional, habituation, and performance subsystems

in it? What is the purpose of the theory? What are the major assumptions of the theory? (see Table 8-3).

Importance of Activities

The most obvious similarity among these six theorists' premises is the focus on the *importance of activities, tasks, and occupations for human functioning*. Humans are not idle creatures—they are active, moving, stimulus-seeking beings who act on, interact with, and seek to alter their surroundings.

Fidler posited that purposeful activity is the core of occupational therapy (Fidler & Fidler, 1978). She saw the use of activity as a communication process whereby thoughts and feelings are expressed nonverbally. Object relationships—that is, relationships with the nonhuman environment—are important for human development and functioning (Fidler & Fidler, 1963).

Mosey (1970) described the therapist's *use* of activity in various frames of reference for practice, rather than the nature of activity, tasks, and occupations for normal human function. As did Fidler, Mosey described activity therapies as those therapies that provide action-oriented interaction to help the mentally ill patient.

Activities, according to Llorens (1976), facilitate human growth and development by enabling one to explore the environment, establish relationships, acquire knowledge, and adapt successfully to one's world.

Ayres (1972a) described children's gross motor play activities in terms of sensory integrative properties and the organizing effects of movement in human neural functioning. Movement requires the integration of all the senses, is mediated at all levels of the neuroaxis, and generates important tactile, proprioceptive, kinesthetic, and vestibular sensations.

Taking a broad viewpoint, Reilly (1962) viewed humans as occupational beings who have an intrinsic need to act on and master their environment and to do so in ways that are in keeping with social role expectations. Meaning as a social being is derived through successful role performance whereby the individual is able to develop those skills necessary to meet role demands. One is satisfied with life and feels reinforced by one's society when one can perform in expected ways.

Building on Reilly's work, Kielhofner (1985) proposed that humans are occupational beings who interact as open systems with the environment. As open systems, humans are active, goal-directed, purposeful creatures who take in information and energy from the environment (intake), use this information or energy for self-maintenance or to initiate further interaction with the environment (throughput), act or produce interaction with the environment (output), and monitor and alter responses on the basis of feedback from the environment.

In summary, Fidler said that "doing is becoming," Mosey advocated action-oriented interactions, Llorens described activity in the OT process of facilitating developmental progression, Ayres focused on the importance of movement for neutral integration, and Reilly and Kielhofner described the occupational nature of humans.

Human Competence

These six theorists agreed that, *through action on and interaction with the environment, humans grow and develop those skills and abilities that enable them to be competent members of a society and to gain a sense of self and social worth.*

Fidler (Fidler & Fidler, 1963) spoke of the interaction of competence, mastery, adaptation, and self-esteem. Through interaction with objects in the environment, humans respond to an innate drive to explore and master their environment. Through action-oriented experiences, humans test skills; clarify relationships; develop and integrate sensory, motor, cognitive, and psychological functions; become socialized to cultural norms and roles; and gain competence as social beings. The skills one develops through "doing" help one become competent in self-care, provide intrinsic gratification, and afford one the means to care for others. Skill development is influenced both by the environment and the individual's biological makeup.

Similarly, Mosey (1973) stated that, through engagement in activity, humans learn to perform life tasks necessary to meet their own needs and the demands of living in their community. Interaction with the nonhuman environment enables the individual to acquire the skills necessary for the performance of life tasks. Mosey defined life tasks as requiring not only the performance of manual skills but also interpersonal relationships, work roles, and recreation.

In Llorens' (1970) outline of ten premises for the OT process, she states that humans naturally develop and master skills, abilities, and relationships simultaneously and chronologically across all areas of development (premises 1-4). This development is fostered by the interaction of the individual's genetic makeup and the environment (premises 5, 6).

Ayres' (1972a) sensory integration theory addressed the development of competence in humans in terms of learning and neural processes. She proposed that, because learning occurs in the brain and is dependent on neural processes, learning disabilities reflect dysfunction in neural functioning. The brain takes in information through the senses; thus integration and processing of sensory information are necessary for learning. The body senses (tactile, proprioceptive, kinesthetic, and vestibular) develop first and provide a basis for the development of visual and auditory systems. Subcortical functions develop first ontogenetically and phylogenetically and provide a basis for the development of cortical, conscious processes. Thus, Ayres considered the body senses and subcortical neural developmental processes to be important for the development of human competency.

Reilly (1974) viewed competency in terms of social role performance, particularly occupational role performance. Occupational roles develop in childhood through play, chores, and schooling as the child acquires the adaptive skills and interactive skills needed as a competent adult worker. Play and social recreation are important throughout life because they promote manipulatory and social skills necessary for role performance and provide socially accepted outlets for aggression.

In his human occupation model, Kielhofner (1985) proposed that the human open system includes three hierarchical subsystems: the volitional, habituation, and performance subsystems. The volitional subsystem addresses the human drive for competence and mastery and includes the motivation and belief in one's ability to act (personal causation) and the development of interests and values. In the habituation subsystem, one develops habits and roles for efficient coping with daily life experience. Underlying the habituation subsystem is the performance subsystem, which includes motor, process, and communication skill development through symbolic, neurologic, and musculoskeletal components. These subsystems interact with the environment in an input-throughput-output feedback process, as noted above, to bring about occupational role functioning.

In summary, these six theorists proposed that human-environment interaction is the mechanism for the development of skills to master the environment and perform as competent members of a society. Fidler said that through doing one becomes competent. Mosey offered her organization of various frames of reference for conceptualizing skill development through activity. Llorens described interaction with the environment as crucial for human development. Ayres posed the relationship of learning to effective interaction with the environment through sensory systems and motor functioning. To Reilly, interaction with the environment in a play-work continuum was necessary for role skill development. Kielhofner viewed humans as open systems interacting with the environment for adaptive functioning.

OT Clinical Practice

A fourth similarity of these OT theorists is the view that, *just as activity is used to acquire skills, it can also be used therapeutically—to restore, regain, or renew skills.*

To Fidler (Fidler & Fidler, 1963) occupational therapy in psychiatry was a communication process involving the psychodynamics of activities and therapeutic relationships. By engaging in activities, patients come to express their emotions and thoughts, learn to interact effectively with the nonhuman environment, and develop skills.

Mosey (1970) provided practical guidelines for the use of activity in therapy. She described the use of work-related, recreational, and creative tasks for improving psychosocial functioning. Activities therapy is a way to use everyday interactions and activities to help persons function in the broader community.

Llorens (1970, 1976) described OT as a facilitation process that assists the individual to achieve and master the tasks of living presented at various life stages. The therapist functions as an enculturation agent to bridge the gap between the patient's functioning level and the level that is socially age expected. Occupational therapy can facilitate the closure of developmental gaps and prevent further dysfunction through the judicious analysis, selection, and use of activities and interpersonal relationships (premises 9, 10).

Ayres' (1972a) sensory integrative therapy used carefully selected motor and sensory activities applied in a developmental sequence to elicit increasingly adaptive sensory and motor responding.

According to Reilly (1974), disease states run counter to the development of life role skills and result in role dysfunction and dissatisfaction. Occupational therapy promotes life satisfaction and self-actualization through the restoration of abilities needed for occupational role functioning.

Occupational therapy, according to Kielhofner (1985), addresses breakdowns in the human/environment open system interaction by identifying occupational role dysfunction and providing remediation at the subsystem level (performance, habituation, or volitional) required to restore or enhance occupational role functioning.

Summary

Although these theorists present a variety of ideas and concepts that are enriched and embellished through their exploration of many issues in the profession, they repeatedly return to a few central themes: the view of humans as occupational beings, mastery of the environment through skill development, the ability of humans to affect their own state of health, and the therapeutic value of tasks, activities, and occupations. It would appear that substantial work has been done to provide us with a working body of knowledge that can be confirmed through clinical practice and research, leading to refined theory building in occupational therapy.

CLINICAL APPLICATION

Evaluation Tools

Most of the theorists developed evaluation tools for OT practice, many of which were originally developed for use in mental health occupational therapy. All of the theorists advocated the use of the therapist's observations and informal assessments as well (see Table 8-4).

Fidler constructed clinical observation tools for use in psychosocial evaluation: the Projective Diagnostic Battery, the Object History, the Play History, and the Lifestyle Performance Profile (1982). Mosey developed survey instruments for group interaction, self-care, child care work, and recreation. An activity configuration for analysis of time spent in various activities throughout the day and questionnaires based on Fidler's work were also devised by Mosey (1973).

In Llorens' framework (1976) for practice that spanned infancy through adulthood and aging, she advocated testing, evaluation, and observation to determine the developmental level of the patient.

Reilly (1974) advocated the case method approach for patient treatment. Direct observations, testing, interview, and history taking were used for

Table 8-4 Clinical Application of Theory

Theorist	Evaluation	Treatment	Patient Population and Setting
Fidler	Projective Diagnostic Battery Object History Play History Lifestyle Performance Profile Patient questionnaires Guidelines for program development	Activity Analysis Prescriptive use of activities Task groups Nonverbal communication Object relations	Adult psychiatry Institutional and community settings
Mosey	Survey instruments: group interaction; self care; child care; work; and recreation Activity Configuration Questionnaires based on Fidler's work	Use of groups Body image treatment Activities therapy	Adult and adolescent psychiatry Institutional and community settings
Llorens	Developmental Analysis, Evaluation and Intervention Schedule (DAEIS) Sequential Client Care Record (SCCR)	Age-appropriate activities Interpersonal relationships	All developmental age groups, disabilities, and settings
Ayres	Southern California Sensory Integration Tests, Postrotary Nystagmus Test Sensory Integration and Praxis Test Ayres' clinical observations	Sensory integrative therapy, tactile, proprioceptive, vestibular, and kinesthetic emphasis Use of scooter boards, net hammock, and suspended swings	Learning disabled children in schools and community clinics
Reilly	Observation, history, and interview techniques	Use of arts, crafts, toys, games, and leisure activities	Applicable to all age and disability groups and settings, but focuses on adults in the community
Kielhofner	Observation, history, interview, and projective assessments	Therapy principles for treatment planning	Applicable to all age and disability groups and settings but roots are in psychosocial dysfunction

evaluation and clinical problem solving and to accommodate individual patient variations. Evaluation results were examined to identify patterns of success and failure, learning style, level of function, and to provide data for formulating an action plan.

Kielhofner (1985) edited a textbook that specifically applied the model of human occupation to five disability areas and included an assessment library of observation, history, interview, and projective assessment tools. The instruments (most were nonstandardized) were selected for applicability to Kielhofner's human occupation model, and many were in use before the publication of the model. Development of tools for the model is now underway.

In contrast to these theorists, a substantial portion of Ayres' work has been devoted to the development of standardized testing instruments for use in OT evaluation of learning disabled children; these tests include the *Southern California Sensory Integration Tests* (1972b), the *Southern California Postrotary Nystagmus Test* (1975), and, more recently, the *Sensory Integration and Praxis Tests* (1987). Sensory integration tests brought occupational therapy into the realm of psychometric testing, requiring therapists' adherence to standard administration and scoring procedures.

Treatment

OT treatment approaches developed by these theorists were predominantly based in mental health occupational therapy. Fidler's clinical contributions include her prescriptive use of activities, suggestions for the use of task groups, and use of activities in nonverbal communication and object relations work in mental health (Fidler & Fidler, 1954, 1963). Mosey regarded clinical practice as the scientific application of theory. The use of five types of groups (1973), treatment of distorted body image (1969), and guidelines for activities therapy in mental health (1973) comprise the specific treatment approaches introduced by Mosey.

Activities and relationships that are in keeping with the patient's age and life roles can be used to facilitate development, according to Llorens (1976). Her early work was in child psychiatry, although her developmental model is applicable across age and dysfunction categories.

Reilly's students applied her theory in various therapy settings, especially mental health, as described later in the section on dissemination.

Although so far primarily applied in psychosocial areas (Barris, Kielhofner & Watts, 1983), Kielhofner's model (1985) provided a framework for conceptualizing OT evaluation and treatment across patient categories.

An exception to these theories that began in mental health occupational therapy is Ayres' sensory integrative therapy. It uses equipment and devices aimed at generating bodily sensations of tactile, proprioceptive, kinesthetic, and vestibular sensation. Ayres (1972a) developed the use of the scooter board, net hammock, and suspended swings of various types, which require adequate clinical space designed to accommodate this kind of equipment safely.

SCOPE AND COMPLEXITY

Scope addresses the range of the theory. Does it apply to all of occupational therapy or only to a part? Does it seek to explain the profession as a whole or to focus on one aspect of the profession? Is the theory a closed theory, or does it allow for expansion and further development? The review of *complexity* explores the number of concepts in each theory, the intensity of study needed to understand the theory, and its implications and the internal consistency of the theory.

Scope

As a group, these theories address the entire range of population ages, settings, and disabilities seen in OT practice, although the scope of each theory does differ. Fidler's contribution to the body of knowledge in the field is perhaps most appropriately viewed in terms of various constructs for OT practice. She provided theoretical formulations for psychoanalytically based occupational therapy in psychiatry and expanded these to include new knowledge through the years. In addition, her work influenced the development of two other theorists reviewed in this book, Mosey and Llorens.

In scope, Mosey has helped articulate the wholeness of occupational therapy and its parts by presenting frameworks for viewing the profession and what we are using and doing. She provided (1) frameworks for structuring and thinking about the OT profession (1968, 1970); (2) a taxonomy for identifying the elements of the profession (1981); and (3) therapy approaches for OT in mental health (1973, 1986).

The scope of Llorens' work included all of occupational therapy, but has been most applicable to pediatrics where more is known about developmental processes than in adulthood and aging. Llorens (1976) provided a way to conceptualize OT practice, to explain what occupational therapy is, and to be able to teach this to students. Because her work is a point of view for the field and embodies beliefs about the field, it could be considered a paradigm. However, Llorens presented her work more as a view of occupational therapy for practice than as a paradigm for the profession.

Sensory integration theory addressed a portion of the field of occupational therapy, occupational therapy for children with learning disabilities (Ayres, 1972a). Ayres' sensory integration theory was developed for the child who has no demonstrable deficits but is having difficulty learning. It was not developed to address neurologic deficits, such as those encountered in mental retardation or cerebral palsy. Yet, principles for understanding sensory and motor functioning and for treatment have been found to be useful for several patient populations.

Reilly's work (1962) is considered a paradigm because she attempted to articulate the idea underlying the field of occupational therapy. She imposed order on multidisciplinary information to proclaim the particular features of the profession. Reilly's paradigm provides her grand-scale perception of the exciting uniqueness of occupational therapy.

Kielhofner's development of Reilly's paradigm stems from his position that there is a critical need to have a mutually agreed-on paradigm. Going beyond Reilly, Kielhofner (1985) provided a comprehensive model for dealing with the complexity of the occupational aspects of humans in a clinical situation. His model includes a framework for evaluation, treatment, and research.

Complexity

Fidler's work has been most valuable in articulating the *constructs* of object relationships, doing and becoming, competence, and mastery. These have *not* been reassembled into a complex and cogent theoretical framework that interrelates the various constructs, yet they express elements of OT practice. Fidler has consistently advocated the articulation of OT theory. She has stated that the fundamental concept underlying occupational therapy is viable, but unless it is developed, it will be usurped by other professions.

Mosey progressively expanded and modified her theoretical contributions in a continued quest for a model for the profession. A prolific theorizer, Mosey's work has been complex, yet her ideas have been presented in a logical and orderly way. However, terminology in some of her synthesis works is sometimes awkward, perhaps due to the difficulty of clearly presenting distillations of the ideas of other theorists. Terminology in recent works has been clearly defined and used consistently. She has developed original ideas as her perceptions have been refined through her relentless examination of ideas underlying OT theory.

Llorens provided ten premises for OT practice that are succinctly stated, comprehensive, and internally consistent. She has continued to refine the application of these concepts in later works.

Ayres' complex theory of sensory integration requires knowledge of neuroscience and thoughtful study of the theory for thorough understanding. Her reliance on neuroscience literature requires the reader to have a background in neurophysiology and neuropsychology. Concepts are consistently and logically presented, building on one another. Terminology is well developed and used consistently throughout.

Although Reilly's ideas were simply and consistently presented, an understanding of her theory requires thoughtful study and careful reading of her writings. Because the theory is a macroview of the profession, some readers may find it difficult to bring it from the the realm of the theoretical to the practical.

Kielhofner's paradigm of work and his model of human occupation demonstrated his belief in the need to develop an academic discipline for occupational therapy through research and theory development. Thorough study is necessary to grasp the model in its complexity. He developed new meanings for existing terms and brought new terms into the field, which has led to some confusion and criticism (Labovitz & Miller, 1986).

In summary, these six theorists demonstrate a valiant commitment to writing the ideas that form the basis for the profession and the principles that guide OT intervention. Fidler presented constructs for OT practice; Mosey, conceptual frameworks for the profession, for OT practice in mental health, and for theory building; Llorens, a conceptualization of the OT practice process; Ayres, a research-based theory for OT practice in pediatrics; Reilly, a paradigm; and Kielhofner, a paradigm and a comprehensive practice model. The theories are intricate and complex in their own ways and are deserving of careful study for appreciation of the depths of knowledge offered.

DISSEMINATION, VALIDATION, AND FURTHER DEVELOPMENT

Throughout their careers, the six theorists have consistently disseminated their ideas, hypotheses, and findings through writings, teachings, and presentations. They have also attempted to validate their theories and develop their ideas further through research and clinical application (See Table 8-5).

Dissemination

As a group, these theorists have written 18 books and published 212 articles and other scholarly writings. All of them have served as OT educators, and most of them have shared their ideas through workshops and presentations. Fidler has written 3 books and 22 articles and has disseminated her ideas through workshops, lectures, clinical teaching, supervision, and service to the AOTA. Mosey has written 5 books and 11 papers and has disseminated her concepts through OT graduate education and workshops. Many of Llorens' 66 publications and much of her teaching in workshops and graduate and undergraduate OT programs reflect aspects of her developmental theory. Ayres has published three books, 52 articles, 22 test instruments, and 4 professional films. She has informed students and therapists about sensory integration theory through workshops and clinical training in her Ayres Clinic. Reilly's theories have been disseminated through her writings (16 articles and 1 book) and through her students' works. As a scholar, Reilly's goal was to enable students to learn to think critically, utilize logical thought processes, and develop qualitative, quantitative, and historical perspectives. Kielhofner has produced 48 papers and 3 books, the most prolific writer for his age of the theorists reviewed and the only example of dissemination through extensive collaborative authorship. He also teaches in workshops and classrooms.

Validation

Validation efforts vary among these theorists: some have validated their ideas empirically through years of clinical practice, others have conducted research, and some have stimulated others to do research.

Fidler derived her ideas from, and tested them through, clinical practice. Although she has not conducted research, she advocated that occupational therapists study activities according to a standardizing process to search for the meaning of activity and its application in the field.

Similarly, Mosey advocated research to test theories and theoretical foundations, but has not conducted research herself. She proposed research as indirectly related to practice and to practice frames of reference. The role of research in theory building should be to contribute to the theoretical base and body of knowledge. Research findings then trickle down to frames of reference for practice, having modified the theoretical base. Thus, clinical practice is based on theoretical foundations that are modified by research.

Llorens' nearly two decades of clinical practice contributed to the formulation of her ideas for a developmental theory of occupational therapy. She conducted research in child psychiatry and the use of her OT record system and has been instrumental in promoting research through her leadership role in the AOTF as well. Her Sequential Client Care Record (SCCR) and case study methods are clinical research data gathering tools, and she has coordinated their use with therapists in various states in the nation.

Table 8-5 Theory Dissemination, Research, and Application/Development of Theory by Others

	Dissemination				
	Publications		Presentations		
Theorist	*Books*	*Articles*	*How, what*	**Research**	**Application/ Development**
Fidler	OT psychiatry OT theory Activities Professional issues	OT psychiatry	Workshops Clinical teaching Group process OT psychiatry Program design Management Activities		
Mosey	OT theory OT psychiatry Activity	OT theory OT psychiatry Activity	OT education Workshops Frames of reference Activity		
Llorens	Developmental theory for OT OT in child psychiatry Consultation in community OT record system	Black culture Cognitive-perceptual-motor dysfunction	OT education Developmental theory	Emotionally disturbed children OT record system AOTF	

Ayres	Sensory integration theory, dysfunction, testing, and treatment		Workshops OT education Clinical teaching Sensory integration Treatment	Sensory integration: learning disabled, autistic, aphasic	Sensory integration international Adult psychiatry Aphasia Mentally Retarded Cerebral Palsy Hyperactivity
Reilly	Work-play continuum	OT education OT profession	OT education Play Work OT education OT profession		Roles Play Work Interests Motivation Curriculum design Temporal adaptation Occupational behavior theory Assessment
Kielhofner	Human Occupation Theory and Application		OT education Workshops Model of human occupation	Human occupation Psychosocial problems Adolescents Delinquency Elderly Mentally retarded adults Assessment and instrument development	Learning disabilities Alcoholics Retarded adults Spinal cord injury Elderly Assessment and instrument development

To construct sensory integration theory, Ayres conducted numerous research projects. The most prolific researcher of these six theorists, Ayres' research efforts span more than two decades. Her work includes test instrument development and treatment efficacy studies with learning disabled children and, more recently, with autistic and aphasic children.

The focus of OT research, according to Reilly, should be to study the nature of occupation from a developmental perspective. Thus, research should focus on achievement, creativity, aptitude, and interest patterns in relationship to occupations and activities. Because of Reilly's influence a tradition of OT scholarly productivity has endured at USC for many years, and Reilly's students have been responsive to that tradition.

With the model of human occupation now well described, Kielhofner and his colleagues and students are undertaking research based on the model. This research is aimed at the development of assessments and testing of treatment based on the model.

Development of the Theory by Others

Further application, research, and development have occurred in sensory integration theory, occupational behavior theory, and human occupation theory. Ayres' sensory integration theory has spawned more research efforts by clinicians and students than has any other theory to date. Therapists have applied the treatment principles to several patient populations, including children with mental retardation and other developmental disabilities, hyperactivity, aphasia, and autism and to adult psychiatry. Supporters of her work established what is now Sensory Integration International (SII), a nonprofit corporation that supports sensory integration research and disseminates the theory. The faculty of SII comprises therapists from throughout the nation who conduct workshops to teach sensory integration theory and test administration and interpretation to occupational therapists in the United States and abroad.

Reilly's students have been instrumental in researching and applying her theory through (1) the development of survey, interview, observation, and history tools; (2) the description of roles and occupational stages, the influence of interests and motivation, and the play-work continuum; and (3) sequences and variables for clinical practice for use with psychiatric patients, juvenile delinquent disabled adolescents, the mildly mentally retarded, physically adolescents, and in geriatrics. Her ideas about OT curriculum design have been incorporated into curriculum designs based on occupation (Levine, 1984). Her work profoundly influenced Kielhofner's development of a theory of human occupation.

The most recent of the theories developed, Kielhofner's model of human occupation has stimulated research in the last decade, most of it since 1980. His students and colleagues have researched the human occupation model with several patient groups, including learning disabled children, alcoholics, retarded adults, spinal cord injured patients, and the elderly. Other research efforts have addressed assessment and instrument development.

Although their work has influenced the thinking of occupational therapists, Fidler's, Mosey's, and Llorens' theories have not been developed through an identifiable body of research or through an identified group of researchers. However, these theorists' works are cited in the literature when reference is made to basic ideas of occupational therapy and have been included in theory compilations (Clark & Allen, 1985; Reed, 1984). As did Reilly, these theorists synthesized OT theory from theories in other fields and made it possible for the development of theory from within the field, as Kielhofner has done.

All of these theorists generously shared their ideas through written and spoken communications. They have consigned their hypotheses and conceptualizations to the rest of the profession for use, examination, and improvement.

FUTURE DIRECTIONS

This review of six major OT theories reveals gaps in theory development when one considers the two main patient treatment areas that comprise OT practice. Patients treated in OT are generally classified as (1) adolescent, adult, and aging persons with physical disabilities or psychosocial dysfunction and (2) infants and children with developmental or pediatric problems. The theories of Fidler, Mosey, Reilly, and Kielhofner focus on adolescents and adults with psychosocial dysfunction. Llorens' and Ayres' theories are considered pediatric theories. Llorens' developmental theory and, more recently, Kielhofner's model of human occupation encompass all OT clinical areas, including psychosocial dysfunction and physical disabilities and all age groups. However, a theory originating in OT practice with adolescent, adult, and aging persons with physical disabilities has not been developed. This is interesting, considering that the physical disabilities patient population comprises more than 40 percent of the patients served (AOTA, 1985a).

This is not to say that OT practice in physical disabilities is not theory-based, for it is. Pre-OT theories of Rood, Bobath, Brunnstrom, and Kabat and Voss underlie OT evaluation and treatment in this area. In addition, OT textbooks have been organized to reflect three conceptual categories for OT evaluation and treatment in physical disabilities—neurodevelopmental, biomechanical, and rehabilitative approaches (Trombly, 1983)—or to reflect the OT process in physical disabilities (Pedretti, 1981). These textbooks incorporate theoretical and practical knowledge from anatomy, neuroscience, kinesiology, physical science, muscle physiology, and medicine and combine it with OT principles of activity analysis, self-care, and functional adaptation to provide a rich array of techniques for OT intervention in physical disabilities. However, the theoretical basis for OT practice in physical disabilities has not been extracted from pre-OT theories nor formulated into conceptual models or frames of reference for practice in physical disabilities. Kielhofner's human occupation model for the profession as a whole certainly encompasses physical disabilities and geriatrics, although the model did not originate from questions in this clinical area. Whether theory development is needed to address practice in physical disabilities just as Fidler and Mosey developed theory for psychosocial dysfunction or whether existing or new OT theories for the entire profession can and should adequately encompass this clinical area is a question for the future. In either case, posing theory to speculate about phenomena in physical disabilities remains to be done.

Lewin (1947) described three stages of theory development: (1) speculative, in which theory is proposed to explain phenomena; (2) descriptive, which involves research to quantify phenomena and for theory testing; and (3) constructive, in which new theory is devised through revision of existing theory and through the use of facts versus speculation. Occupational therapy theory development is now at stages one and two.

Fidler, Mosey, Llorens, Ayres, Reilly, and Kielhofner have all proposed rationales for the profession's existence and/or explanations of OT practice. Through her efforts to quantify sensory integrative phenomena and to test her ideas, Ayres' research has brought OT theory into stage two. Other theorists have contributed to this stage. Fidler and Mosey have been research advocates. Llorens, through her SCCR, provided a method for clinical case study data collection. Reilly's students conducted research for instrument development and to explain constructs of occupational behavior theory. Kielhofner and colleagues have recently engaged in research of the model of human occupation. Theories described in this book have begun to be validated through research.

Although the field of occupational therapy has begun a serious attempt to articulate and quantify phenomena of concern, much remains to be done to test the theories described in this book and to validate frames of reference and theoretical formulations that exist in the field but are beyond the scope of this book. In this book alone are contained innumerable research ideas, and within its literature, possible research directions are limitless. Occupational therapy is on the threshold of developing research traditions, identifying research processes, and claiming research areas that will help us begin to test our ideas scientifically. This era will give us the research know-how and clearer descriptions of "what OT is" that will serve as a basis for bringing OT theory development to stage three: theory construction. Hudson's thoughts, as expressed in the *American Journal of Occupational Therapy* in 1954, on the nature of research, provide a challenge to each of us as occupational therapists: "It is exciting to realize that we are all on a scientific frontier that has hardly been penetrated—that the opportunities for individual contribution to knowledge are endless" (Hudson, 1954, p. 150).

REFERENCES

American Occupational Therapy Association. (1979). *TOTEMS, Training Occupational Therapy Management in the Schools.* Rockville, MD: Author.

American Occupational Therapy Association. (1985a). *Occupational therapy manpower: A plan for progress.* Rockville, MD: Author.

American Occupational Therapy Association. (1985b). *PIVOT, Planning and Implementing Vocational Readiness in Occupational Therapy.* Rockville, MD: Author.

American Occupational Therapy Association. (1985c). *Education data survey.* Rockville, MD: Author.

American Occupational Therapy Association. (1986a). *ROTE, Role of Occupational Therapy with the Elderly.* Rockville, MD: Author.

American Occupational Therapy Association. (1986b). *SCOPE, Strategies, Concepts and Opportunities for Program Development and Evaluation.* Rockville, MD: Author.

Ayres, A.J. (1963). The development of perceptual motor abilities: As a theoretical basis for treatment of dysfunction. *American Journal of Occupational Therapy, 6,* 221–225.

Ayres, A.J. (1972a). *Sensory integration and learning disorders.* Los Angeles: Western Psychological Services.

Ayres, A.J. (1972b). *Southern California Sensory Integration Tests.* Los Angeles: Western Psychological Services.

Ayres, A.J. (1975). *Southern California Postrotary Nystagmus Test.* Los Angeles: Western Psychological Services.

Ayres, A.J. (1979). *Sensory integration and the child.* Los Angeles: Western Psychological Services.

Ayres, A.J. (1987). *Sensory Integration and Praxis Tests.* Los Angeles: Western Psychological Services, In press.

Barris, R., Kielhofner, G., & Watts, J.H. (1983). *Psychosocial occupational therapy.* Laurel, MD: Ramsco Publishing Company.

Chinn, P.L., & Jacobs, M.K. (1983). *Theory and nursing—A systematic approach.* St. Louis: CV Mosby, Co.

Clark, P.N., & Allen, A.S. (1985). *Occupational therapy for children.* St. Louis: CV Mosby Co.

Duldt, B.W., & Griffin, K. (1985). *Theoretical perspectives for nursing,* Boston: Little, Brown & Co.

Fidler, G.S. (1948). Psychological evaluation of occupational therapy activities. *American Journal of Occupational Therapy, 1,* 284–287.

Fidler, G.S. (1966). Learning as a growth process: A conceptual framework for professional education. *American Journal of Occupational Therapy, 20,* 1–8.

Fidler, G.S. (1982). The lifestyle performance profile: An organizing frame. In B. Hemphill (Ed.), *The evaluative process in psychiatric occupational therapy.* Thorofare, NJ: Charles B. Slack.

Fidler, G.S., & Fidler, J.W. (1954). *Introduction to psychiatric occupational therapy.* New York: Macmillan Company.

Fidler, G.S., & Fidler, J.W. (1963). *Occupational therapy: A communication process in psychiatry*. New York: Macmillan Company.

Fidler, G.S., & Fidler, J.W. (1978). Doing and becoming: Purposeful action and self actualization. *American Journal of Occupational Therapy, 32,* 305–310.

Hopkins, H.L. (1983). An historical perspective on occupational therapy. In H.L. Hopkins & H.D. Smith (Ed). *Willard and Spackman's occupational therapy,* (6th ed.) (pp. 3–29) Philadelphia: JB Lippincott, Co.

Hudson, B. (1954). What is research. *American Journal of Occupational Therapy, 8,* 140–141 and 150.

Kielhofner, G. (Ed.). (1983). *Health through occupation: Theory and practice in occupational therapy.* Philadelphia: FA Davis Company.

Kielhofner, G. (Ed.). (1985). A model of human occupation. Baltimore: Williams & Wilkins.

Labovitz, D.R. & Miller, R.J. (1986). Commentary: Organization of knowledge in occupational therapy: A proposal and a survey of the literature. *Occupational Therapy Journal of Research, 6,* 85.

Levine, A.E. (1984, May). *A design for an entry-level curriculum based on occupation.* Paper presented at the meeting of the American Occupational Therapy Association Commission on Education, Kansas City, Missouri.

Lewin, K. (1947) *Principles of topological psychology.* New York: McGraw-Hill.

Light, S. & Reilly M. (1943). The correlation of physical therapy and occupational therapy. *Occupational Therapy and Rehabilitation. 22,* 171–175.

Llorens, L.A. (1970). Facilitating growth and development: The promise of occupational therapy. *American Journal of Occupational Therapy, 24,* 93–101.

Llorens, L.M. (1973). (Ed.). *Consultation in the Community: Occupational Therapy in Child Health.* Dubuque, Iowa: Kendall-Hunt, Publishers.

Llorens, L.A. (1976). *Application of a developmental theory for health and rehabilitation.* Rockville, MD: American Occupational Therapy Association.

Llorens, L.A. (1982). *Occupational therapy sequential client care record manual.* Laurel, MD: Ramsco Publishing Company.

Llorens, L.A., & Rubin, E.Z. (1967). *Developing ego functions in disturbed children: Occupational therapy in Milieu.* Detroit: Wayne State University Press.

Meleis, H.I. (1985). *Theoretical nursing: Development and progress.* Philadelphia: JB Lippincott.

Mosey, A.C. (1968). Recapitulation of ontogenesis: A theory for practice of occupational therapy. *American Journal of Occupational Therapy, 22,* 426–432.

Mosey, A.C. (1969). Treatment of pathological distortion of body image. *American Journal of Occupational Therapy, 23,* 413–416.

Mosey, A.C. (1970). *Three frames of reference for mental health.* Thorofare, New Jersey: Charles B. Slack.

Mosey, A.C. (1973). *Activities therapy.* New York: Raven Press.

Mosey, A. (1974). An alternative: The biopsychosocial model. *American Journal of Occupational Therapy, 28,* 137–140.

Mosey, A.C. (1981). *Occupational therapy: Configuration of a profession,* New York: Raven Press.

Mosey, A.C. (1986). *The psychosocial components of occupational therapy.* New York: Raven Press.

Pedretti, L.W. (1981). *Occupational therapy practice skills for physical dysfunction.* St. Louis: CV Mosby Co.

Reed, K.L. (1984). *Models of practice in occupational therapy.* Baltimore: Williams & Wilkins.

Reed, K.L., & Sanderson, S.R. (1980). *Concepts of occupational therapy.* Baltimore: Williams & Wilkins.

Reilly, M. (1958). An occupational therapy curriculum for 1965. *American Journal of Occupational Therapy, 12,* 293–299.

Reilly, M. (1962). Occupational Therapy can be one of the great ideas of 20th century medicine. *American Journal of Occupational Therapy, 10,* 1–9.

Reilly, M. (1974) (Ed.). *Play as exploratory learning.* Beverly Hills, CA: Sage Publishers.

Reilly, M. (1984). The issue is—The importance of the client versus patient issue for occupational therapy. *American Journal of Occupational Therapy, 38,* 407–408.

Trombly, C.A. (1983). *Occupational therapy for physical dysfunction.* Baltimore: Williams & Wilkins.

Index

About the Authors

B. Rosalie Johanna Miller graduated from Earlham College in 1966 and earned a certificate in occupational therapy from the University of Pennsylvania two years later. After several years of practice in mental health she went to Boston University for her master's degree in OT. In 1978 she earned a PhD. in education from the University of Florida. She served on the faculty in OT at the University of Florida for 3 1/2 years before moving to New York City to join the OT faculty at New York University. She has published and made presentations in her areas of interest that include the chairperson's role; OT history, philosophy, theory and research; integrative education; and feminist theory, particularly as it applies to the predominantly female "helping professions".

Kay W. Sieg earned her B.S. in occupational therapy in 1964 and her M.Ed. in special education in 1970 from the University of Florida. After practicing in pediatrics for a number of years, she joined the faculty at the University of Florida, and then became chairperson in 1984. She is currently enrolled in a doctoral program in special education. Ms. Sieg is a member of the faculty of Sensory Integration International, and is neurodevelopmental treatment (NDT) certified. She has presented nationally in sensory integration workshops, developed videotapes for teaching the sensory integration tests, and participated in the national standardization project for the sensory integration and praxis test. Publications include results of her research on developmental reflexes and tactile localization as well as articles on a variety of other topics.

Ferol Menks Ludwig earned her B.S. degree in occupational therapy and her master's degree in human development and family relations from Ohio State University. She worked in mental health until joining the faculty at the University of Florida in 1973. In 1983 she became coordinator of the school of OT at the Houston Center of Texas Woman's University. She is the creator of the simulation board game "All About Aging," and has published and presented on topics such as projective tests, mid-life and aging issues, and nontraditional students; and served as an author and expert panel member for Project ROTE I and II. She is currently in private practice in Phoenix, Arizona in mental health and grerontic OT and is involved in consultation on program development, education, and research.

Susan Denegan Shortridge is the owner and president of Developmental Health Care Services, Inc. After earning her bachelor's degree in occupational therapy from the University of Florida in 1977 and her master's in OT in 1978, she taught at the University of Florida for three years. She has published in the area of pediatric growth and development. Her practice specialty is the treatment of oral motor dysfunction.

Julia Van Deusen earned master's and doctoral degrees from the University of Southern California in 1963 and 1971, respectively. Her practice expertise is in the area of physical disabilities. She has published and done extensive research primarily on the relationship of perceptual dysfunction to deficits in self-care in adults. She has been on the faculties in occupational therapy at Howard University and at the University of Wisconsin. Currently she is an associate professor at the University of Florida.